FOOD INSECURITY AND DISEASE

FOOD INSECURITY AND DISEASE

Editor

Rubem Dalca

scitus academics

Food Insecurity and Disease
Edited by **Rubem Dalca**

ISBN: 978-1-68117-729-8
Library of Congress Control Number: 2016958844

616, Corporate Way, Suite 2, 4766,
Valley Cottage, NY 10989

www.scitusacademics.com

Notice

Printed in United States of America on Acid Free Paper

PREFACE

Food insecurity is a public health problem affecting both adults and children. Food insecurity and disease are intimately connected. Food insecurity refers to the inability to afford enough food for an active, healthy life. Numerous studies have shown associations between food insecurity and adverse health outcomes among children. Food insecurity among children and adults has adverse health effects, including increased rates of iron-deficiency anemia, acute infection, chronic illness, and developmental and mental health problems.

Food Insecurity and Disease summarizes the literature on the link between food insecurity and the following: diet, weight gain, and chronic disease, among children and adults. Presents a framework for considering how the lived experience of household food insecurity may potentiate the development of chronic disease by activating the stress response among individuals at critical developmental periods in a food-impoverished environment. The association between food insecurity and clinical evidence of diet-sensitive chronic disease, including hypertension, hyperlipidemia, and diabetes is examined.

This book contends the need to expand the framing of food security to include not just quantity of food but also its nutritional quality, the wider social context and environmental dimensions. By using such a framing, food insecurity would encompass both a lack of food and a lack of good nutrition. This informative compilation will provide comprehension on these important issues for students, researchers and practitioners in food security and environmental studies..

TABLE OF CONTENTS

1

THE QUALITY OF ORGANICALLY PRODUCED FOOD

Ewa Rembiałkowska[1, 2], Aneta Załęcka[1, 2], Maciej Badowski[1] and Angelika Ploeger[3, 2]

[1] Warsaw University of Life Sciences, Faculty of Human Nutrition and Consumer Sciences, Poland

[2] International Organic FQH Research Association,

[3] Kassel University, Department of Organic Food Quality and Food Culture, Germany

1. INTRODUCTION

Organic farming began to develop in the modern world as a response to intensified farming and industrial agriculture, using synthetic fertilizers, chemical pesticides, introduction of monocultures into large areas, the separation the animal husbandry from plant production and using heavy machinery. All of this leads both to environmental degradation, and on the other hand, the overproduction of food. At the same time the food quality decreases continuously with regard to nutritional value, which is also the effect of strongly developed food technology.

Regulations specifying the conditions of organic crop and animal production are very strict, which results in high quality of agricultural products. The same applies to the processing scheme, however the techniques are not regulated so far (only few ones, such as radiation and genetic modifications, are banned in organic food processing). While conventional processing is based on several hundred different types of food additives (colorings, stabilizers, enhancers, etc.), the organic food processing allows only few dozen of additives, which usually are natural substances. This is a particularly difficult situation for organic farmers, who are obliged to maintain the quality of their products without using chemicals. However, the consumers' health is essential.

2. FOOD QUALITY

The quality of food products is a subject of many debates, which result in different definitions of this term. The definition of food quality is constantly changing. Initially it was represented by the quantitative/measurable parameters. Nowadays more and more popular is the holistic approach to the problem of quality. Vogtmann (1991) adopted a food quality evaluation approach including analytical and holistic criteria. According to this approach, the organic food quality assessment should be focused on all aspects and from all possible points of view, i.e. holistic model. Kahl et al., (2010a) analyzed the current status of organic food quality in relation to potential quality claims. They concluded, that a model is missed, which can be applied in scientific research as well as in practice. Furthermore they identified a gap between consumer expectations on the quality of the food and what can be guaranteed by regulation so far. Recently Kahl et al., (2012) published a model for organic food quality, taking into account a conceptual background which consists of the different (historical) sources as IFOAM standards, EC-Regulations and consumer understanding. A central part of this model is the evaluation, which should take part on different levels. As am essential part, organic food quality consists of product and process related aspects, which can be described by criteria and measured by parameters. This holistic or systemic view brings all different criteria together: technological value, nutritional value, sensory value as well as biological value and ethical indicators.

The technological value refers to the distinctive features of food products in light of the requirements of different interest groups. For individual participants of the food production chain (producers, processors, distributors and consumers) different features may be the most important distinguishing parameters, depending on the specific purpose for which the food product is intended.

The sensory quality is represented by a set of features assessed by humans by the use of standarized tests, based on human senses: taste, smell, touch, vision and hearing. Among these criteria, the appearance plays an important role in the assessment of raw materials and finished products, along with other organoleptic characteristics such as taste, smell or texture. Sensory quality is of great importance because it affects the process of making a choice when buying food. Sensory evaluation of food products is based on two main methods. The first one is to assess the desirability, acceptance and consumer preferences assessed in so-called 'consumer tests'. The second method is to evaluate the product based on defined criteria and by a specially trained person (so-called 'sensory panel'). The results are analyzed statistically.

The nutritional value can be considered as the minimum content of food contaminants (pesticide residues, nitrates, heavy metals, etc.) at the optimum content of valuable ingredients (vitamins, mineral elements, protein, etc.)

Interestingly the quality of organic food is mainly measured by standard single compound detection through analytical methods. In order to follow the holistic view on agriculture, also the evaluation of the food should be more holistic than reductionistic. Kahl et al., (2010 b) discussed several approaches and methods for this purpose. The biocrystallization method seems to be most encouraging in this direction (Kahl et al., 2009, Szulc et al., 2010, Busscher et al., 2010a,b).

Another question, related to organic food quality is, how authentic the food is. Authenticity can be understood in two ways. First one is represented by the sense of product traceability, when it is possible to verify whether the characteristics of the product actually correspond to characteristics that are attributed to him. For instance, research conducted to determine whether the products offered on the market as organic really come from organic production (Kahl et al., 2010b). Therefore, it is needed to find methods that would enable tracing of all "biography of the product" in a fast and simple way. It would be an efficient tool for controlling the products offered on the market. Here an European project, bringing several approaches together is currently working on this topic (www.http://www.coreorganic2.org/Upload/CoreOrganic2/Document/Leaflet_AuthenticFood_2012.pdf) and the second approach authenticity can be understood as a counterweight to the growing trend of food globalization. More and more people look for food from safe sources, produced locally by the well-known manufacturers. Nowadays, food is transported from long distances, from the place of production by the place of processing up to the point of sale. As a result, consumers look for products less intensively processed, derived from known safe sources such as buying locally and directly from the farmer. The average food transport route from the place of production to the place of consumption in America is approximately 2,000 km (Wilkins and

Gussow, 1997). There are scientific studies showing that it is possible to satisfy the nutritional needs of consumers with the State of New York based mainly on food produced locally. On the other hand, local agriculture in this state disappeared almost completely, although most consumers of the State of New York evaluated the local varieties of vegetables and fruits better (Wilkins and Gussow, 1997). The active opposition against food globalization is represented by the movement called "slow food" - to support food production which is an alternative to "fast food".

The biological value defines the impact of food on human health. This criterion is based on the holistic approach to the food quality and on the belief that the knowledge of the chemical composition of foods is not sufficient to determine the relationship between the consumed food and the human health. At the same time health is understood not only as the absence of disease, but also as the well-being, fertility and vitality. So far, several scientific studies have been conducted with regard to this issue, but only on laboratory animals (mice, rats and rabbits). Due to many obstacles of a formal, logistic and economic nature, very few studies assessing the direct impact of organic food on human health have been carried out.

The ethical value of food quality comprise three aspects: the aspect of environmental impact, the socio-economic aspect and the farm animal welfare.

One of the main factors determining the quality of products is the quality of the environment. We can expect the best crop quality only where the air, soil, ground-and surface water meet the required quality standards. Legal regulations on organic farming does not provide specific guidance on the definition of the quality of the agricultural environment where organic production can take place. However, the guidelines elaborated by various associations of organic farming may specify requirements in this field. Organic farmers are required to maintain the environment in good condition and should try to support the cycle approach. The organic production methods are focused on the protection of all environmental components against the pressure of the agricultural aspects. Environmental impact of organic and conventional farming was researched by Tyburski and Żakowska-Biemans (2007). The authors point out that organic farming consumes less energy, which is of great importance. Nowadays, when the world is focused on energy crisis, organic agriculture achieves lower energy consumption rates because it does not apply fertilizers and pesticides, whose production requires high energy inputs. In addition, high energy lead to large emissions of greenhouse gases and the conventional farming is a very large emission source of them. Therefore, organic plant production significantly contributes to reducing greenhouse gas emissions. Furthermore, conventional agriculture leads to eutrophication and pollution of water resources, i.a. by the use of pesticides (Tyburski and Żakowska-Biemans, 2007). The biological diversity resulting from the spatial complexity of organic agricultural landscape supports three important functions: an ecological function, which is to maintain biological diversity and homeostasis; the production function, based on prevention, rather than fighting diseases and pests; and the function of the health and welfare, which results from the fact that humans are an integral part of the environment and can exist only through the harmonious coexistence with nature. Contact with nature is essential for mental health, and mental health is the foundation of physical health.

The choice of agricultural products, which are produced, processed and sold under conditions of equality and social justice is becoming increasingly popular among EU consumers. So-called "fair trade" principles implemented within developing countries are very important. By boycotting companies that do not follow the socioeconomic rules, the consumers may have a positive impact on reducing social inequalities, which are common in the production, processing and sale of agricultural products within tropical countries. Consumers have the choice because of the wide access to information about companies in the food trade market.

Furthermore, environmentally aware consumers are now more and more convinced that the methods of animal husbandry are important even during making decisions about purchasing food products. The reason is the suffering of animals, which is a result of very inappropriate conditions of animal husbandry (crowding, aggression, disease).

3. PLANT PRODUCTS

3.1. Harmful Substances

Pesticides are a group of synthetic compounds which do not occur in nature, and are introduced into environment as a deliberate human decision. Use of pesticides can increase the profitability of crops, protecting them against pests and diseases. However, the applied chemicals do not affect only the target organisms. Their residues accumulate in plants and move along the food chain, including the human body. Depending on the dose consumed by a man with the contaminated food, the consequences include various health effects. In order to reduce the adverse impact of pesticides on human health, the

Maximum Residue Limit (MRL) of pesticide, which may be present in food, has been established. MRL is usually established by testing of pesticides on rats. It is believed that the consumption of pesticides below the MRLs does not impose a health risk. However, pesticides even in low concentrations are known or suspected to be the cause of many diseases and health problems including birth defects and cancer (BMA, 1992; Howard, 2005). The main problem is that the MRLs for pesticides are usually determined by testing of individual active substances (each one) on rats for a relatively short period of time. Almost nothing is known about the effects of consuming a total of potentially hundreds of different pesticides during the whole lifetime and associated actions resulting from synergistic mixtures of pesticides. This reaction is named in literature as a 'cocktail effect'. According to Howard (2005), the most recommended way to protect ourselves is to avoid consuming all of pesticides, especially in case of pregnant women, nursing mothers and young children up to 3 years. In 1994-1999 Baker et al., (2002) analyzed in the USA the fruit and vegetables from the three types of production (organic, integrated and conventional) for pesticide residues content. According to the results, the percentage of organic crops with a known presence of pesticide residues was approximately three times lower compared to conventional crops, and about two times lower compared to the raw materials from integrated agriculture (see Figure 1). Most samples with pesticide residues were found in conventional celery, spinach, pears and apples.

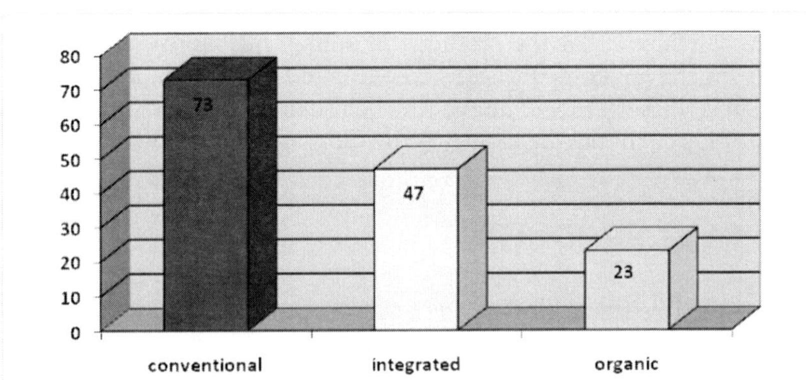

Figure 1. The comparison of contamination of agricultural crops with pesticide residues in the USA (in %) (Baker et al., 2002)

According to Lairon (2010), who reviewed the reports of French Agency of Food Safety and recent studies, from 94 to 100 per cent of organic foodstuffs contain no pesticide residues. In 1995-2001 similar survey was conducted in Belgium. The results revealed, that the percentage of organic crops contaminated with pesticides was 12%, whereas in the case of conventional crops this percentage reached 49% (AFSCA-FAVV, 2001). Research carried out in Poland gave a surprising result, as the highest percentages of crops containing pesticide residues were found in integrated agriculture, i.e. 47% (2005) and 48% (2006). Conventional agriculture presented the intermediate state between the other two management systems - 28% of raw materials in 2005 and 21% in 2006 contained pesticide residues. Crops derived from organic production were contaminated at a level of 5% (2005) and 7% (2006), which were the lowest among all three systems. The detected residues of pesticides in organic fruits and vegetables result from its unauthorized use (Gnusowski and Nowacka, 2007), which indicates the imperfect control system of organic farms conducted by certification bodies. Such situations occur not only in Poland but in all countries worldwide. It should be noted that those cases are rare and in general organic raw materials present much lower pesticide residue level compared to conventional ones. Therefore, it is expected that a diet based on organic products should result in lower levels of pesticides in breast milk and human tissues. A few studies support this hypothesis. It was found in France that pesticide residues in human breast milk decreased significantly with increasing share of organic food (from 25% to 80%) in the daily diet of lactating women (Aubert, 1987). Similar results were obtained by comparing the content of organophosphorus pesticide residues in blood and urine of children fed organically vs. conventionally (Curl et al., 2003). Body fluids of children on conventional diet contained six times more pesticide residues than children on organic diet. These results indicate that consumption of organic products can significantly reduce the risk of excess pesticide intake with food and thus improve public health.

Each year the European Food Safety Authority (EFSA) publishes a report on monitoring of pesticide contamination in the market food in 27 European Union member states and two EFTA countries (Norway and Iceland). For several years, the report has also included the studies on organic food.

According to the report for 2007, the percentage of organic food products containing residues of pesticides at levels exceeding the MRL value was much lower than for conventional products. A similar result was obtained in 2008 (see Figure 2).

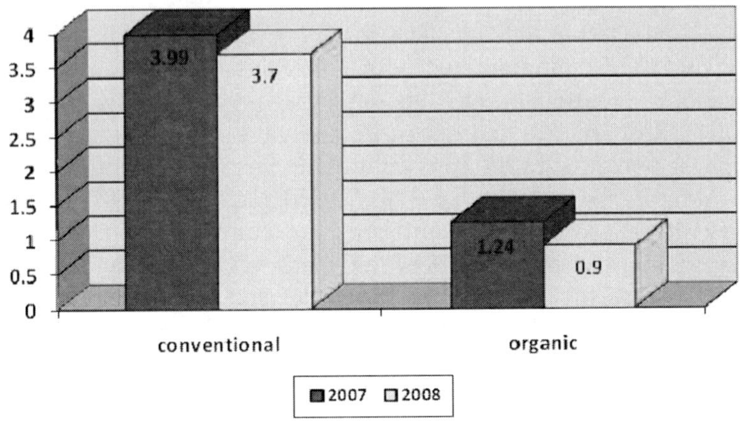

Figure 2. Samples with pesticide residues above the MRL in European food (%) (EFSA, 2009; 2010)

A number of studies clearly indicate a higher content of nitrates and nitrites in conventionally produced crops compared to organic ones. According to Lairon (2010) organic vegetables contain approximately 50% lower levels of nitrites when compared to conventional ones. This is the result of the treatment with synthetic, readily soluble nitrogen fertilizers, that is absorbed in large quantities through the root system and leads to accumulation of nitrates in the leaves and other plant organs. The organic system allows using organic fertilizers, which also contain nitrogen, but in organically bound form. When they reach the soil, followed by further decomposition of the fertilizer by soil microorganisms and by edaphon, the complex organic-mineral compound (humus) is formed. The plants get nitrogen from the humus only when they need it, so there is little possibility of excessive accumulation of nitrate in plant organs (Vogtmann, 1985). This is important for human health because the nitrates are converted into nitrites, which can cause a dangerous condition known as methemoglobinemia in case of infants, young children and older people (Mirvish, 1993). Furthermore, nitrite can react with amines to form carcinogenic and mutagenic nitrosamines, causing gastrointestinal cancers and leukemia (Szponar and Kierzkowska, 1990). This process is dangerous not only for children but also for adults of any age. Many authors compared the nitrate content in organic vs. conventional crops in the following species: white cabbage (Wawrzyniak et al., 2004; Rutkowska, 1999; Rembiałkowska, 2000), red cabbage (Rutkowska, 1999), potatoes (Hajslova et al., 2005;Rembiałkowska, 2000; Rembiałkowska, 1998), lettuce (Guadagnin et al., 2005), beetroot

(Leszczyńska, 1996; Rembiałkowska, 2000), parsley (Rutkowska, 1999), carrot (Rembiałkowska, 1998; Rutkowska, 1999; Rembiałkowska, 2000), celery (Wawrzyniak et al., 2004), Pac Choy Chinese cabbage (Wawrzyniak et al., 2004). After averaging the results of the above studies and application of a formula by Worthington (2001): (CONV-ORG) / ORG x 100%, conventional crops contain an average of 148.39% more nitrate than organic crops. The highest levels of nitrate were found in red beetroots, because they exhibit the tendency of nitrate accumulation in roots. Therefore, despite their high nutritional value we should pay particular attention to the production system, as the best choice is the organic agriculture. The data presented above provide a basis to conclude that organic system helps to reduce the intake of nitrates and nitrites by the human body.

Heavy metals such as cadmium, lead, arsenic, mercury and zinc are introduced into the food chain from various sources: industry, transport, municipal waste and agriculture. For example, mineral phosphate fertilizers used in conventional agriculture can introduce cadmium into plant crops, as well as the metal industry and transportation cause cadmium contamination of soil and crops. Therefore, there are no clear differences in the heavy metal content between organic and conventional raw materials. Some of the studies confirm the higher levels of heavy metals in conventional crops, whereas other authors show the opposite results (Rembiałkowska, 2000). Problem to be solved is whether organic farming (composting, increasing of soil organic matter, increasing soil pH, etc.) can reduce the intake of heavy metals by crops.

Mycotoxins are toxic compounds produced by fungi of the groups of *Aspergillus, Penicillium* and*Fusarium*, which are found in food products (Kouba, 2003). Production of mycotoxins depends primarily on temperature, humidity and other environmental conditions. The effect of mycotoxins consumption on human health is negative, as they perform carcinogenic properties and affect negatively the immune system. More and more studies are currently carried out in order to compare the content of mycotoxins in food products, as the consumers are becoming more aware of aspects concerning food safety. The content of mycotoxins in organic products is discussed all over the world, as the use of fungicides in organic farming is prohibited. The most important question is whether the system of agricultural production has an impact on the development of mycotoxins. Studies comparing the mycotoxins content in organic vs. conventional products show comparable amounts in both types of products, sometimes indicating lower content of mycotoxins in organic products. Spadaro et al., (2006) and Versari et al., (2007) confirmed lower amounts of mycotoxins in organic products compared to conventional ones. Even if the level of mycotoxins in organic products is higher, the differences are small and do not exceed acceptable levels (Gottschalk et al., 2007; Jestoi, 2004; Pussemier, 2004; Maeder et al., 2007). According to Lairon (2010), organic cereals contain similar levels of mycotoxins as conventional cereals. An important case is wheat, which is a commonly consumed grain in European countries (mostly in the form of bread and pasta), and may be contaminated with mycotoxins. For this reason, much research is done to ensure the food security of winter wheat. The studies revealed that the level of damage caused by *Fusarium* and the concentration of mycotoxins were lower in case of organic crops. Environmental factors have comparable impact on the content of mycotoxins as the use of varieties with high resistance (Wieczyńska, 2010).

3.2. Bioactive Substances

The nutritional value of food depends primarily on the appropriate content of compounds necessary for the proper functioning of the human body. The content of phytochemicals in plant foods is a major concern in the current food science. Secondary plant metabolites play a critical role in human health and may have a very high nutritional value (Lundegårdh and Mårtensson, 2003). Phenolic compounds are of particular interest because of their potential antioxidant activity and other healthy properties, including properties that may prevent cancer (Brandt and Mølgaard, 2001). Therefore the content of the secondary metabolites from the group of phenolic compounds in plant foods is of great interest, as more and more scientific studies are focused on comparing their content in organic and conventional products.

Secondary plant metabolites are substances naturally synthesized by the plant, but usually do not take direct part in the creation of its cells. They are usually produced as a reaction to exposure of the plant on the external stimuli, performing the functions of physiological changes regulators in case of pests attack or other stress factors (Brandt and Mølgaard, 2001). These substances include antioxidants, which protect the organism against the effects of many external factors and reduce the risk of civilization diseases (Di Renzo et al., 2007).

Plant secondary metabolites can be basically divided into compounds that do not contain nitrogen phenolic compounds, such as phenolic acids, flavonoids (six classes of them: flavones, flavonols, flavanones, flavanols, isoflavones, anticyanides) and terpenoids (e.g. tetraterpenes, carotenes, xanthophylls) and nitrogen-containing compounds (alkaloids, amines, non-protein amino acids, glycosides, glucosinolates).

Mostly discussed are flavonoids, which constitute a large group of several thousand different compounds and play an important role in healthcare, performing many functions in the human body (Bidlack, 1998). Flavonoids present strong antioxidant activity, they chelate metals, affect the immune system e.g. by inhibiting tumor growth, prevent arteriosclerosis, strengthens blood vessel walls, reduce blood clot formation and thus reduce the risk of stroke, have a protective effect for vitamin C increasing its effectiveness; prevent some bacterial and viral infections (Bidlack, 1998).

According to Brandt et al., (2011), who conducted a meta-analysis of the published comparative studies of the content of secondary metabolites in organic vs. conventional crops, organic ones contain 12% higher levels of favorable secondary metabolites than corresponding conventional fruits and vegetables.

In most studies comparing organic vs. conventional raw materials with respect to the content of secondary metabolites, the total amount of polyphenols is analysed, with no breakdown for individual compounds belonging to this group. To express the content of polyphenols in the plant, the conversion can be used, such as tannic acid (Carbonaro et al., 2002). The content of flavonoids or flavonols themselves can be expressed as equivalent amounts of quercetin (Rembiałkowska et al., 2003a and b;Young et al., 2005; Hallmann and Rembiałkowska, 2006). Moreover, Anttonen et al., (2006) analysed the organic and conventional strawberries with respect to individual substances: quercetin and kaempherol belonging to flavonols. As a separate group of polyphenolic compounds, the anthocyanins are tested in plant foods by many authors (Rembiałkowska et al., 2003 b; Rembiałkowska et al., 2004;Hallmann and Rembiałkowska, 2006; Tarozzi et al., 2006). Polyphenol content is compared by some authors as a dry matter of the product. However in most cases the content in the fresh plant product is analysed. Anyway, all of the analyzed studies - except one (Anttonen et al., 2006), which showed lower levels of one substance (kaempherol) in organic compared to conventional strawberries - indicate a significant advantage of fruits (apples, apple juice, stewed apple, peaches, pears, blackberries, strawberries, frozen strawberries, red oranges) derived from organic production (Weibel et al., 2000;Carbonaro and Mattera, 2001; Carbonaro et al., 2002; Asami et al., 2003; Rembiałkowska et al., 2003a; Rembiałkowska et al., 2004; Weibel et al., 2004; Rembiałkowska et al., 2006; Anttonen et al., 2006; Tarozzi et al., 2006). After averaging the results of the above research and application of a formula by Worthington (2001): (CONV-ORG) / ORG x 100% organic fruits contain on average 44.7% more polyphenols than conventional ones.

The studies performed on vegetables are also conducted with respect to the total polyphenol content, with no breakdown for individual substances. The comparative research shows that organic vegetables (frozen corn, tomatoes, Pac Choi Chinese cabbage, lettuce, red peppers and onions) contain significantly more polyphenols than conventional vegetables (Asami et al., 2003; Rembiałkowska et al., 2003b; Young et al., 2005; Hallmann et al., 2005; Hallmann and Rembiałkowska, 2006). After averaging the results of the above research and application of a formula by Worthington (2001): (CONV-ORG) / ORG x 100% organic vegetables contain on average 57.4% more polyphenols than conventional ones.

Carotenoids are another group of secondary metabolites of plants, characterized by strong antioxidative properties. They include over 600 pigments, which give the plants yellow, orange and red color. Carotenoids are also found in green leafy vegetables, but their color is masked by the green chlorophyll. The best-known carotenoid is beta-carotene found in many orange and yellow fruits and green leafy vegetables. Lycopene gives tomatoes intensive red color. Lutein and zeaxanthin make corn yellow. Carotenoids play an important role for human health, as they lower the blood cholesterol level, and thus favorably affect the heart. Moreover, they support the immune system - especially beta-carotene, which stimulates the increased number of lymphocytes. Carotenoids also exhibit antitumor activity, mainly thanks to its antioxidant properties (Stracke et al., 2008).

The comparative studies performed with respect to total carotenoid content in organic and conventional vegetables revealed the highest differences in case of pepper (Perez-Lopez et al., 2007). Slightly higher content of carotenoids (1.13%) was also found in organic tomatoes (Caris-Veyrat et al., 2004;Toor et al., 2006; Rickman Pieper and Barrett, 2009; Juroszek et al., 2009). The content of beta-carotene in organic carrots was higher, according to research by Abele (1987). By contrast Warman and Havard (1997) confirmed a lower content of beta-carotene in organic carrots. However, research by Caris-Veyrat et al., (2004) showed over 40% more beta-carotene in organic tomatoes.

The comparative studies conducted in the Organic Food Department of Warsaw University of Life Sciences confirmed significantly higher amount of beta-carotene in organic tomatoes and peppers (Rembiałkowska et al., 2003b; Hallmann et al., 2005; Hallmann et al.,

2007), lutein in organic pepper (Hallmann et al., 2005; Hallmann et al., 2007) and total carotenoids in organic peppers (Hallmann et al., 2007; Hallmann et al., 2008; Hallmann and Rembiałkowska, 2008 a). However, higher lycopene content in organic material were found only in tomato juice (Hallmann and Rembiałkowska, 2008 b), whereas less lycopene in organic tomatoes and green peppers were found in comparison to conventional crops (Hallmann et al., 2005; Hallmann et al., 2007; Rembiałkowska et al., 2005;Hallmann and Rembiałkowska, 2007a and b; Hallmann and Rembiałkowska, 2008a).

The group of favourable antioxidants include also vitamin C, which performs fundamental metabolic functions in the human body. First of all it ensures the proper functioning of the immune system. Furthermore, it supports the biosynthesis of collagen, accelerates the process of wound healing and development of bones. In addition, it participates in the metabolism of fats, cholesterol and bile acids, regenerates vitamin E and other low molecular antioxidants such as glutathione and a has a stabilizing effect in relation to the flavonoids. Vitamin C exhibits bacteriostatic properties and even bactericidal activity against some pathogens. It supports the absorption of non-haem iron and is involved in the production of red blood cells. Vitamin C inhibits the formation of carcinogenic nitrosamines, thus it reduces the negative effect of nitrate intake (Mirvish, 1993).

Except two studies, which confirmed lower vitamin C content in organic frozen corn (Asami et al., 2003) and organic tomatoes (Rembiałkowska et al., 2003b), most of the results revealed that organic crops were characterized by a higher content of vitamin C: spinach (Schuphan, 1974; Vogtmann et al., 1984), celery (Schuphan, 1974; Leclerc et al., 1991), kale (Schuphan, 1974), cabbage (Rembiałkowska, 1998; Rembiałkowska, 2000), lettuce (Schuphan, 1974), leek (Lairon et al., 1984), potatoes (Schuphan, 1974; Petterson, 1978; Fischer and Richter, 1984; Rembiałkowska and Rutkowska, 1996; Rembiałkowska, 2000; Hajslova et al., 2005), Swiss chard (Moreira et al., 2003), onion (Hallmann and Rembiałkowska, 2006), tomatoes (Rembiałkowska et al., 2003b; Rembiałkowska et al., 2005; Hallmann et al., 2005), pepper (Hallmann et al., 2005; Hallmann et al., 2007), apples (Rembiałkowska et al., 2003a) and oranges (Rapisarda et al., 2005). After averaging the results of the above research and application of a formula by Worthington (2001): (CONV-ORG) / ORG x 100% organic materials contain on average 32.2% more vitamin C than conventional products. Recent meta-analysis of the various vitamins in vegetables and fruits showed that the organic raw materials contained on average 6.3% more vitamins than conventional raw materials, but the difference was not statistically significant (Hunter et al., 2011).

Summary of studies comparing the mineral content in organic vs. conventional vegetables (Worthington, 2001) indicates a higher content of minerals (iron, magnesium and phosphorus) in organic crops. According to the author, a possible reason of a higher content of mineral elements in organic raw materials is associated with a higher content of microorganisms in organically cultivated soil. The microorganisms generate compounds that support plants in introducing active substances adsorbed by soil minerals, making them more available for plant roots. Recent meta-analysis of mineral content showed that organic fruits and vegetables contain an average 5.5% more minerals than conventional ones (Hunter et al., 2011), and the difference was statistically significant. This was found with respect to boron, copper, magnesium, molybdenum, potassium, phosphorus, selenium, sodium and zinc. According to Lairon (2010), organic plant products contain higher concentrations of iron and magnesium, which can be explained with abovementioned factors.

There are several studies confirming the higher content of total sugars in organic fruits and vegetables, including carrots, beets, red beets, potatoes, spinach, kale, cherries, red currants and apples (Zadoks, 1989; Rembiałkowska, 1998; Rembiałkowska et al., 2004; Rembiałkowska, 2000; Hallmann and Rembiałkowska, 2006; Hallmann et al., 2007). The higher sugar content is associated with higher technological quality (for instance in case of sugar beet) and also with the higher sensory quality (taste). In research carried out both by consumers and by the trained panel, vegetables and fruits produced organically are often better evaluated in terms of their sensory properties (Rembiałkowska, 2000). Numerous studies based on the food preferences were also performed on rats. The results revealed better sensory properties of organic materials (Maeder et al., 1993; Velimirov, 2001; Velimirov, 2002). Rats that were fed both with organic and conventional food presented the tendency to choose organic carrots (81% of animals) and organic wheat (68%). Smaller differences were found in the choice of apples and red beets from organic farming, which, however, were also more likely to be selected by more than half (58%) of rats.

Several studies carried out so far (Rembiałkowska, 2000; Worthington, 2001) confirmed lower total amount of protein in organic crops compared to conventional. However, the protein quality (considered as the content of essential amino acids) were found to be higher in organic crops. According to Worthington (2001), nitrogen derived from each type of fertilizer affect the quantity and quality of proteins produced by plants. A large amount of nitrogen available to plants increases the production of proteins, and reduces carbohydrate production. Furthermore, proteins produced in response to high levels of nitrogen, present lower amounts of essential amino acids, e.g. lysine, and therefore represent lower nutritional value for consumers.

The higher technological value of organic plant products results from higher dry matter content, so that organic products perform better storage quality (Bulling, 1987; Rembiałkowska, 2000). Samaras (1978) confirmed that the main impact on the amount of weight loss after storage of vegetables is the type of fertilizer applied to them. All tested root vegetables (carrots, turnips, beets and potatoes), which were grown with organic fertilizer were characterized by much lower storage losses. The higher storage losses of vegetables grown with mineral fertilizer may be associated with a higher content of water absorbed by the plant, along with easily soluble mineral compounds. The average storage losses of crops grown with mineral fertilizers were 46.4% of the initial mass, whereas in case of crops grown with organic fertilization the losses were 28.9% (Samaras, 1978). Bulling (1987) made a set of studies comparing the differences in the storage losses between organic and conventional vegetables and fruits. Average values for the organic raw materials tested in 53 different studies were found to be 10% lower than for conventional crops. These properties are important both from nutritional and economic point of view. The hypothesis that plant materials from organic production is better to store was also confirmed by Benbrook (2005). Higher dry matter content of organic raw materials were observed in carrots (Velimirov, 2005), apples (Weibel, 2004; Rembiałkowska et al., 2004), potatoes (Rembiałkowska, 2000), strawberries (Reganold et al., 2010). However, Gąstoł et al., (2009) found lower dry matter content of organic apples and black currant than in conventional ones.

4. ANIMAL PRODUCTS

Principles of organic animal husbandry refer to animal welfare (indoor farm density, access to open air, the presence of natural bedding, the possibility of movement), the nutrition (prohibition on synthetic feed additives) and rearing conditions (choice of breed, conditions of weaning and slaughter). Furthermore, organic livestock production is carried out without the use of antibiotics (except the situations, when the life of animal is endangered and there are no other therapeutic agents available), hormones, genetically modified organisms and their products. Organically reared animals can be fed only with organic materials.

A key factor determining the quality of animal products is the animal feed, which in case of organic agriculture involves the use of seasonal grazing and cutting down on feed concentrates, which is beneficial for the content of bioactive substances in meat and milk.

4.1. Meat

Meat derived from organic farming perform desirable nutritional properties, such as favorable ratios of fatty acids. This means the lower content of saturated and monounsaturated fatty acids, the higher content of polyunsaturated fatty acids, and a lower ratio of n-6 fatty acids to n-3 fatty acids. The meat produced organically exhibits also lower total fat content, which has been confirmed for: beef (Enser et al., 1998; Pastushenko et al., 2000), pork (Hansen et al., 2006; Bee et al., 2004; Nilzen et al., 2001;Kim et al., 2009), sheep (Fisher et al., 2000; Enser et al., 1998), lamb (Angood et al., 2007), poultry (Castellini et al., 2002). The studies conducted on poultry revealed different results, as higher content of saturated fatty acids was found in organic meat. However, it exhibited lower content of monounsaturated fatty acids and higher levelpolyunsaturated fatty acids. In turn, results obtained by Walshe et al., (2005) confirmed higher total fat content in organic beef, but comparable fatty acid composition in both types of meat. Research carried out on rabbit meat by Pla (2008) and Combes et al., (2003a) revealed a lower total fat content in meat derived from organically reared rabbits. However, Lebas et al., (2002) obtained opposite results.

Figure 3 below presents the comparison of fatty acid profile of *M. longissimus* muscle between organic and conventional pork derived from Korean black pigs (Kim et al., 2009).

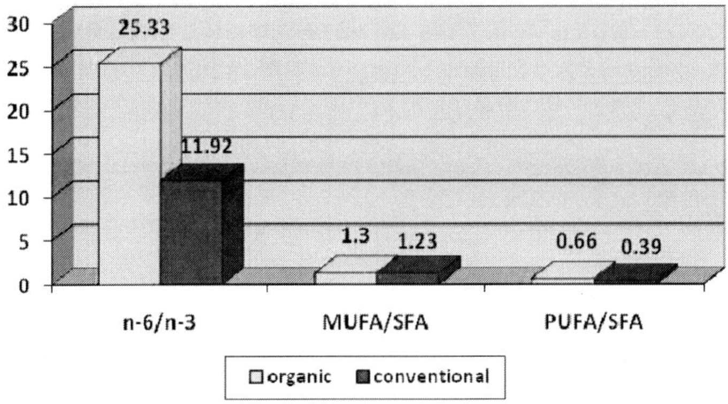

Figure 3. Fatty acid profile of organic and conventional pork from Korean black pigs (Kim et al., 2009)

Most of the studies confirm a higher content of intramuscular fat in organic meat, which was found in beef (Woodward and Fernandez, 1999), pork (Sundrum and Acosta, 2003; Millet et al., 2004), mutton (Fisher et al., 2000). The higher intramuscular fat content is associated with better sensory quality of meat from organic production. Only research done by Olsson et al., (2003) indicated a lower content of intramuscular fat and a lower lean body mass in organic pork.

As far as sensory quality is concerned, the darker meat color was identified in the case of organic pork (Kim et al., 2009; Millet et al., 2004) and sheep (Fisher et al., 2000). Research conducted by Fisher et al., (2000) found that organic lamb meat is preferred much more than conventional because of the sensory properties. Castellini et al., (2002) demonstrated with the sensory profile that the organic poultry is more juicy and acceptable than conventional. According to Combes et al., (2003b), the organic rabbit meat is softer than conventional. The sensory assessment done by Pla (2008) confirmed that organic rabbit meat exhibited more liver flavor and less anise and grass taste.

The adverse properties of organic meat include the lower carcass weight (lower daily weight gains), which has been confirmed for beef (Woodward and Fernandez, 1999), pork (Sundrum and Acosta, 2003; Hansen et al., 2006) and poultry (Castellini et al., 2002). However, study performed by Millet et al., (2004) indicated a higher weight gains of organic pigs in comparison to conventional ones.

Organic meat is also characterized by poor storage quality (high levels of TBARS), which was confirmed by analyses conducted on beef (Walshe et al., 2005), pork (Hansen et al., 2006; Nilzen et al., 2001), mutton (Fisher et al., 2000) and poultry (Castellini et al., 2002).

4.2. Milk

Cow's milk is very variable with respect to fat content. This fraction is formed in about 95%by triacylglycerols, which are composed of fatty acids whose chain length and degree of saturation determine the nutritional value of milk fat. Saturated fatty acids are considered as a factor adversely affecting the human health, because they contribute to the development of arteriosclerosis (Pfeuffer and Schrezenmeir, 2000) and increased levels of blood cholesterol, which leads to cardiovascular diseases (Haug et al, 2007). Among the unsaturated fatty acids, the n-3 ones pose beneficial effects on the human organism. N-3 acids affect positively the nervous system, as well as they reduce the risk of diabetes and cardiovascular diseases (Horrobin, 1993; Hu et al., 1999). The important parameter of milk quality is also the ratio of unsaturated fatty acids n-6:n-3. If the content of the first group of acids is too high, the risk of inflammation, thrombosis, and autoimmune symptoms is increased. The most important fatty acid among the n-3 acids is alpha-linolenic acid (LNA), while linoleic acid (LA) occurs in the largest quantities among the n-6 acids. As for monounsaturated fatty acids, oleic acid is the predominant one, amounting to about ¼ of the total weight of fatty acids. It supports the functioning of n-3 and n-6 acids, preventing them from oxidation, and lowers cholesterol and acts antineoplastic (Ip, 1997; Kris-Etherton et al., 1999; Mensink et al., 2003). A special place in the composition of cow's milk is conjugated linoleic acid (CLA). Cow's milk is the main source of the isomers of this compound in the human diet (Haug et al., 2004). The most important isomer (constituting about 90% of CLA) is *cis-9 trans-11*, preventing the development of cancer, heart disease and stimulating the immune system (Whigham et al., 2000). It is called rumenic acid because the rumen is the place of its synthesis from linoleic acid. Other CLA isomers (*trans-7 cis-9*, *trans-10 cis-12* and *trans-9 cis-11*) counteract obesity (by reducing fat and increasing muscle mass) and support the treatment of diabetes (Taylor and Zahradka, 2004). The content of CLA in milk fat is affected by a number of factors. First of all, it depends on the feed given to animals (Parodi, 1999), followed by seasonal variations (Parodi, 1977), the endogenous synthesis of trans-vaccenic acid (TVA) (Griinari et al., 2000) and oxidation of linoleic acid (LA) during processing (Ha et al., 1989).

The research comparing the quality of milk from different production systems is based on the analysis of particular differences in the composition of fatty acids (Molkentin and Giesemann, 2007; Butler et al., 2008). According to the results of Ellis et al., (2006) organic milk can be characterized with a significantly higher content of polyunsaturated fatty acids, including n-3 acids (the difference in comparison to conventional milk was over 60%). The ratio of n-6: n-3 was consequently lower, which is favorable from a health point of view. Moreover, the amount of polyunsaturated fatty acids relative to monounsaturated ones was found higher. The detailed results are presented in table 1. Similar conclusions were also drawn by Butler and Leifert (2009) who confirmed that the value of the ratio of n-6: n-3 in organically produced milk does not exceed 1.25, while in the conventional milk is above 2.5.

Table 1. Differences in fatty acid composition between organic and conventional milk (Ellis et al., 2006)

% FA	Conventional milk	Organic milk
SFA	67,25 ± 3,54	68,13 ± 3,51
MUFA	**27,63 ± 2,94**	**26,19 ± 3,01**
PUFA	**3,33 ± 0,66**	**3,89 ± 0,61**
total n-3	**0,66 ± 0,22**	**1,11 ± 0,25**
total n-6	1,68 ± 0,46	1,68 ± 0,44
TVA	1,75 ± 1,09	2,06 ± 0,96
CLA	0,58 ± 0,34	0,65 ± 0,28

Qualitative changes in milk, resulting from the application of ecological production system, can be also identified in the concentration of CLA (Bergamo et al., 2003; Szente et al., 2006). A study by Butler et al., (2008) revealed that its amount may be higher by up to 60% compared to the content in the conventional milk. Research byJahreis et al., (1996) confirms that the organic production of milk contributes to increased concentrations of CLA, TVA and LNA. This was also indicated by research byChin et al., (1992), Lin et al., (1995), Prandini et al., (2001), particularly in relation to CLA content in cow's milk and buffalo milk. However, few studies showed no difference in the amount of CLA between milk from both production systems (Ellis et al., 2006; Toledo et al., 2002).

Antioxidants, especially vitamin E and carotenoids, are another advantage for the consumption of organically produced milk. Their content was found higher in milk from cows from organic husbandry and this corresponds to the fact that the feeding of such cattle is based on green forage pasture (Nielsen et al., 2004; Butler et al., 2008). This has been also confirmed by the research conducted within the project QLIF (Quality Low Input Food). The level of antioxidants in organic milk was almost double compared to conventional milk (QLIF, 2008).

Palupi et al., (2012) carried out a meta-analysis of comparative studies related to the nutritional quality of organic and conventional dairy products. The authors' approach used the Hedges' d effect size method with regard to the results obtained by various authors in the last three years. The meta-analysis confirmed, that compared to conventional dairy products, organic ones exhibit significantly higher content of protein, alpha-linolenic acid, conjugated linoleic acid, transvaccenic acid, docosapentanoic acid, eicosapentanoic acid and the total n-3 fatty acids. Furthermore, the n-3:n-6 ratio was found to be significantly higher in organically produced dairy products (0,42 vs. 0,23).

Organic production implies the abandonment of the use of mineral supplements, making the content of these components generally higher in conventionally produced milk. This has been confirmed byCoonan et al., (2002), who found the deficiencies of copper, selenium, zinc, iodine and molybdenum in the organic milk. Kuusela and Okker (2007) explain this as a result of a low content of trace elements in soil within organic farms. The use of synthetic fertilizers, which increase the concentration of macro- and microelements in soil are not permitted in organic farming. The crops, which have grown within such soil, are as a consequence a poor feed for animals with respect to these components, which contributes to their deficiency in milk. However, few studies showed a higher calcium content in organically produced milk (Lund and Algers, 2003; Zadoks, 1989).

Apart from the abovementioned benefits milk of organic production has one more advantage over the conventional milk. This is a prohibition on the use of antibiotics, which are often routinely given by conventional farmers to farm animals for the purposes of prevention. In the certified organic farms such practices are prohibited. The issue of the impact of antibiotics in conventionally fed cows on the resistance of the human body to these antibiotics is still a topic of discussion. The use of synthetic hormones and genetically modified feed ingredients is also not allowed in organic system. For this reason, the residues listed above, which are frequently detected in conventional dairy products, are negligible in milk from organic production. Research conducted by

USDA (United States Department of Agriculture) confirmed this hypothesis by detecting the presence of pyretroid pesticides in 27% of conventional milk samples. Among the organic samples, only one contained a low level of these substances, while others were completely free of these contaminants (Benbrook, 2005). The analysis of heavy metals in both types of milk showed no differences between the samples, detecting low contamination of all samples (Gabryszuk et al., 2008).

Sensory quality assessments of organic and conventional milk are very rare and so far inconclusive. Research by Zadoks (1989) showed greater acceptability of conventional milk among consumers. The predominant factor responsible for this result was the peculiar smell of cow's milk, much more intense in the case of organic milk. Today's consumers are not used to such properties, preferring generally available in the market milk with a neutral smell. Croissant et al., (2007) found that consumers felt more grassy and animal smell in milk derived from organic production compared to typical conventional milk, but only when the temperature of milk was 15°C. No differences between milk from both systems were found at a temperature of milk of 7°C. The authors concluded that there are clear differences between the smell and quality of milk from organic and conventional systems, but this has no effect on consumer acceptance.

5. CONCLUSIONS

The favorable high nutritional value of food depends not only on the appropriate content of compounds necessary for the proper functioning of the human body and the low content of harmful substances. According to studies cited here, the nutrient content in plant raw materials in most cases is higher when they come from organic farming. This includes the compounds belonging to the desirable antioxidants: vitamin C, phenolic compounds, carotenoids, as well as sugars and dry matter. The latter two components both contribute to higher technological value and reduction of storage losses. Furthermore, they significantly increase the palatability of organic fruits and vegetables. As a result, the flavor of organic products may be more intense compared to conventional materials, so that consumers evaluate the taste of organic materials as more typical, characteristic of the plant, which is also confirmed by preference tests performed on animals.

In terms of pesticides and nitrates from the consumer point of view raw materials from organic production are certainly safer than conventional. The level of mycotoxins is dependent not only on the production system, but is also affected by storage and weather conditions. Studies show that there are no significant differences in the content of cereals with mycotoxins between organic and conventional products.

Meat derived from organically reared animals exhibit positive quality characteristics, such as favorable ratios of fatty acids and low total fat content. Organic meat is also better evaluated according to their sensory qualities, which is associated with a higher intramuscular fat content. The unfavorable properties of organic meat include lower carcass weight (lower daily weight gain), and inferior storage quality (high levels of TBARS).

Milk from organic production is characterized by a favorable fatty acid composition (including a high content of CLA), high levels of vitamins and antioxidants, acting an important part health-oriented prevention. However, due to the ban on the use of mineral supplements and fertilizers in organic farming, milk from organic production may be characterized by the deficiency of some macro- and micronutrients. Moreover, milk from organically reared animals can be worse evaluated by consumers because of the specific organoleptic characteristics, especially the smell.

According to Dangour et al., (2010) and Huber et al., (2011), the higher nutritional value of organic foodstuffs cannot be simply considered as an evidence, that consumption of organic food contributes to the improvement of consumers' health. Based on the research carried out so far, no clear relationship between nutritional value and health effects can be defined. Evidence for such effects are still lacking, therefore more developed studies are needed to determine the nutrition-related health effects that result from the consumption of organic products.

ACKNOWLEDGEMENTS

We are very grateful to dr Johannes Kahl from University of Kassel, Dep. Organic Food Quality and Food Culture for his careful pre-review and amendments.

REFERENCES

1. U. Abele, 1987Produktqualität und Düngung- mineralisch, organisch, biologisch-dynamisch. Angewendte Wissenschaft (Schriftenreihe des Bundesministers für Ernährung, Landwirtschaft und Forsten), Heft 345.

2. AFSCA-FAVV,2001Chemical safety of organically produced foodstuffs. Report from the scientific committee of the Belgian federal agency for the safety of the food chain (AFSCA-FAVV), Brussels.

3. K. M. Angood, J. D. Wood, G. R. Nute, F. M. Whittington, S. I. Hughes, P. R. Sheard, 2008A comparison of organic and conventionally-produced lamb purchased from three major UK supermarkets: Price, eating quality and fatty acid composition. Meat Science 78176184

4. M. J. Anttonen, K. I. Hoppula, R. Nestby, M. J. Verheul, R. O. Karjalainen, 2006Influence of fertilization, mulch color, early forcing, fruit order, planting date, shading, growing environment, and genotype on the contents of selected phenolics in strawberry (Fragaria × ananassaDuch.) fruits. J Agric Food Chem, 5426142620

5. D. K. Asami, Y. Hong, J. , D. M. Barrett, A. E. Mitchell, 2003Comparison of the Total Phenolic and Ascorbic Acid Content of Freeze-Dried and Air-Dried Marionberry, Strawberry, and Corn Grown Using Conventional, Organic, and Sustainable Agricultural Practices. J. Agric. Food Chem., 5112371241

6. C. Aubert, 1987Pollution du lait maternel, une enquete de Terre vivante. Les Quatre Saisons du Jardinage, 423339

7. B. P. Baker, C. M. Benbrook, E. Groth, K. L. Benbrook, 2002Pesticide residues in conventional, integrated pest management (IPM)-grown and organic foods: insights from three US data sets. Food Additives and Contaminants, 19427446

8. G. Bee, G. Guex, W. Herzog, 2004Free-range rearing of pigs during the winter: Adaptations in muscle fiber characteristics and effects on adipose tissue composition and meat quality traits. J. Anim. Sci. 8212061218

9. C. M. Benbrook, 2005FAQS on Pesticides in Milk. Organic Center.Calculated from USDA's Pesticide Data Program.

10. P. Bergamo, E. Fedele, L. Iannibeli, G. Marzillo, 2003Fat-soluble vitamins contents and fatty acid composition in organic and conventional Italian dairy products. Food Chemistry 82625631

11. W. W. Bidlack, 1998Functional Foods. Biochemical and Processing Aspects. G. Mazza, red. Lancaster, PA: Technomic Publishing Co., Inc., 437

12. BMA,1992The BMA guide to pesticides, chemicals and health. Report of science and education. British Medical Association, UK.

13. K. Brandt, J. P. Molgaard, 2001Organic agriculture: does it enhance or reduce the nutritional value of plant foods? J. Sci. Food Agric. 81924931

14. K. Brandt, C. Leifert, R. Sanderson, C. J. Seal, 2011Agroecosystem Management and Nutritional Quality of Plant Foods: The Case of Organic Fruits and Vegetables. Critical Reviews in Plant Sciences 30177197

15. W. Bulling, 1987Qualitätsvergleich von "biologisch" und "konventionell" erzeugten Feldfruchten. Regierungspräsidium, Stuttgart.

16. G. Butler, C. Leifert, 2009Effect of organic production methods on product quality and animal health and welfare; why are there differences? Proceedings of the conference on Improvement of quality of animal products obtained in sustainable production systems with special reference to bioactive components and their benefit for human health, 1415May 2009, Jastrzębiec, 88-93.

17. G. Butler, J. H. Nielsen, T. Slots, C. Seal, M. D. Eyre, R. Sanderson, C. Leifert, 2008Fatty acid and fat-soluble antioxidant concentrations in milk from high- and low-input conventional and organic systems: seasonal variation. Journal of the Science of Food and Agriculture 8814311441

18. M. Carbonaro, M. Mattera, 2001Polyphenoloxidase activity and polyphenol levels in organically and conventionally grown peach (Prunuspersica L., cv. Regina bianca) and pear (Pyruscommunis L., cv. Williams). Food Chemistry, 72419424

19. M. Carbonaro, M. Mattera, S. Nicoli, P. Bergamo, M. Cappelloni, 2002Modulation of antioxidant compounds in organic vs. conventional fruit (Peach, Prunuspersica L, and Pear, Pyruscommunis L.). J Agric Food Chem 5054585462

20. C. Caris-Veyrat, M. J. Amiot, V. Tyssandier, D. Grasselly, M. Buret, M. Mikolajczak, J. C. Guilland, C. Bouteloup-Demange, P. Borel, 2004Influence of organic versus conventional agricultural practice on the antioxidant microconstituent content of tomatoes and derived purees; consequences on antioxidant plasma status in humans. J Agric Food Chem, 5265036509

21. C. Castellini, C. Mugnai, Bosco. A. Dal, 2002Effect of organic production system on broiler carcass and meat quality. Meat Sci. 60219225

22. S. F. Chin, W. Liu, J. M. Storkson, Y. L. Ha, M. W. Pariza, 1992Dietary sources of conjugated dienoic isomers of linoleic acid, a newly recognized class of anticarcinogens. Journal of Food Composition and Analysis, 5185197

23. S. Combes, F. Lebas, H. Juin, L. Lebreton, T. Martin, N. Jehl, L. Cauquil, B. i. Darche, M. A. Corboeuf, 2003bComparaison lapin " Bio "/ lapin standard : Analyses sensorielles et tendretemecanique de la viande. 10emes Journées de la Recherche Cunicole, Paris, 137140

24. S. Combes, F. Lebas, L. Lebreton, T. Martin, N. Jehl, L. Cauquil, B. Darche, M. A. Corboeuf, 2003aComparison lapin " Bio "/ lapin standard : Caractéristique des carcasses et composition chimique de 6 muscles de la cuisse. Proc. 10emes Journées de la Recherche Cunicole, Paris, 133136

25. C. Coonan, C. Freestone-Smith, J. Allen, D. Wilde, 2002Determination of the major mineral and trace element balance of dairy cows in organic production systems. W: Proceeding of Organic Meat and Milk from Ruminants (Red.Kyriazakis, Zervas), Athens, October 4-6, 2002, EAAP Publication, 106

26. A. E. Croissant, S. P. Washburn, L. L. Dean, M. A. Drake, 2007Chemical Properties and Consumer Perception of Fluid Milk from Conventional and Pasture-Based Production Systems. Journal of Dairy Science, 901149424953

27. C. L. Curl, R. A. Fenske, K. Elgethun, 2003Organophosphate pesticide exposure of urban and suburban preschool children with organic and conventional diets. Environ Health Perspect. 111377382

28. A. D. Dangour, K. Lock, A. Hayter, A. Aikenhead, E. Allen, R. Uauy, 2010Nutrition-related health effects of organic foods:systematic review. Am J Clin Nutr 92203210

29. L. Di Renzo, D. Di Pierro, M. Bigioni, V. Sodi, F. Galvano, R. Cianci, 2007Is antioxidant plasma status in humans a consequence of the antioxidant food content influence? European review for medical and pharmacological Sciences, 185192

30. EFSA Journal,2010Scientific Report of EFSA, 2008 Annual Report on Pesticide Residues according to Article 32 of Regulation (EC) 396European Food Safety Authority. European Food Safety Authority (EFSA), Parma, Italy, 8(6): 1646.

31. EFSA Scientific Report,2009Annual Report on Pesticide Residues according to Article 32 of Regulation (EC) 396Prepared by Pesticides Unit (PRAPeR) of EFSA (Question No EFSA-Q-2008-714), 305, 1-106.

32. K. A. Ellis, G. T. Innocent, D. Grove-White, P. Cripps, W. G. Mc Lean, C. V. Howard, M. Mihm, 2006Comparing the fatty acid composition of organic and conventional milk. Journal of Dairy Science 8919381950

33. M. Enser, K. G. Hallett, B. Hewett, G. A. J. Fursey, J. D. Wood, G. Harrington, 1998Fatty acid content and composition of UK beef and lamb muscle in relation to production system and implications for human nutrition. Meat Sci. 49329341

34. A. Fischer, C. Richter, 1984Influence of organic and mineral fertilizers on yield and quality of potatoes. (W:) The Importance of Biological Agriculture in a World of Diminishing Resources (Red.Vogtmann H, Boehncke E, Fricke I). Witzenhausen.VerlagsgruppeWeiland, 1984: 236 248.

35. A. V. Fisher, M. Enser, R. I. Richardson, J. D. Wood, G. R. Nute, E. Kurt, L. A. Sinclair, R. G. Wilkinson, 2000Fatty acid composition and eating quality of lamb types derived from four diverse breedx production system. Meat Sci. 55141147

36. M. Gabryszuk, K. Słoniewski, T. Sakowski, 2008Macro- and microelements in milk and hair of cows from conventional vs. organic farms. Animal Science Papers and Reports 26 (3), 199-209.

37. M. Gąstoł, I. Domagała-Świątkiewicz, M. Krośniak, 2009Właściwości prozdrowotne produktów i przetworów uzyskanych metodą ekologiczną i konwencjonalną-analiza porównawcza. Uniwersytet Rolniczy im. Hugona Kołłątaja w Krakowie, 3032

38. B. Gnusowski, A. Nowacka, 2007Pozostałości środków ochrony roślin w polskich płodach rolnych pochodzących z różnych systemów gospodarowania. FragmentaAgronomica 3 (95), 121-125.

39. C. Gottschalk, J. Barthel, G. Engelhardt, J. Bauer, K. Meyer, 2007Occurrence of type A trichothecenes in conventionally and organically produced oats and oat products. Mol.Nutr. FoodRes., 5115471553

40. J. M. Griinari, B. A. Corl, S. H. Lacy, P. Y. Chouinard, K. V. V. Nurmela, D. E. Bauman, 2000Conjugated linoleic acid is synthesized endogenously in lactating dairy cows by Δ9-desaturase. Journal of Nutrition, 13022852291

41. S. G. Guadagnin, S. Rath, F. G. R. Reyes, 2005Evaluation of the nitrate content in leaf vegetables produced through different agricultural systems. Food Additives and Contaminants, 221212031208

42. Y. L. Ha, N. K. Grimm, M. W. Pariza, 1989Newly recognized anticarcinogenic fatty acids: identification and quantification in natural and processed cheese. Journal of Agricultural and Food Chemistry, 377581

43. J. Hajslova, V. Schulzova, P. Slanina, K. Janne, K. E. Hellenas, Ch. Andersson, 2005Quality of organically and conventionally grown potatoes: Four-year study of micronutrients, metals, secondary metabolites, enzymic browning and organoleptic properties. Food Addit. Contam. 22514534

44. E. Hallmann, E. Rembiałkowska, 2006Zawartość związków antyoksydacyjnych w wybranych odmianach cebuli z produkcji ekologicznej i konwencjonalnej. Journal of Research and Applications in Agricultural Engineering 51 (2), 42- 46.

45. E. Hallmann, E. Rembiałkowska, 2007aZawartość związków bioaktywnych w owocach papryki z uprawy ekologicznej i konwencjonalnej. ŻywienieCzłowieka i Metabolizm, XXXIV, 538543

46. E. Hallmann, E. Rembiałkowska, 2007bComparison of the nutritive quality of tomato fruits from organic and conventional production in Poland. Proceedings of the 3rd International Congress of the European Integrated Project Quality Low Input Food (QLIF) (Red. U. Niggli i in.), University of Hohenheim, Germany, March 20-23: 131-135

47. E. Hallmann, E. Rembiałkowska, 2008aThe content of selected antioxidant compounds in bell pepper varieties from organic and conventional cultivationbefore and after freezing process. Proceedings of the Second Scientific Conference of the International Society of Organic Agriculture Research (ISOFAR) (Red.D. Neuhoff I in.).Modena, 18-20 June, 2

48. E. Hallmann, E. Rembiałkowska, 2008bOcena wartości odżywczej i sensorycznej pomidoróworaz soku pomidorowego z produkcji ekologicznej i konwencjonalnej. Journal of Research and Applications in Agricultural Engineering, 53/ 38895

49. E. Hallmann, E. Rembiałkowska, L. Kaproń, 2005Zawartość związków bioaktywnych w pomidorach i papryce z uprawy ekologicznej i konwencjonalnej. Wybrane zagadnienia ekologiczne we współczesnym rolnictwie. Monografia, PIMR, Poznań, tom 2258263

50. E. Hallmann, E. Rembiałkowska, A. Szafirowska, K. Grudzień, 2007Znaczenie surowców z produkcji ekologicznej w profilaktyce zdrowotnej na przykładzie papryki z uprawy ekologicznej. Roczniki PZH 2007, 58/17782

51. E. Hallmann, M. Sikora, E. Rembiałkowska, 2008Porównanie zawartości związków przeciwutleniających w owocach papryki świeżej i mrożonej pochodzącej z uprawy ekologicznej i konwencjonalnej. PostępyTechnikiPrzetwórstwaSpożywczego, 18/13033

52. L. L. Hansen, C. Cludi-Magnussen, S. K. Jensen, H. J. Andersen, 2006Effect of organic production system on performance and meat quality. Meat Sci. 74605615

53. N. Hassold-Piezunka, 2003Eignung des Chroma-Boden-Tests zur Bestimmung von Kompostqualität und Rottegrad. Pracadoktorska.Universität Oldenburg.

54. A. Haug, A. T. i. Hostmark, O. M. Harstad, 2007Bovine milk in human nutrition-a review. Lipids in Health and Disease 6, 25 (www.lipidworld.com/content/6/I/25).

55. A. Haug, O. Taugbol, E. S. Olsen, A. S. Biong, O. M. Harstad, 2004Milk fat in human nutrition. Studies in dairy cows with special reference to CLA. Animal Science Papers and Reports, 223

56. D. F. Horrobin, 1993Fatty acid metabolism in health and disease: the role of delta-6desaturase. American Journal of Clinical Nutrition 57, 732S-736S.

57. V. Howard, 2005Pesticides and Health. W: A lecture at the Congress: "Organic Farming, Food Quality and Human Health". 56January 2005, Newcastle, UK.

58. F. B. Hu, M. J. Stampfer, J. E. Manson, E. B. Rimm, A. Wolk, G. A. Colditz, C. H. Hennekens, W. C. Willett, 1999Dietary intake of {alpha}-linolenic acid and risk of fatal ischemic heart disease among women. American Journal of Clinical Nutrition 69(5), 890- 897.

59. M. Huber, E. Rembiałkowska, D. Średnicka, S. Bügel, L. P. L. van de Vijver, 2011Organic food and impact on human health: Assessing the status quo and prospects of research. Wageningen Journal of Life Sciences 58103109

60. D. Hunter, M. Foster, J. O. Mc Arthur, R. Ojha, P. Petocz, S. Samman, 2011Evaluation of the Micronutrient Composition of Plant Foods produced by Organic and Conventional Agricultural Methods. Critical Reviews In Food Science and Nutrition, 51571582

61. C. Ip, 1997Review of the effects of trans fatty acids, oleic acid, n-3 polyunsaturated fatty acids, and conjugated linoleic acid on mammary carcinogenesis in animals. American Journal of Clinical Nutrition 66, 1523S-1529S.

62. G. Jahreis, J. Fritsche, H. Steinhart, 1996Monthly variations of milk composition with special regards to fatty acids depending on season and farm management systems-conventional versus ecological. Fett/Lipid, 98365369

63. M. Jestoi, M. C. Somma, M. Kouva, P. Veijalainen, A. Rizzo, A. Ritieni, K. Peltonen, 2004Levels of mycotoxins and sample

cytotoxicity of selected organic and conventional grain-based products purchased from Finnish and Italian markets. Mol.Nutr. FoodRes, 48299307

64. P. Juroszek, H. M. Lumpkin, R. Yang, Y. , D. R. Ledesma, C. , H. , 2009Fruit Quality and Bioactive Compounds with Antioxidant Activity of Tomatoes Grown On-Farm: Comparison of Organic and Conventional Management Systems. Journal of the Agricultural and Food Chemistry, 5711881194

65. J. Kahl, N. Busscher, A. Ploeger, 2010Questions on the Validation of Holistic Methods of Testing Organic Food Quality. Biological Agriculture and Horticulture, 278194

66. D. H. Kim, P. N. Seong, S. H. Cho, J. H. Kim, J. M. Lee, C. Jo, D. G. Lim, 2009Fatty acid composition and meat quality traits of organically reared Korean native black pigs. Livestock Science 120200996102

67. M. Kouba, 2003Quality of organic animal products. Livestock Production Science, 803340

68. P. M. Kris-Etherton, T. A. Pearson, Y. Wan, R. L. Hargrove, K. Moriarty, V. Fishell, T. D. Etherton, 1999High-monounsaturated fatty acid diets lower both plasma cholesterol and triacylglycerol concentrations. American Journal of Clinical Nutrition 70100915

69. I. Kummeling, C. Thijs, M. Huber, L. P. van de Vijver, B. E. Snijders, J. Penders, F. Stelma, R. van Ree, Brandt. P. A. van den, P. C. Dagnelie, 2008Consumption of organic foods and risk of atopic disease during the first 2 years of life in the Netherlands. Br. J. Nutr. 99(3), 598-605.

70. E. i. Kuusela, L. Okker, 2007Influence of organic practices on selenium concentration of tank milk-a farm study. Journal of Animal and Feed Sciences 16, Suppl. I, 97101

71. D. Lairon, E. Termine, S. Gauthier, M. Trouilloud, H. Lafont, J. Hauton, Ch, 1984Effects of Organic and Mineral Fertilization on the Contents of Vegetables in Minerals, Vitamin C and Nitrates, W: The Importance of Biological Agriculture in a World of Diminishing Resources. Proc. (Red.H.Vogtmann i in.), 5th IFOAM Conference, Verlagsgruppe, Witzenhausen.

72. D. Lairon, 201, 2010Nutritional quality and safety of organic food.A review.Agron Sustain Dev 303341

73. F. Lebas, L. Lebreton, T. Martin, 2002Statistics on organic production of rabbits on grassland. Cuniculture 1647480

74. J. Leclerc, M. L. Miller, E. Joliet, G. Rocquelin, 1991Vitamin and Mineral Contents of Carrotand Celeriac Grown under Mineral or Organic Fertilization, Biological Agriculture and Horticulture, 7339348

75. T. Leszczyńska, 1996Azotany i azotyny w warzywach pochodzących z upraw konwencjonalnych i ekologicznych, Bromat. ChemiaToksykol., 293289293

76. H. Lin, T. D. Boylston, M. J. Chang, L. O. Luedcke, T. D. Shultz, 1995Survey of the conjugated linoleic acid contents of dairy products. Journal of Dairy Science, 7823582365

77. V. Lund, B. Algers, 200, 2003Research on animal health and welfare in organic farming- a literature review.Livestock Production Science. 805568

78. B. Lundegardh, A. Martensson, 2003Organically Produced Plant Food Evidence of Health Benefits. Soil and Plant Sci., 53315

79. P. Maeder, D. Hahn, D. Dubois, L. Gunst, T. Alföldi, H. Bergmann, M. Oehme, R. Amado, H. Schneider, U. Graf, A. Velimirov, A. Fließbach, U. Niggli, 2007Wheat quality in organic and conventional farming: results of a 21 year field experiment, J. Sci. Food Agric. 8718261835

80. P. Maeder, L. Pfiffner, U. Niggli, U. Balzer, F. Balzer, K. Plochberger, A. Velimirov, J. Besson-M, 1993Effect of three farming systems (bio-dynamic, bio-organic, conventional) on yield and quality of beetroot (Beta vulgaris L. var. esculenta L.) in a seven year crop rotation. Acta Hor., 3391031

81. R. P. Mensink, P. L. Zock, A. D. i. Kester, M. B. Katan, 2003Effects of dietary fatty acids and carbohydrates on the ratio of serum total to HDL cholesterol and on serum lipids and apolipoproteins: a meta-analysis of 60 controlled trials. American Journal of Clinical Nutrition 77114655

82. S. Millet, M. Hesta, M. Seynaeve, E. Ongenae, S. De Smet, J. i. Debraekeleer, G. P. J. Janssens, 2004Performance, meat and

carcass traits of fattening pigs with organic versus conventional hausing and nutrition. Livest. Prod. Sci. 87109119

83. S. S. Mirvish, 1993Vitamin C inhibition of N-nitroso compounds formation. Am. J. Clin. Nutr. 57598599

84. J. Molkentin, A. Giesemann, 2007Differentiation of organically and conventionally produced milk by stable isotope and fatty acid analysis. Analytical and Bioanalytical Chemistry 388(1), 297-305.

85. M. R. Moreira, S. I. Roura, C. E. Del Valle, 2003Quality of Swiss chard produced by conventional and organic methods. Lebensm.-Wiss. U.-Technol., 36135141

86. J. H. Nielsen, T. Lund-Nielsen, L. Skibsted, 2004Higher antioxidant content in organic milk than in conventional milk due to feeding strategy. DARCOFenews, Newsletter from Danish Research Centre for Organic Farming, 3 (http://www.darcof.dk/enews/sep04/milk.html).

87. V. Nilzen, J. Babol, P. C. Dutta, N. Lundeheim, A. C. Enfält, K. Lundstrom, 2001Free range rearing of pigs with access to pasture grazing- effect on fatty acid composition and lipid oxidation products. Meat Sci. 58267275

88. V. Olsson, K. Andersson, I. Hansson, K. Lundström, 2003Differences in meat quality between organically and conventionally produced pigs. Meat Sci. 64 (3), 287-297.

89. E. Palupi, A. Jayanegara, A. Ploeger, J. Kahl, 2012Comparison of nutritional quality between conventional and organic dairy products: a meta-analysis. J Sci Food Agric 2012.

90. P. W. Parodi, 1977Conjugated octadecadienoic acids of milk fat. Journal of Dairy Science, 6015501553

91. P. W. Parodi, 1999Conjugated linoleic acid and other anticarcinogenic agents of bovine milk fat. Journal of Dairy Science, 8213391349

92. V. Pastushenko, H. Matthes, D. , T. Hein, Z. Holzer, 2000Impact of cattle grazing on meat fatty acid composition in relation to human health. Proc. 13th IFOAM Sci. Conf., Basel, s. 693.

93. A. J. Perez-Lopez, M. I. Fortea, F. M. Del Amor, A. Serrano-Martinez, E. Nunez-Delicado, 2007Influence of agricultural

practices on the quality of sweet pepper fruits as affected by the maturity stage. J Sci Food and Agric, 8720752080

94. B. D. Petterson, 1978A Comparison between the Conventional and Biodynamic Farming Systems as Indicated by Yields and Quality, W: International IFOAM Conference- Towards a Sustainable Agriculture- Sissach.

95. M. Pfeuffer, J. Schrezenmeir, 2000Bioactive substances in milk with properties decreasing risk of cardiovascular disease. British Journal of Nutrition 84 (1), 155-159.

96. M. Pla, 2008A comparison of the carcass traits and meat quality of conventionally and organically produced rabbits. Livestock Science 115112

97. A. Prandini, D. Geromin, F. Conti, F. Masoero, A. Piva, G. Piva, 2001Survey on the level of conjugated linoleic acid in dairy products. Italian Journal of Food Science, 13243253

98. L. Pussemier, Y. Larondelle, C. Peteghem, A. Huyghebaert, 2006Chemical safety of conventionally and organically produced food stuffs: a tentative comparison under Belgian conditions. Food control, 61421

99. QLIF (Quality Low Input Food),2008www.qlif.org

100. P. Rapisarda, M. L. Calabretta, G. Romano, F. Intrigliolo, 2005Nitrogen Metabolism Components as a Tool To Discriminate between Organic and Conventional Citrus Fruits. J. Agric. Food Chem., 2005, 53 (7), 2664-2669.

101. J. Reganold, P. Andrews, J. Reeve, L. Carpenter-Boggs, Ch. Schadt, R. Alldredge, C. Ross, N. Davies, J. Zhou, 2010Fruit and Soil Quality of Organic and Conventional strawberry Agroecosystems. PlusOne, 5/ 9123137

102. E. Rembiałkowska, 1998Badania porównawcze jakości zdrowotnej i odżywczej marchwi i białej kapusty z gospodarstw ekologicznych i konwencjonalnych. Rocz. AR Pozn. CCCIV, Ogrod., 27257266

103. E. Rembiałkowska, 2000Zdrowotna i sensoryczna jakość ziemniaków oraz wybranych warzyw z gospodarstw ekologicznych. Fundacja Rozwój SGGW, Warszawa.

104. E. Rembiałkowska, M. Adamczyk, E. Hallmann, 2003aJakość sensoryczna i wybrane cechy jakości odżywczej jabłek z produkcji ekologicznej i konwencjonalnej. Bromat.Chem. Toksykol., 363340

105. E. Rembiałkowska, M. Adamczyk, E. Hallmann, 2004Porównanie wybranych cech wartości odżywczej jabłek z produkcji ekologicznej i konwencjonalnej, Bromat. Chem. Toksykol-Suplement, 201207

106. E. Rembiałkowska, E. Hallmann, M. Adamczyk, J. Lipowski, U. Jasińska, L. Owczarek, 2006Wpływ procesów technologicznych na zawartość polifenoli ogółem oraz potencjał przeciwutleniający przetworów (soku i kremogenu) uzyskanych z jabłek pochodzących z produkcji ekologicznej i konwencjonalnej. Żywność, Technologia Jakość, 1(46), Suplement, 121126

107. E. Rembiałkowska, E. Hallmann, A. Szafirowska, 2005Nutritive quality of tomato fruits from organic and conventional cultivation. Culinary Arts and Sciences V. Global and National Perspectives. (Red. Edwards, J.S.A., Kowrygo, B., Rejman, K.). 193202

108. E. Rembiałkowska, E. Hallmann, G. Wasiak-Zys, 2003bJakość odżywcza i sensoryczna pomidorów z uprawy ekologicznej i konwencjonalnej. Żywienie Człowieka i Metabolizm, 30893899

109. E. Rembiałkowska, B. Rutkowska, 1996Comparison of sensory, nutritional and storage quality of potatoes from ecological and conventional farms. W: Proc. of the 5th International Conf. "Quality for European Integration" (Red. Szafran M., Kozioł J., Małecka M.), Poznań, 382385

110. Pieper. J. Rickman, D. M. Barrett, 2009Effects of organic and conventional production systems on quality and nutritional parameters of processing tomatoes. J Sci Food Agric, 89177194

111. G. Rutkowska, 1999Badania zawartości azotanów i azotynów w warzywach uprawianych ekologicznie i konwencjonalnie. Przem. Spoż. 64749

112. J. Samaras, 1978Nachernteverhalten unterschiedlich geduengter Gemusearten mit besonderer Berucksichtigung physiologischer und mikrobiologiscer Parameter. Schriftenreihe "Lebendige Erde" Darmstadt.

113. W. Schuphan, 1974Nutritional value of crops as influenced by organic and inorganic fertilizer treatments- Qualitas Plantarum-Pl.Fds.hum.Nutr.XIII, 4333358

114. D. Spadaro, A. Ciavorella, S. Frati, A. Garibaldi, M. L. Gullino, 2008Occurrence and level of patulin contamination in conventional and organic apple juices marketed in Italy. Poster na konferencji: Cultivating the Future Based on Science: 2nd Conference of the International Society of Organic Agriculture Research ISOFAR, Modena, Italy, June 1820

115. B. A. Stracke, C. E. Rüfer, A. Bub, K. Briviba, S. Seifert, C. Kunz, B. Watzl, 2008Bioavailability and nutritional effects of carotenoids from organically and conventionally produced carrots in healthy men, Br. J. Nutr. Forthcoming, 19

116. A. Sundrum, A. Y. Acosta, 2003Nutritional strategies to improve the sensory quality and food safety of pork while improving production efficiency within organic framework conditions. Report of EU-project, Improving Quality and Safety and Reduction of Costs in the European Organic and 'Low Input' Supply Chain, CT-2003 506358.

117. V. Szente, S. Szakaly, Z. S. Bukovics, O. Szigeti, Z. S. Polereczki, O. Szekely, S. Z. Berke, G. Y. Takacs, Farkas. R. Nagyne, Z. Szakaly, 2006 The role of CLA content of organic milk in consumers' healthcare. Materiały konferencyjne Joint Organic Congress, Odense, Denmark (www.orgprints.org/7207/).

118. L. Szponar, E. Kierzkowska, 1990Azotany i azotyny w środowisku oraz ich wpływ na zdrowie człowieka. Post.Hig. Med. Dośw. 44327350

119. A. Tarozzi, S. Hrelia, C. Angeloni, F. Morroni, P. Biagi, M. Guardigli, G. Cantelli-Forti, P. Hrelia, 2006 Antioxidant effectiveness of organically and non-organically grown red oranges in cell culture systems. Eur J Nutr45152158

120. G. C. Taylor, P. Zahradka, 2004 Dietary conjugated linoleic acid and insulin sensitivity and resistance in rodent models. American Journal of Clinical Nutrition 79 (Supl.6), 1164S-1168S.

121. P. Toledo, A. Andren, L. Bjorck, 2002Composition of raw milk from sustainable production systems. International Dairy Journal 127580

122. R. K. Toor, G. P. Savage, A. Heeb, 2006Influence of different types of fertilizers on the major antioxidant components of tomatoes. J Food Comp Anal, 192027

123. J. Tyburski, S. Żakowska-Biemans, 2007Wprowadzenie do rolnictwa ekologicznego. Wydawnictwo Szkoły Głównej Gospodarstwa Wiejskiego, Warszawa.

124. A. Velimirov, 2001Ratten bevorzugen Biofutter. Oekologie & Landbau 1171921

125. A. Velimirov, 2002Integrative Qualitaetsmethoden im Zusammenhang mit der P-Wert Bestimmung. Tagungsband 9. Internationale Tagung Elektrochemischer Qualitaetstest, 30.05.-01.06.2002, Institut fuer Gemuesebau und Blumenproduktion, Mendel-Universitaet.

126. A. Velimirov, 2005The consistently superior quality of carrots from one organic farm in Austria compared with conventional farms. 15th IFOAM Organic World Congress "Researching and Shaping Sustainable Systems", Adelaide, 21.-23.

127. A. Versari, G. P. Parpinello, A. U. Mattioli, 2007Survey of Patulin Contamination in Italian Apple Juices from Organic and Conventional Agriculture. J of Food Technology, 52143146

128. H. Vogtmann, 1985Ökologischer Landbau- Landwirtschaft mit Zukunft. Pro Natur Verlag, Stuttgart.

129. H. Vogtmann, 1991W: Lassen J. Paper- Food Quality and the Consumers. 1993.

130. H. Vogtmann, A. T. Temperli, U. Kunsch, M. Eichenberger, P. Ott, 1984Accumulation of nitrates in leafy vegetables grown under contrasting agricultural systems. Biol Agric Hort, 2, 51 68.

131. B. E. Walshe, E. M. Sheehan, C. M. Delahunty, P. A. Morrissey, J. P. Kerry, 2006Composition, sensory and shelf life stability analyses of Longissimus dorsi muscle from steers reared under organic and conventional production systems. Meat Science 73319325

132. P. R. Warman, K. A. Havard, 1997Yield, vitamin and mineral contents of organically and conventionally grown carrots and cabbage. Agriculture, Ecosystems and Environment, 61155162

133. A. Wawrzyniak, J. Hamułka, M. Gołębiewska, 2004Ocena zawartości azotanów (V) i azotanów (III) w wybranych warzywach uprawianych konwencjonalnie i ekologicznie. Bromatologia i Chemia Toksykologiczna, 4341345

134. F. P. Weibel, R. Bickel, S. Leuthold, T. Alfoldi, 2000Are organically grown apples tastier and healthier? A comparative field study Rusing conventional and alternative methods to measure fruit quality. Acta. Hortic., 7417427

135. F. P. Weibel, D. Treutter, A. Haseli, U. Graf, 2004Sensory and health related quality of organic apples: a comparative field study over Tyree years using conventional and holistic methods to assess fruit quality. 11th International Conference on Cultivation Technique and Phyotpathological Problems in Organic Fruit Growing; LVWO: Weinsberg, Germany, 185195

136. L. D. Whigham, M. E. Cook, R. L. Atkinson, 2000Conjugated linoleic acid: implications for human health. Pharmacological Research 42(6), 503-10.

137. J. Wieczyńska, 2010rodowiskowe uwarunkowania występowania mikotoksyn w pszenicy ekologicznej i konwencjonalnej. SGGW, Warszawa.

138. J. L. Wilkins, J. D. Gussow, 1997Regional Dietary Guidance: Is the Northeast Nutritionally Complete? Agricultural Production and Nutrition. Proceedings of an International Conference, Boston, Massachusetts, Tufts University, Medford, MA 02155, March 19-21, 1997: 23-33.

139. B. W. Woodward, M. I. Fernandez, 1999Comparison of conventional and organic beef production systems II. Carcass characteristics. Livestock Prod. Sci. 61225231

140. V. Worthington, 2001Nutritional Quality of Organic Versus Conventional Fruits, Vegetables, and Grains, The Journal of Alternative and Complementary Medicine72

141. J. E. Young, X. Zhao, E. E. Carey, R. Welti, S. Yang-S, W. Wang, 2005Phytochemical phenolics in organically grown vegetables. Mol. Nutr. Food Res. 4911361142

142. J. C. Zadoks, 1989Development of Farming Systems, Pudoc, Wageningen.

2

FOOD INSECURITY, FOOD CHOICES, AND BODY MASS INDEX IN ADULTS: NUTRITION TRANSITION IN TRINIDAD AND TOBAGO

Martin C Gulliford, Deepak Mahabir and Brian Rocke

Department of Public Health Sciences, King's College London, Nutrition and Metabolism Division, Ministry of Health, Laventille, Trinidad and Tobago.

ABSTRACT

Background This study evaluated whether food insecurity and obesity were associated in a population sample in Trinidad.

Methods A sample was drawn of 15 clusters of households, in north central Trinidad. Resident adults were enumerated. A questionnaire was administered including the short form Household Food Security Scale (HFSS). Heights and weights were measured. Analyses were adjusted for age, sex, and ethnic group.

Results Data were analysed for 531/631 (84%) of eligible respondents including 241 men and 290 women with a mean age of 47 (range 24–89) years. Overall, 134 (25%) of subjects were classified as food insecure. Food insecurity was associated with lower household incomes and physical disability. Food insecure subjects were less likely to eat fruit (food insecure 40%, food secure 55%; adjusted odds ratio [OR] = 0.60, 95% CI: 0.36–0.99, $P = 0.045$) or green vegetables or salads (food insecure 28%, food secure 51%; adjusted OR = 0.46, 95% CI: 0.27–0.79, $P = 0.005$) on ≥5–6 days per week. Body mass index (BMI) was available for 467 (74%) subjects of whom 41 (9%) had BMI <20 kg/m^2, 157 (34%) had BMI 25–29 kg/m^2, and 120 (26%) had BMI ≥30 kg/m^2. Underweight (OR = 3.21, 95% CI: 1.17–8.81) was associated with food insecurity, but obesity was not (OR = 1.08, 95% CI: 0.55–2.12).

Conclusions Food insecurity was frequent at all levels of BMI and was associated with lower consumption of fruit and vegetables. Food insecurity was associated with underweight but not with present obesity.

Keywords: Obesity, body mass index, food insecurity, socioeconomic status, food intake, Trinidad and Tobago, West Indies

The health transition in middle-income countries is associated with falling mortality rates and the emergence of non-communicable diseases as the main causes of death.[1] As the importance of undernutrition declines, obesity has emerged as a significant public health problem.[2,3] The reasons for the increase in obesity are not fully understood but decreasing levels of physical activity and increasing availability of foods high in fat or refined carbohydrate are thought to be important contributing factors.[3,4]

In low-income countries, obesity is associated with affluence but in high-income countries obesity is more often associated with lower socioeconomic status.[5] This observation suggests that, in a more food-abundant environment, socioeconomic factors such as education and income level may modify the relationship between food availability and obesity. In the middle-income countries, these relationships are less consistent. Obesity may be associated with affluence in some situations but with poverty in others.[6] Underweight and obesity may sometimes co-exist in the same neighbourhoods,[7] or even in the same households.[8] These findings suggest an apparent paradox that obesity may exist in households that are food insecure.[9] It has been suggested that limited availability of food may lead to obesity.[9] This might occur if food insecurity leads to the consumption of obesity promoting types of food,[9] or to overeating when food becomes available, or to metabolic changes that permit more efficient use of energy.[10]

Food insecurity has been defined as the 'limited or uncertain availability of nutritionally adequate and safe foods, or limited or uncertain ability to acquire acceptable foods in socially acceptable ways'.[11] The concept of food insecurity includes problems with the quantity and quality of the food available, uncertainty about the supply of food, and experiences of going hungry.[12] Blumberg *et al.*[13] recently described a short form of the Household Food Security Scale (HFSS) which includes six items. These concern experiences of cutting the size of meals or skipping meals because of lack of money for food, being hungry but not eating because of an inability to afford food, food not lasting and not having enough money to buy more, and being unable to afford balanced meals. According to this instrument, respondents are classified as food insecure if they give affirmative responses to two of the six items.

In the Caribbean region in 2000, the per capita GNP of the English speaking countries ranged from US$2440 in Jamaica to US$4980 in Trinidad and Tobago and US$9280 in Barbados.[14] These figures contrast with values of US$24 500 in the UK and US$34 260 in the USA.[14] Food security continues to be a significant concern for public policy in the Caribbean. According to the UN Food and Agriculture Organization, 13% of the Trinidad and Tobago population were undernourished in 1997–1999.[15] Most attention has been directed at the nutritional status of children and the need to provide meals in school to increase dietary intakes in order to improve nutritional and educational outcomes.[16,17]However, in children in Trinidad and Tobago, overweight, as well as underweight, appears to be prevalent.[18] Obesity in adults is also important in the Caribbean region. Beckles *et al.* found that between 27% and 32% of women in Port of Spain, Trinidad were obese.[19] Rotimi *et al.*found that the prevalence of obesity in populations of West African descent increased with increasing economic development. Using the criterion of body mass index (BMI) ≥31.1 kg/m^2 for men and BMI ≥32.3 kg/m^2 for women, the prevalence of obesity was 10.3% in men and 30.1% in women in Barbados.[20]

In the Eastern Caribbean, a study of the relationship between food insecurity and BMI in adults is both relevant and feasible because both conditions are likely to be common. We carried out a population survey in Trinidad with the aim of evaluating the prevalence of both food insecurity and obesity, and the relationship between them. We evaluated associations of food insecurity with general health, food choices, physical activity levels, and socioeconomic status.

METHODS

Sample and subjects

We took a sample of approximately 300 households based on the resources available for the survey. The sample was drawn by the Central Statistical Office. The target area was one of the constituencies in north central Trinidad which was considered to provide a good representation of the ethnic and socioeconomic characteristics of the population of Trinidad and Tobago. The area includes a range of settings from a relatively affluent residential suburb of the capital, to areas with small houses on the lower slopes of the northern range characterized by poverty and overcrowding. The area has traditionally been involved in agriculture including market gardening, but this has declined as residential areas spread. There are also good numbers of fruit trees (mango, citrus etc.). A two-stage sampling procedure was used. At the first stage, 15 out of the 66 enumeration districts (ED) in the constituency were selected. This was done by ranking the ED according to size (number of households) then, after a random start, ED were systematically selected. At the second stage, a cluster of approximately 20 households was randomly selected from the clusters in each ED. The fieldworkers visited each household, enumerated all adults, and invited adults aged ≥25 years to participate in the survey. The study received research ethics committee approval and subjects gave written informed consent to participation.

Questionnaire

Subjects were asked to complete an interview-administered questionnaire. This included items on food choices, food security, cigarette smoking, alcohol use, physical activity, general health, and socioeconomic variables. The questionnaire was administered by trained interviewers who usually work on surveys for the Central Statistical Office. Many of the questionnaire items were adapted, with permission, from the report of the Health Survey for England 1994.[21]

The short form of the HFSS was included as described by Blumberg *et al.*[13]This instrument is also referred to as the food security core module.[22] We found that the six items were readily understood in face-to-face interviews. A short food frequency questionnaire was included. Subjects were asked how often they ate the following groups of foods: sweet biscuits or cake; fruit; green vegetables and salads; fish (including shellfish); sweets or chocolate; burgers, fried chicken or pizzas; beans, peas lentils etc.; ground provisions including yam, cassava, potatoes, dasheen, edoes etc.; roti; and rice. Categories used were more than once a day, once every day, 5–6 days a week, 3–4 days a week, 1–2 days a week, at least once a month, less than once a month, rarely or never. For analysis, for foods that were consumed frequently the categories were reduced to eaten ≥5–6 days a week or not, and for less frequently consumed foods, categories were reduced to eaten at least weekly or not. Cigarette smoking was analysed using the categories non-smoker, ex-smoker, and current smoker. Physical activity levels were analysed using two global questions from the NHANES I study:[23] 'Do you get much exercise in things you do for recreation (sport, walking for exercise, anything like that) or hardly any exercise or in between?' and 'In your usual day, aside from recreation are you physically very active, moderately active or quite inactive?' Responses to these questions were strongly associated with more detailed questions concerning recreational, work, and household activities. The questionnaire included the following item concerning physical limitation from the SF12: 'During the last 4 weeks, were you limited in the kind of work or other regular daily activities you do, as a result of your physical health?'[24] Subjects were also asked about the monthly income of their household using ten categories ranging from ≤TT$200 (US$33.3) to ≥TT$51 201 (US$8533.5). For analysis the lowest three, and highest four, categories were combined. Subjects were asked 'How would you describe your ethnic group?' Responses were classified into the categories, 'African', 'Indian', 'white', 'Chinese', 'mixed', 'other', or 'not known'. This represented a shortened form of the categories used in the Trinidad and Tobago national census.[25] For analysis the categories were further reduced to 'Afro-Trinidadian', 'Indo-Trinidadian', 'Mixed', and 'Other and not known'. Subjects were also asked about the water supply in the home, whether the head of the household was male or female, the number of adults and children in the home, their personal educational attainment, and employment status, as described previously.[18]

Measurements

Measurements of height and weight were taken by the nutritionists and food demonstrators from the Nutrition Division of the Ministry of Health. The measurement procedures generally followed those used in the Health Survey for England 1994.[21] Height was measured using a portable stadiometer (Seca 'Leicester' height pole). Values were recorded to the last complete 0.1 cm and 0.05 cm was added at the time of analysis to correct the bias. Weight was measured using portable electronic scales (Soehnle) to the nearest 0.1 kg. Waist and hip circumferences were measured using tape measures.

The waist was defined as the midpoint between the lower rib margin and the iliac crest, and the hips as the maximum circumference over the buttocks.[21] Two measurements were made but if these two measurements differed by >2 cm then a third measurement was taken. Subjects were measured in light clothing but without shoes. Fieldworkers also noted whether there was any difficulty recording any of the measurements.

Analysis

For these analyses, age was taken as the difference between the date of birth and the measurement date. For 11 cases where date of birth not available, the reported age last birthday plus one half was used. Underweight was defined as a BMI <20 kg/m^2. Overweight was defined as BMI ≥25 kg/m^2 and obesity as BMI ≥30 kg/m^2. In order to allow for the sampling design, random effects logistic regression models were fitted using the statistical package MLwiN version 1.10.[26,27] A three-level model was specified with individuals nested within households, and households within clusters of households. Logistic regression models were fitted using first order maximum quasi-likelihood estimation because penalized quasi-likelihood estimation did not lead to convergence.[26] *P*-values were obtained by comparing the coefficient with its standard error in the three-level model. Intraclass correlation coefficients (ICC) were estimated by restricted maximum likelihood. The ICC at household level were estimated allowing for the effect of cluster of households. Adjusted means were obtained from a random effects model allowing for clustering by household only, using the 'xtreg' command with the maximum likelihood option in Stata.[28]

RESULTS

There were approximately 300 households listed, and 631 adults aged ≥25 years were enumerated. Questionnaire data were obtained for 548 (87%) subjects. Among the 15 clusters, the response rates ranged between 56% and 100% with middle class areas giving lower response rates. Measurements were obtained for 482 (76%) subjects. Two subjects for whom data were collected were aged 23.8 and 24.8 years respectively but these were included in the analyses. The mean age was 46.8 years (SD 14.1 years, range 23.8–89.1 years). There were 250 men and 298 women. The ICC for food insecurity was 0.60 at household level and 0.14 at cluster level. Ethnicity (ICC = 0.36) and household income (ICC = 0.13) were also correlated within clusters of households.

Table 1 shows the responses obtained for the six items of the HFSS, together with the distribution of summed affirmative responses. Of the 548 respondents, 17 had missing data for all items on the HFSS. These cases were excluded, and the remaining analyses were confined to 531 (84%) of subjects with data for food security with measurements available for 467 (74% total). Of these, 134 (25%) were classified as being food insecure. Among 77 subjects with missing values for income, 7 (9%) were food insecure compared with 127/454 (28%) with known income levels. In 64 subjects with missing values for BMI, 10 (16%) were food insecure compared with 124/467 (27) with known BMI.

Table 1. Responses to individual items on the Household Food Security Scale

	Total (531)
a) Affirmative responses to individual items	
Cut size of meals or skipped meals	93 (18)
If yes, how often (almost every month/some months)	70 (13)
Ate less because not enough money	75 (14)
Hungry but couldn't afford food	31 (6)
Food didn't last and no money for more (often/sometimes)	109 (21)
Couldn't afford to eat balanced meals (often/sometimes)	162 (31)
b) Summed affirmative responses	
0	339 (64)
1	58 (11)
2	44 (8)
3	25 (5)
4	22 (4)
5	27 (5)
6	16 (3)

Table 2 shows the prevalence of food insecurity according to demographic, socioeconomic, and household characteristics. Odds ratios (OR) were estimated after adjusting for age, gender, and ethnic group. Food insecurity was not associated with age or gender, but subjects of Indo-Trinidadian ethnicity were less likely to be food insecure than Afro-Trinidadians in this sample. This difference remained after additional adjustment for household income (OR = 0.25, 95% CI: 0.13–0.49). After adjusting for age, sex, and ethnicity, there was a strong negative association between household income and food insecurity (test for trend $P < 0.001$). Food insecurity was strongly associated with the presence of physical limitation ($P = 0.001$). This association was not explained by adjusting for income, in addition to age sex and ethnic group (adjusted OR = 3.12, 95% CI: 1.55–6.27). There was evidence of a negative association between increasing educational attainment and food insecurity (test for trend, $P = 0.005$). However, food insecurity was not associated with employment status, the type of water supply in the home, or whether the head of household was male or female. There was little evidence of a trend towards increasing food insecurity with increasing number of children in the family ($P = 0.176$).

Table 2. Distribution of food insecurity according to social and demographic factors. Figures are frequency (percentage)

		Food insecure/Total (%) 134/531 (25)	Odds ratio (95% CI)[a]
Gender	Men	59/241 (24)	–
	Women	75/290 (26)	1.18 (0.76–1.68)
Age group	<35	38/129 (29)	–
	35–44	32/138 (23)	0.88 (0.46–1.68)
	45–54	28/110 (25)	1.00 (0.50–1.97)
	55–64	22/82 (27)	1.23 (0.60–2.51)
	≥65	14/69 (20)	0.80 (0.36–1.78)
	Not known	0/3 (0)	–
Ethnic group	Afro-Trinidadian	69/155 (45)	–
	Indo-Trinidadian	32/246 (13)	0.31 (0.16–0.58)
	Mixed	31/106 (29)	0.56 (0.29–1.07)
	Other and not known	2/24 (8)	0.19 (0.04–0.84)
Monthly household income (US$)	≤133	35/72 (49)	–
	≤267	32/91 (35)	0.48 (0.21–1.13)
	≤533	26/110 (24)	0.32 (0.13–0.75)
	≤1067	29/89 (33)	0.52 (0.21–1.27)
	>1067	5/92 (5)	0.08 (0.02–0.27)
	Not known	7/77 (9)	0.15 (0.05–0.45)
Education	Primary	54/167 (32)	–
	Secondary	62/230 (27)	0.61 (0.34–1.10)
	Technical	9/27 (33)	0.81 (0.28–2.35)
	University	5/84 (6)	0.18 (0.06–0.54)
	Not known	4/23 (17)	0.38 (0.10–1.44)
Employment	Paid employment	86/334 (26)	–
	Looking for work	8/15 (53)	1.65 (0.48–5.72)
	Home duties	16/69 (23)	0.93 (0.42–2.04)
	Retired	15/74 (20)	0.70 (0.27–1.81)
	Disabled	6/16 (38)	1.98 (0.54–7.30)
	Other and not known	3/23 (13)	0.58 (0.14–2.41)
Physical Limitation	No	102/456 (22)	–
	Yes	31/74 (42)	2.96 (1.54–5.68)
	Not known	1/1	–

	Not known	1/1	–
Piped water in home	Yes	101/450 (22)	–
	No	33/77 (43)	1.58 (0.70–3.57)
	Not known	0/4 (0)	–
Head of household	Man	88/392 (22)	–
	Woman	46/133 (35)	1.74 (0.97–3.11)
	Not known	0/6 (0)	–
No. of children	0	50/224 (22)	–
	1	33/97 (34)	1.28 (0.62–2.63)
	2	25/105 (24)	1.01 (0.49–2.11)
	3	7/26 (27)	1.25 (0.38–4.07)
	≥4	18/38 (47)	2.20 (0.82–5.91)
	Not known	1/41 (2)	–

[a] Adjusted for age, gender, and ethnic group only.

Subjects who were food insecure were less likely to be frequent consumers of fruit or green vegetables or salads (Table 3). The single item of the HFSS to which affirmative responses were given most frequently was in response to the statement 'We couldn't afford to eat balanced meals'. Table 4 shows the association between this item and frequent consumption of fruit or vegetables. There was evidence of a trend to less frequent consumption of fruit and vegetables with decreasing ability to afford balanced meals. There were no differences according to food insecurity for consumption of rice, bread, legumes, fish, confectionery, or 'fast foods' (Table 3). Subjects who were food insecure tended to be more likely to eat 'ground provisions' (yam, cassava, potatoes, dasheen, edoes etc.) at least weekly. There were no differences in smoking habits or recreational exercise habits according to food security but the food insecure were more likely to report that they were 'quite inactive' in terms of non-recreational activity. However, this association was mostly accounted for by additionally adjusting for physical limitation (adjusted OR = 1.81, 95% CI: 0.79–4.14, $P = 0.162$).

Table 5 shows the mean values for anthropometric variables according to food insecurity for men and women, after adjusting for age and ethnicity. In the food insecure group mean weights and heights tended to be slightly lower, but this was only confirmed statistically for height in women. The distribution of the sample by BMI category is shown in Table 6. Overall, 55% of men and 62% of women were overweight or obese, and 21% of men and 29% of women were obese. The distribution of food insecurity according to BMI category is shown in Table 7. Food insecurity was common at all levels of BMI. However, the lowest frequency of food insecurity was at intermediate BMI levels (BMI 20.0–24.9 kg/m^2 in women and 25.0–29.9 kg/m^2 in men). After adjusting for age, gender, and ethnicity, compared with those of normal BMI, the relative odds of being underweight were higher for those who were food insecure (Table 8). However, food insecurity was not associated with an increased relative odds of overweight or obesity. There was no statistical evidence for an interaction between gender and BMI group in their association with food insecurity. There was no clear association between household income and BMI category (Tables 7 and 8).

Table 3. Food choices, smoking, and exercise habits according to level of food insecurity. Figures are frequency (percentage)

Food choices	Food secure (397)	Food insecure (134)	Odds ratio[a] (95% CI)	*P*-value
Whether eaten at least 5–6 days a week				
Fruit	218 (55)	53 (40)	0.60 (0.36–0.99)	0.045
Green vegetables and salad	202 (51)	37 (28)	0.46 (0.27–0.79)	0.005
Rice	254 (64)	87 (65)	0.96 (0.57–1.61)	0.874
Bread or bread rolls	272 (69)	84 (63)	0.74 (0.43–1.25)	0.260
Legumes (beans, peas, or lentils)	173 (44)	67 (50)	1.07 (0.64–1.77)	0.795
Whether eaten at least weekly				
Ground provisions[b]	253 (64)	103 (77)	1.70 (0.96–3.01)	0.069
Fish (including shellfish)	255 (64)	70 (52)	0.66 (0.40–1.10)	0.109
Sweets, chocolate etc.	116 (29)	31 (23)	0.78 (0.44–1.38)	0.388
Sweet biscuits or cakes	161 (41)	47 (35)	0.98 (0.59–1.63)	0.930
Burgers, fried chicken, or pizzas	106 (27)	40 (30)	1.23 (0.71–2.12)	0.460
Smoking habit				
Non-smoker	260 (65)	76 (57)	–	
Ex-smoker	92 (23)	25 (19)	0.73 (0.40–1.34)	0.310
Current smoker	44 (11)	33 (25)	1.53 (0.77–3.03)	0.229
Not known	1 (0)	0 (0)	–	
Recreational physical activity				
Much exercise	162 (41)	44 (33)	–	
Hardly any exercise	151 (38)	66 (49)	1.49 (0.88–2.53)	0.142
In between	82 (21)	22 (16)	0.86 (0.44–1.69)	0.670
Not known	2 (1)	2 (1)	–	
Non-recreational physical activity				
Physically very active	141 (36)	38 (28)	–	
Moderately active	207 (52)	75 (56)	1.53 (0.89–2.62)	0.121
Quite inactive	42 (11)	19 (14)	2.29 (1.04–5.07)	0.041
Not known	7 (2)	2 (1)	–	

[a] Adjusted for age, gender, and ethnic group.

[b] Yam, cassava, potatoes, dasheen, edoes etc.

Table 4. Consumption of fruit and vegetables in relation to whether subjects could afford to eat balanced meals. Figures are frequency (percentage)

Could not afford balanced meals	Total	Eaten ≥5–6 days per week	
		Fruit	Vegetables and salads
Often	24	6 (25)	5 (21)
Sometimes	138	64 (46)	43 (31)
Never	369	201 (54)	191 (52)
P-value[a]		0.034	<0.001

[a] Test for trend from three-level model.

Table 5. Mean values (standard error) for anthropometric variables adjusted for age and ethnicity, by sex and food security

	Mean (standard error) adjusted for age and ethnicity		
	Food secure	Food insecure	*P*-value
Men			
No.	146	52	
Height (cm)	171 (0.64)	170 (1.07)	0.301
Weight (kg)	77.2 (1.28)	74.9 (2.24)	0.398
Body mass index (kg/m^2)	26.2 (0.39)	25.9 (0.67)	0.618
Waist circumference (cm)	93.4 (1.03)	91.5 (1.75)	0.335
Hip circumference (cm)	102.3 (0.84)	100.5 (1.41)	0.268
Waist hip ratio	0.91 (0.01)	0.91 (0.01)	0.702
Women			
No.	197	72	
Height (cm)	159 (0.42)	157 (0.72)	0.032
Weight (kg)	70.0 (1.22)	67.7 (2.08)	0.356
Body mass index (kg/m^2)	27.5 (0.46)	27.3 (0.78)	0.792
Waist circumference (cm)	88.6 (0.89)	88.4 (1.51)	0.927
Hip circumference (cm)	105.4 (0.87)	104.2 (1.48)	0.489
Waist hip ratio	0.84 (0.01)	0.85 (0.01)	0.473

Table 6. Distribution of body mass index category by gender. Figures are frequency (percentage)

Body mass index (kg/m^2)	Men (198)	Women (269)	Total (467)
<20.0	14 (7)	27 (10)	41 (9)
20.0–24.9	75 (38)	74 (28)	149 (32)
25.0–29.9	68 (34)	89 (33)	157 (34)
≥30.0	41 (21)	79 (29)	120 (26)

Table 7. Distribution of food insecurity and household income according to body mass index category. Figures are frequency (percentage)

		Body mass index category				
	All	<20.0	20.0–24.9	25.0–29.9	≥30.0	Not known
Men	241	14	75	68	41	43
Food insecure	59	6 (43)	22 (29)	12 (18)	12 (29)	7 (16)
Household income (US$ per month)						
≤133	32 (13)	3 (21)	11 (15)	10 (15)	5 (12)	3 (7)
≤267	40 (17)	3 (21)	12 (16)	10 (15)	9 (22)	6 (14)
≤533	46 (19)	3 (21)	14 (19)	15 (22)	9 (22)	5 (12)
≤1067	46 (19)	2 (14)	15 (20)	14 (21)	7 (17)	8 (19)
>1067	45 (19)	2 (14)	9 (12)	11 (16)	7 (17)	16 (37)
Not known	32 (13)	1 (7)	14 (19)	8 (12)	4 (10)	5 (12)
Women	290	27	74	89	79	21
Food insecure	75	8 (30)	16 (22)	25 (28)	23 (29)	3 (14)
Household income (US$ per month)						
≤133	40 (14)	3 (11)	9 (12)	16 (18)	11 (14)	1 (5)
≤267	51 (18)	8 (30)	8 (11)	15 (17)	15 (19)	5 (24)
≤533	64 (22)	3 (11)	20 (27)	16 (18)	21 (27)	4 (19)
≤1067	43 (15)	4 (15)	13 (18)	14 (16)	11 (14)	1 (5)
>1067	47 (16)	5 (19)	14 (19)	17 (19)	7 (9)	4 (19)
Not known	45 (16)	4 (15)	10 (14)	11 (12)	14 (18)	6 (29)

Table 8. Relative odds of under- or overweight in relation to food insecurity and household income. Figures are odds ratios (95% CI) for body mass index (BMI) category compared with normal weight (BMI 20.0–24.9 kg/m2)

	Odds ratio (95% CI)[a]		
	Underweight (BMI <20.0)	Overweight or obese (BMI ≥25.0)	Obese (BMI ≥30.0)
Food insecurity	3.21 (1.17–8.81)[c]	1.05 (0.61–1.79)	1.08 (0.55–2.12)
Household income[b]	0.78 (0.56–1.07)[d]	0.87 (0.73–1.05)	0.86 (0.69–1.07)

[a] Adjusted for age, sex, and ethnic group. BMI 20.0–24.9 as reference.
[b] Test for linear trend.
[c] $P = 0.024$.
[d] Allowing for clustering by household only because of non-convergence with three-level model.

DISCUSSION

At the community level, food insecurity and obesity were common and often coexisted. At the level of the household and individual, low income and physical limitation were strongly associated with food insecurity. The economic situation of a substantial minority of households appeared to restrict their food choices. Consistent with this, 31% of the sample reported that they 'sometimes' or 'often' could not afford to eat balanced meals and food insecurity was associated with lower consumption of green vegetables and salads. This hypothesis that food insecurity and obesity might be associated was not supported in these cross-sectional data because food insecurity was common at every level of BMI, and there was no clear association between food insecurity and obesity.

Limitations of study

The main limitation of the study related to the size and structure of the sample. We aimed to sample an area that could be considered typical of the socioeconomic conditions of Trinidad and Tobago. However, compared with previous national studies, this sample included a higher proportion with university education and a lower proportion without piped water supply in the home.[18] The overall response rate was satisfactory but the response rate tended to be somewhat lower in more affluent areas which could have positively biased the assessment of the prevalence of food insecurity. In addition, data for household income were not obtained for 16%, and BMI for 24%, of initial responders. The strengths of the survey were the carefully standardized instruments which were administered by trained staff. The HFSS has been extensively studied in the US.[29] As Trinidad and Tobago is an English speaking country, we used the scale without modification in order to allow comparability of results. We did not attempt to specifically evaluate the questionnaire for use in Trinidad and Tobago. However, the unexplained ethnic differences in food insecurity might raise the possibility of cultural differences in response to this instrument.

Comparison with other work

Survey data suggest that up to 12% of US households may experience some food insecurity,[11] although a smaller proportion experience food insecurity with hunger.[11,12] Recent studies have associated food insecurity with BMI. Olson reported analyses of data for 193 women living in rural locations in New York state. She found that the mean BMI of women living in food insecure households was higher than for women living in food secure households. Only for women with severe food insecurity was BMI lower than for the food secure.[30] In a nationally representative sample of 6506 men and women in Finland, Sarlio-Lahteenkorva and Lahelma found that thin people showed the most food insecurity but obese subjects reported fearing or experiencing running out of money for food, and buying cheaper foods because of financial restrictions more frequently than subjects with normal BMI.[31] In data from a national US survey of food intakes, Townsend *et al.* found an association between food insecurity and overweight in women but not men.[32] Alaimo*et al.*[10] found that food insufficiency was associated with overweight in older white US girls but not in African American or Mexican American children. These studies provide preliminary evidence that food insecurity may be surprisingly frequent in high-income countries, and may be associated either with thinness or with obesity. Our results suggest that food insecurity may be more frequent in the setting of a middle-income country.

In a study from the US, Casey *et al.*,[33] found that children from low-income food insufficient families consumed less fruit. Tarasuk[34] found that Canadian women from food insecure households reported lower consumption of vegetables, fruit, and meat than women from food secure households. Kendall *et al.*[35] reported decreasing consumption of fruit and vegetables with increasing food insecurity in a rural area in New York state. These observations are consistent with our data which showed that subjects who were food insecure were less likely to eat fruit or vegetables and salads frequently.

In a study from Argentina, Aguirre observed that consumption of fruit and vegetables accounted for 19% of food consumption among the highest income quintile but 14% in the lowest income quintile.[36] She noted that the price of 500 g lettuce would buy 700 g beef or 1.5 kg of pasta or 1.4 kg of bread. The price structure of food appeared to promote the consumption of foods with higher energy content. Consumption of vegetables has been negatively associated with obesity in some studies.[37]Bell and Rolls found that in women, consumption of energy dense foods gave a 20% higher energy intake but with similar ratings for hunger or fullness.[38] Data from NHANESIII showed that consumption of energy-dense nutrient-poor foods accounted for higher energy intakes and reduced compliance with dietary recommendations.[39]

Physical limitations may prevent people gaining access to food both directly by reducing their ability to acquire food, and indirectly by influencing their ability to work and obtain income. Our results showed a strong association between food insecurity and physical limitation. Physical limitations also accounted for the lower levels of physical activity among those who were food insecure. It was difficult to account for the marked ethnic difference observed for food insecurity, which was not explained by differences in household income. It is possible that there are cultural differences in perception and reporting of food insecurity, and this possibility makes the application of more objective measures of food supply desirable.

Nutrition transition

Our results show that even in a relatively affluent middle-income country perceptions of food insecurity may be widespread, especially among those on low incomes, but at the same time obesity is also an important problem. Middle income countries are considered to be engaged in a process of nutrition transition[40] through which widespread under-nutrition is gradually replaced by a situation in which dietary intakes and physical activity patterns predispose to the development of obesity and associated non-communicable disorders. Current economic policies aim to promote economic development and thus reduce the conditions in which food insecurity is found. However, liberalization of trade may have the effect of increasing the importation of processed foods, or used cars, thereby perhaps contributing to the development of obesity. Popkin[40] has observed that key questions concern how potentially unfavourable health outcomes of these processes may be avoided, prevented, or reversed.

CONCLUSIONS

In Trinidad, food insecurity was common in association with low income and physical limitation. There was evidence that subjects who were food insecure, or who were unable to afford to eat a balanced diet, were less likely to consume fruits and vegetables or salads frequently. Overweight and obesity were frequent in all groups but there were no clear associations between either food insecurity, or household income, and obesity.

Any relationship between food security and obesity is likely to evolve over time. Future studies might therefore use prospective designs at key stages of the life course, in order to provide further insights into these relationships, which appear to be particularly relevant in middle-income country settings.

KEY MESSAGES

- Obesity is increasing in middle-income countries but the reasons for the increase are not fully understood.
- Some studies from high-income countries have suggested that food insecurity may be associated with obesity.
- We evaluated food insecurity and body mass index in a population sample of adults in Trinidad and Tobago.
- In this sample, 25% of subjects were food insecure and 60% were overweight or obese. Compared with food secure subjects, people who were food insecure showed an increased relative risk of underweight, but food insecurity was as frequent in those of normal weight as in those who were overweight or obese.
- Food insecurity was associated with underweight but not with present obesity in these cross-sectional data.

ACKNOWLEDGMENTS

The authors thank the Chief Medical Officer of Trinidad and Tobago for permission to report this work. We also thank the staff of the Central Statistical Office for help in drawing the sample and for advice on conducting the survey, the Principal Medical Officer (Community

Services), and the staff of the Nutrition Division for their skill and dedication in working on the survey.

REFERENCES

1. Gribble JN, Preston SH. *The Epidemiological Transition. Policy and Planning Implications for Developing Countries.* Washington DC: National Academy Press, 1993.

2. Popkin BM. The nutrition transition and obesity in the developing world. J Nutr 2001;131:871S–73S.

3. World Health Organization. *Obesity: Preventing and Managing the Global Epidemic.* Report of a WHO Consultation. WHO Technical Report Series No. 894. Geneva: World Health Organization, 2000.

4. Harnack LJ, Jeffrey RW, Boutelle KN. Temporal trends in energy intake in the United States: an ecologic perspective. Am J Clin Nutr 2002;71:1478–84.

5. Sobal J, Stunkard AJ. Socioeconomic status and obesity: a review of the literature. Psychol Bull 1989;105:260–75.

6. Monteiro CA, Conde WL, Popkin BM. Independent effects of income and education on the risk of obesity in the Brazilian adult population. J Nutr2001;131:881S–86S.

7. Doak CM, Adair LS, Monteiro C, Popkin BM. Overweight and underweight coexist within households in Brazil, China and Russia. J Nutr 2000;130:2965–71.

8. Florencio TM, Ferreira HS, de Franca AP, Cavalcante JC, Sawaya AL. Obesity and undernutrition in a very-low-income population in the city of Maceio, northeastern Brazil. Br J Nutr 2001;86:277–84.

9. Dietz WH. Does hunger cause obesity? Pediatrics 1995;95:766–67.

10. Alaimo K, Olson CM, Frongillo EA Jr. Low family income and food insufficiency in relation to overweight in US children: is there a paradox? Arch Pediatr Adolesc Med 2001;155:1161–67.

11. Carlson SJ, Andrews MS, Bickel GW. Measuring food insecurity and hunger in the United States: Development of a national

benchmark measure and prevalence estimates. J Nutr 1999;129:510S–06S.

12. Alaimo K, Briefel RR, Frongillo EA Jr, Olson CM. Food insufficiency exists in the United States: results from the third National Health and Nutrition Examination Survey (NHANES III). Am J Public Health 1998; 88:419–26.

13. Blumberg SJ, Bialostosky K, Hamilton WL, Briefel RR. The effectiveness of a short form of the Household Food Security Scale. Am J Public Health1999;89:1231–34.

14. World Bank. *World Development Indicators Database.* Washington: World Bank, 2001.

15. United Nations Food and Agriculture Organization. The state of food security in the world. **http://www.fao.org/docrep/003/y1500e/y1500e06.htm#P0_3**accessed 15 April 2002.

16. Walker SP, Powell CA, Hutchinson SE, Chang SM, Grantham-McGregor SM. Schoolchildren's diets and participation in school feeding programmes in Jamaica. Public Health Nutr 1998;1:43–49.

17. Gulliford MC, Mahabir D, Rocke BC, Chinn S, Rona RJ. Free school meals and children's social and nutritional status in Trinidad and Tobago. Public Health Nutr 2002;5:625–30.

18. Gulliford MC, Mahabir D, Rocke B, Chinn S, and Rona RJ. Overweight, obesity and skinfold thicknesses of children of African or Indian descent in Trinidad and Tobago. Int J Epidemiol 2001;30:989–98.

19. Beckles GL, Miller GJ, Alexis SD *et al.* Obesity in women in an urban Trinidadian community. Prevalence and associated characteristics. Int J Obes1985;9:127–35.

20. Rotimi CN, Cooper RS, Ataman SL *et al.* Distribution of anthropometric variables and the prevalence of obesity in populations of west African origin: the International Collaborative Study on Hypertension in Blacks (ICSHIB). Obes Res1995;3**(Suppl.2):**95S–105S.

21. Colhoun H, Prescott-Clarke P. *Health Survey for England 1994.* London: HMSO, 1996.

22. USDA Food and Nutrition and Economic Research Service. Food security/hunger core module.**http://www.ers.usda.gov/briefing/foodsecurity/surveytools/core0699.pdf**accessed 19 November 2002.

23. Gillum RF, Mussolino ME, Ingram DD. Physical activity and stroke incidence in women and men. The NHANES I Epidemiologic Follow-up study. Am J Epidemiol1996;143:860–69.

24. Jenkinson C, Layte R. Development and testing of the UK SF-12. J Health Serv Res Policy 1997;2:14–18.

25. Republic of Trinidad and Tobago. Central Statistical Office. *1990 Population and Housing Census. Vol. 2. Age Structure, Religion, Ethnic Group, Education.*Port of Spain: Office of the Prime Minister. Central Statistical Office, 1994.

26. Goldstein H. *Multilevel Statistical Models.* London: Arnold, 1996.

27. Woodhouse G. *Multilevel Modelling Applications. A Guide for Users of MLn.*London: Institute of Education, University of London, 1998.

28. Stata Corporation. *Stata Reference Manual. Release 7. Vol. 4.* Su-Z. College Station, TX: Stata Corporation, 2001.

29. Frongillo EA. Validation of Measures of Food Insecurity and Hunger. J Nutr1999;129:506.

30. Olson CM. Nutrition and health outcomes associated with food insecurity and hunger. J Nutr 1999;129:521S–24S.

31. Sarlio-Lahteenkorva S, Lahelma E. Food insecurity is associated with past and present economic disadvantage and body mass index. J Nutr 2001;131:2880–84.

32. Townsend MS, Peerson J, Love B, Achterberg C, Murphy SP. Food insecurity is positively related to overweight in women. J Nutr 2001; 131:1738–45.

33. Casey PH, Szeto K, Lensing S, Bogle M, Weber J. Children in food-insufficient, low-income families: prevalence, health, and nutrition status. Arch Pediatr Adolesc Med 2001;155:508–14.

34. Tarasuk VS. Household food insecurity with hunger is associated with women's food intakes, health and household circumstances. J Nutr2001;131:2670–76.

35. Kendall A, Olson CM, Frongillo EA. Relationship of hunger and food insecurity to food availability and consumption. J Am Diet Assoc 1996; 96:1019–24.

36. Aguirre P. Socio-anthropological aspects of obesity in poverty. In: Pena M, Bacallao J (eds). *Obesity and Poverty: A New Public Health Challenge.* Scientific Publication No. 576, pp. 11–22. Washington DC: PAHO/WHO, 2000.

37. Lahti-Koski M, Pietinen P, Heliovaara M, Vartiainen E. Associations of body mass index and obesity with physical activity, food choices, alcohol intake, and smoking in the 1982–1997 FINRISK studies. Am J Clin Nutr 2002;75:809–17.

38. Bell EA, Rolls BJ. Energy density of foods affects energy intake across multiple levels of fat content in lean and obese women. Am J Clin Nutr 2001;73:1018.

39. Kant AK. Consumption of energy-dense, nutrient-poor foods by adult Americans: nutritional and health implications. The Third National Health and Nutrition Examination Survey, 1988–1994. Am J Clin Nutr 2000;72:929–36.

40. Popkin BM. An overview on the nutrition transition and its health implications: The Bellagio meeting. Public Health Nutr 2002;5: 93–103.

3

HOUSEHOLD FOOD INSECURITY, DIET, AND WEIGHT STATUS IN A DISADVANTAGED DISTRICT OF HO CHI MINH CITY, VIETNAM: A CROSS-SECTIONAL STUDY

Thuy Ngoc Vuong[1,2*], Danielle Gallegos[2] and Rebecca Ramsey[2]

[1]Department of Epidemiology, the Institute of Hygiene and Public Health, 159, Hung Phu Street, Ward 8, District 8, Ho Chi Minh City, Vietnam

[2] School of Exercise and Nutrition Sciences, Queensland University of Technology, Victoria Park Avenue, Kelvin Grove, Queensland 4059, Australia

ABSTRACT

Background

Food security exists when all people, at all times, have physical, economic and socially acceptable access to safe, sufficient, and adequately nutritious food in order to meet their dietary needs for an active and healthy life. For high income countries and those experiencing the nutrition transition, food security is not only about the quantity of available food but also the nutritional quality as related to over- and under-nutrition. Vietnam is currently undergoing this nutrition transition, and as a result the relationship between food insecurity, socio-demographic factors and weight status is complex. The primary objective of this study was to therefore measure the prevalence of household food insecurity in a disadvantaged urban district in Ho Chi

Minh City (HCMC) in Vietnam using a more comprehensive tool. This study also aims to examine the relationships between food insecurity and socio-demographic factors, weight status, and food intakes.

Methods

A cross-sectional study was conducted using multi-stage sampling. Adults who were mainly responsible for cooking were interviewed in 250 households. Data was collected on socioeconomic and demographic factors using previously validated tools. Food security was assessed using the Latin American and Caribbean Household Food Security Scale (ELCSA) tool and households were categorized as food secure or mildly, moderately or severely food insecure. Questions regarding food intake were based on routinely used and validated questions in HCMC, weight status was self-reported.

Results

Cronbach's alpha coefficient was 0.87, showing the ELCSA had a good internal reliability. Approximately 34.4% of households were food insecure. Food insecurity was inversely related to total household income (OR = 0.09, 95% CI = 0.04 - 0.22) and fruit intakes (OR = 2.2, 95% CI 1.31 - 4.22). There was no association between weight and food security status.

Conclusions

Despite rapid industrialization and modernization, food insecurity remains an important public health issue in large urban areas of HCMC, suggesting that strategies to address food insecurity should be implemented in urban settings, and not just rural locations. Fruit consumption among food insecure households may be compromised because of financial difficulties, which may lead to poorer health outcomes particularly related to non-communicable disease prevention and management.

Keywords: Household food insecurity Diet Weight Health Vietnam

BACKGROUND

Food and nutrition security exists "when all people at all times have physical, social and economic access to food, which is safe and consumed in sufficient quantity and quality to meet their dietary needs and food preferences, and is supported by an environment of adequate sanitation, health services and care, allowing for a healthy and active life" [1]. Conversely, food insecurity exists when access to or availability of such foods is limited, or when these foods cannot be accessed by socially acceptable means. Of note, is that food security does not only relate to the food quantity but also quality, with the emphasis on foods that promote and maintain health and wellbeing.

Food insecurity may have adverse impacts on the nutritional and health status of individuals [2,3] and these impacts may vary between high income and low to middle income countries. Among children in high income countries, food insecurity may result in deficits in physical and psychological development and lower academic achievement [4,5]. Among adults, food insecurity may be associated with poor dietary choices, and consequently overweight and obesity (primarily among women), poorer health, depression, and an increased risk of diet-related chronic conditions, such as cardiovascular diseases and diabetes [2,6]. In low to middle income countries, food insecurity among adults and children has been associated with poor dietary intakes, malnutrition, and underweight (as opposed to obesity as seen in high income countries). However, as several low to middle income countries begin to undergo the nutrition transition, diet and health factors associated with food insecurity may begin to mimic those of high income countries, resulting in a 'triple burden of disease' in which these countries experience high rates of obesity, chronic disease and mental health issues as well as malnutrition and communicable diseases [7]. Despite this, there exist a limited number of studies investigating the associations between food security, diet and weight status in urban areas, in countries experiencing the nutrition transition [2,7].

Currently, investigations into household food insecurity in Vietnam are limited, relying on indirect indicators such as the poverty rate or Hunger Index [8], in lieu of more direct, comprehensive tools [2,9]. Previous studies have suggested a dissonance between the prevalence of food insecurity estimated by direct methods compared to indirect methods [9,10]. Based on poverty rates, it is estimated that the prevalence of food insecurity among the population of Vietnam in 2009 was around 14% with no reporting of differences between urban and rural areas [11]. In 2002, the rural food poverty rate was estimated at 13.6% compared to 1.9% within urban areas [12]. However, the use of rates of undernourishment as a proxy for food insecurity revealed a prevalence estimate 7% higher compared to the poverty rate [9]. This poses a problem as targeted interventions aimed at those defined conventionally as "poor", could potentially exclude large numbers of food insecure households. It should also be noted that undernourishment only deals with average caloric intake, while food security requires both adequate quantity and quality of foods. In addition, given the paradoxical relationship between food insecurity and overweight/obesity in high income countries which is also likely to be evident in countries undergoing the nutrition transition, the measurement of undernourishment may not accurately reflect food insecurity rates. Thus, there is a need for a more specific assessment of food insecurity in order to assist policy-makers establish equitable and effective public programs.

With economic growth, Vietnam may be able to provide enough food for its population [13]. Given this potential, it could be assumed that food insecurity is no longer an issue, especially in economically developed areas. However, this may not be the case as sufficient amounts of food at the population level do not necessarily guarantee equitable distribution at the household level, both between and within households. Specifically, disadvantaged urban populations may be at risk of food insecurity due to their lack of access to agricultural resources compared to their rural counterparts [14]. Additionally, recent financial crises leading to higher food prices and unemployment in large cities may also increase rates of food insecurity among disadvantaged urban households [14].

Despite the high likelihood of food insecurity among the disadvantaged urban population [13,15], the government has made food security a major agricultural policy aim [16]. As such, most food security policies and programs rightly heavily invest in agriculture to ensure the supply of food for the whole population [13]. These programs frequently prioritize ethnic minority groups (those living in the mountains of the north and in the central highlands who include Khmer Krom, Hoa, Lao, the Mon-Khmer, the Tay) and the disadvantaged in remote and rural areas, because there is an assumption that food insecurity is more prevalent in these areas due to a lack of resources to obtain sufficient quantities of food [8,17]. These programs have effectively increased the amount of food available and as a result improved food access. While it is essential that these policy initiatives need to be maintained at the national level, they may however, be insufficient to ensure equitable access, availability, and affordability for urban poor households.

This research aimed to identify the prevalence of food insecurity among an urban, disadvantaged population in HCMC, using a more comprehensive and direct measure, the Latin American and Caribbean Household Food Security Scale (ELCSA) tool [18]. This tool has been adapted from the USDA Food Security Survey Module (FSSM) [19] and has been applied in countries with similar development indexes to Vietnam [20-22]. In addition, the potential associations between food insecurity and socio-demographic attributes, dietary factors and weight status were also investigated.

METHODS

Ethical approval

This study was approved by the Queensland University of Technology Human Research Ethics Committee (UHREC), Australia (approval number 1100001491) and the Institute of Hygiene and Public Health (IHPH) of HCMC, Vietnam.

Research setting

HCMC is located in the South of Vietnam. It is the largest city with an estimated population of eight million people [23]. District eight (D8) is one of the poorest districts in HCMC with a large number of people living in slums and shanties [24]. In 2011, approximately 5,500 households with 29,504 people in this district lived below the national poverty line [25].

Sample and sampling methodology

Sample size calculations yielded a required sample size of 250 individuals to determine statistically significant differences in rates of food insecurity with 90% power. This assumed a non-response rate of 10% [26].

Two-hundred and fifty adults who were responsible for cooking in their households in D8 were identified and approached using a multi-stage sampling method. The district is divided into 16 wards. Three out of the

16 wards, were randomly selected (Wards 2, 8, and 15) and households were subsequently randomly sampled. The total number of households in each ward was selected by Probability Proportional to Size sampling with 100 households sampled from Wards 2 and 15; and 50 households sampled from Ward 8. The adult responsible for cooking and, where relevant, the youngest child was then selected from each household. A small gift valued at $1AUD was given to participants to thank them for participation.

Data collection

One week in advance of data collection a one day training session in interview techniques and use of the questionnaire was undertaken for 12 students majoring in public health at the Ho Chi Minh City University of Medicine and Pharmacy. These data collectors went door-to-door, in pairs, to undertake the interviews. The interviews were mostly conducted in the evenings after dinner and on the weekends to ensure the majority of participants were present in the household.

Socio-economic and demographic characteristics

Participants' age, gender, ethnicity, level of education, place of birth, household income, and family type were recorded. A household was defined as "people who sleep under the same roof and share food with each other" [27]. To determine place of birth, participants were asked to record the province in which they were born. These were then categorised into "HCMC" and "other". Age of the participant was reported as a continuous variable, then categorised into 18–44 years, 45–54 years, 55–64 years or 65 or older years for analyses. Ethnicity was recorded as either Kinh (the majority group) or "other". Total household income was categorized into " ≤ the poverty line (PVL)" versus " > PVL" according to the PVL for urban areas set by the Ministry of Labour Invalids and Social Affairs (MOLISA) [28]. Urban households who are considered poor have an income of one million VD (AUD 45) or less per month per household [28].

Additionally, ownership of 12 high-value items derived from the Bureau Statistics were used to evaluate household income level [29]. This is an indirect way of assessing household income, however is considered a practical means compared to direct questioning. Each affirmative response to the aforementioned items in the households received a score of one. Values were then summed and households were ranked accordingly as low income (the total score was less than 4), medium income (a score of 4–8), and high (a score of 9–12).

Food security status

Food security status was assessed using the 15-item Latin American and Caribbean Household Food Security Scale (ELCSA), which is a modified version of the USDA FSSM [21]. Households are classified as food insecure if they respond affirmatively to any questions [30]. Households are further categorized as mildly, moderately, and severely food insecure if they have 1–5, 6–10, and 11+ affirmative responses respectively [30].

The English version of the ELCSA was translated into the Vietnamese language and pretested among 30 local people to assess face and content validity, and where required make minor adjustments to wording to improve comprehension before data collection. Although this tool has not yet been formally validated amongst a Vietnamese population, it yielded high internal and external reliability in Mexico, Colombia, Ecuador, Guatemala, El Salvador, Honduras, and Nicaragua [20]. Similar to Vietnam, most of these countries are undergoing the nutrition transition [31] and have similar development indexes [32]. This tool had a reliability of Cronbachs alpha = 0.87 within the current sample, indicating high internal reliability.

Weight status

Weight status was assessed by calculating body mass index (BMI). Participants self-reported their weight and height, which were used to calculate BMI as per the standard equation (weight(kg)/height(m)^2). The Asian specific BMI cutoff of 23.0 kg/m^2 was used to define overweight and obesity among adults [33]. Parental proxy-report was also used to obtain weights and heights for children. BMI was then calculated as per standard protocol and assessed against World Health Organisation child-specific BMI cut-off values to classify children as either underweight/healthy weight or overweight/obese [34].

Vegetable and fruit intakes

Fruit and vegetable intakes were assessed using short-answer questions that asked "How often do you eat vegetable/fruit *per week*?" [2] Responses to this item were categorized into "everyday" and "<

everyday" for the purpose of data analyses. These short-answer intake questions have previously been used in a study to validate food frequency questionnaires among Vietnamese in HCMC [35].

Meat consumption

Participants were asked to report on their usual weekly consumption of processed meats, red meat (pork and beef), fish and other seafood, chicken and other poultry, for example "How many times per week do you eat red meat?" [2] Responses were coded as "Yes" (1–2 times/week + ≥ 3 times/week) and "No" (never/rarely") for analyses.

Fast foods and take-away foods

Take away and fast food consumption was assessed using items measuring the frequency of consumption of sweet sticky rice, fried chicken and potato chips, hamburgers, pizza, and cakes. These foods were the most popular takeaway items consumed in HCMC [35]. Responses were coded as "Yes" (1–2 times/week + ≥ 3 times/week) and "No" (never/rarely").

Soft drink and alcohol

Drinks included items measuring the frequency of consumption of carbonated soft drinks and alcohol asked as separate questions. Responses were coded as "Yes" (1–2 times/week + ≥ 3 times/week) and "No" (never/rarely").

Data analyses

Data were entered into Epi Data 3.0 and analysed using Stata 11.0. Chi-square analyses were used to investigate bivariate associations between food insecurity and the socio-demographic, dietary and weight variables. Binary logistic and multiple linear regressions were then

Table 1. Socio-demographic characteristics of the study sample from District Eight (n = 250) compared to the total population of the HCMC

Characteristics	Total study sample (%)	Total population of HCMC (%)[*]
Age		
18-44	45.0	54.0
45-64	45.0	17.0
≥65	10.0	5.0
Gender		
Female	89.0	52.0
Male	11.0	48.0
Ethnicity		
Kinh	95.0	93.0
Others (Chinese, the Tay, Cham, ect.)	5.0	7.0
Education		*% (Urban population)*[†]
Never went to school	5.2	3.1
Completed primary school (5 years of schooling)	28.0	25.9
Completed secondary school (9 years of schooling)	41.2	46.6
Completed high school (12 years of schooling)	19.6	n/a
Completed college or above (>12 years of schooling)	6.0	15.2
Place of birth		
HCMC	57.2	n/a
Others	42.8	
Settlement time		
≤10 years	26.0	n/a
>10 years	74.0	

[*] The 2010 Viet Nam Population and Housing Census and 2010 Statistical Yearbook of Ho Chi Minh City.

[†]Data for "Education" were unavailable for HCMC, but available for urban areas.

n/a: not available.

applied to investigate associations between food insecurity and diet, and weight factors, that were identified as being significant at the bivariate level, controlling for socio-demographic characteristics.

RESULTS

Socio-demographic characteristics

The demographic characteristics of the sample and the total population of HCMC are summarised in Table 1. The majority of respondents were female, of Kinh (the majority group) ethnicity, had completed secondary school, were married and from households in the medium tertile for income. As the respondents were providing answers at the household level, the higher proportion of women respondents was unlikely to affect the representativeness of the sample.

Food insecurity

Over one-third (34.4%) of households reported some degree of food insecurity. Mildly food insecure households accounted for the highest percentage (21.6%) with 12.0% identifying as moderately food insecure. There was an extremely low proportion (0.8%) of severely food insecure households.

Table 2 summarises the associations between food insecurity and socio-demographic characteristics of the households. At the bivariate level, food insecurity was significantly associated with age ($p = 0.01$), education ($p < 0.01$), settlement time ($p = 0.02$), and total household income ($p < 0.01$) using Chi-square test. After adjustment for appropriate covariates, the only significant association that remained was between food insecurity and total household income. Medium and high income households were 60% and 93% less likely to experience food insecurity respectively, compared to their lower income counterparts ($p < 0.01$).

Table 3 summarises the bivariate and multivariate associations between food insecurity and dietary intakes. At the bivariate level, food insecurity was significantly associated with lower intakes of fruit ($p = 0.02$), processed meat ($p = 0.04$), fresh chicken and other poultry ($p < 0.01$). After adjustment for potential confounders, only intakes of fruit remained associated with food insecurity (OR and 95% CI = 2.2 (1.31 - 4.22).

Table 2. Food insecurity by socio-demographic characteristics among households in District Eight in HCMC (n = 250)

Characteristics	Food insecurity status			
	Food insecure (%)	Food secure (%)	P value**	OR (95% CI)
Age††			0.01*	
18-44	32.5	51.2		1.00
45-64	52.3	41.4		1.63 (0.68-3.94)
≥65	15.1	7.3		1.71 (0.91-4.02)
Gender			0.18	
Male	23.0	77.0		
Female	36.2	63.8		
Education†			0.00*	
Never went to school	4.2	6.8		1.38 (1.09-1.83)
Completed primary school	38.6	21.9		1.41 (1.22-1.63)
Completed secondary school	44.3	39.0		1.27 (1.12-1.44)
Completed high school or above	10.2	34.7		1.00
Ethnicity			0.83	
Kinh	34.0	66.0		
Others	40.0	60.0		
Settlement time‡			0.02*	
≤10 years	82.6	69.5		2.13 (1.08-4.31)
>10 years	30.5	17.4		1.00
Employment			0.25	
Family size			0.95	
Living arrangement			0.19	
Total income by urban poverty lines			0.18	
Total household income by house items§			0.00*	
Low	100.0	0.0		7.28 (2.99-17.69)
Medium	44.0	60.5		3.14 (1.24-4.33)
High	6.7	93.3		1.00

*Significant at $p < 0.05$.
**P-value for chi-square (difference between food secure and food insecure households).
††Adjusted for education.
†Adjusted for age and total income.
‡Adjusted for age.
§Adjusted for age and education.

Weight status and its associations with food security status are summarised in Table 4. Overall, the prevalence of underweight among adults was low at only 8%. Individuals from food insecure households reported higher rates of underweight compared to their food secure counterparts (13.6% versus 8.3% among adults and 43.5% versus 39.6% among children). The prevalence of overweight and obesity among adults was high (approximately 33% and 10% respectively). Among children, the prevalence of overweight and obesity was low (less than 5% among boys and girls). Weight status was not significantly associated with food insecurity among adults or children ($p > 0.05$).

Table 3. Associations between food insecurity and dietary intakes among households in District Eight, HCMC (n = 250)

Dietary intakes	Total sample (%)	Food security status Food insecure (%)	Food secure (%)	p-value**	OR (95% CI)
Fruit intake				0.02*	
Less than everyday	49.2	36.0	9.1		2.2 (1.31 - 4.22)
Everyday	50.8	64.0	90.9		1.00
Vegetable				0.17	
Less than everyday	14.4	18.6	12.2		
Everyday	85.6	81.4	87.8		
Processed meat				0.04*	
Yes	18.4	11.6	21.9		1.00
No	81.6	88.4	78.1		1.88 (0.87 - 4.03)
Red meat (pork, beef)				0.91	
Yes	86.4	86.1	86.6		
No	13.6	14.0	13.4		
Fresh chicken and other poultry				0.00*	
Yes	61.2	50.0	67.1		1.00
No	38.8	50.0	33.0		1.18 (0.65 -2.15)
Fish and other seafood				0.19	
Yes	81.6	86.1	79.3		
No	18.4	14.0	20.7		
Sweet sticky rice				0.76	
Yes	26.8	27.9	26.2		
No	73.2	72.1	73.8		
Cakes				0.88	
Yes	20.4	79.1	79.9		
No	79.6	20.9	20.1		
Fried chicken and potato chips				0.10	
Yes	7.2	3.5	9.1		
No	92.8	96.5	90.8		
Yes	5.2	4.7	5.5		
No	94.8	95.4	94.5		
Pizzas				0.75	
Yes	5.2	5.8	4.9		
No	94.8	94.2	95.1		
Soft drinks				0.50	
Yes	34.4	37.2	32.9		
No	65.6	62.8	67.1		
Beer				0.21	
Yes	23.2	18.6	25.6		
No	76.8	81.4	74.4		
Alcohol				0.39	
Yes	10.4	8.1	11.6		
No	89.6	91.9	88.4		

*Significant at $p < 0.05$.
**P-value for chi-square (difference between food secure and food insecure households).

Table 4. The associations between food insecurity and weight status among households in District Eight, HCMC (n = 250)

		Food security status		
	Total sample (%)	Food insecure (%)	Food secure (%)	p-value**
BMI Adults				0.40
Underweight	8.4	13.6	8.3	
Healthy weight	49.2	56.8	52.3	
Overweight/obesity	42.4	29.5	39.4	
BMI Children				
Male children				0.90
Thinness§	2.6	43.5	39.6	
Healthy weight	93.4	43.5	49.1	
Overweight/obese¶	4.0	13.0	11.3	
Female children				0.79
Thinness§	4.1	61.9	53.9	
Healthy weight	91.8	38.1	42.3	
Overweight/obese¶	4.1	0.0	3.9	

§,¶International BMI cutoff points to define thinness, overweight and obesity in children and adolescents were applied [36].
Statistical significance: $p < 0.05$.
**P-value for chi-square (difference between food secure and food insecure households).

DISCUSSION

Findings of the current study suggest that food insecurity is a salient issue among this disadvantaged urban population of HCMC, identifying a prevalence rate of 34% which is markedly higher than the 14% among the entire Vietnamese population (recorded in the latest national report in 2010), and the 1.9% identified in urban areas in 2002 [37]. This finding supports previous evidence, suggesting that rates of food insecurity are greater among disadvantaged communities than the general population [2,37-39]. It is also consistent with results from countries undergoing the nutrition transition, namely India [40], the Philippines [41], and Guatemala [42], which have suggested that disadvantaged urban populations, and those populations in marginal rural areas, are at risk of food insecurity in countries undergoing the nutrition transition. This finding suggests that the true burden of food insecurity among poor households living in densely populated areas may be as serious as those having inadequate resources to access foods in rural locations and among ethnic minority groups.

Consistent with previous studies, we identified a significant, inverse association between food insecurity and fruit intakes. This association may be explained by changes in food prices. The price of food has increased significantly since the 2008 global food crisis [43], in particular fruit prices have risen sharply between 2006 and 2011 in HCMC. Urban households who are economically vulnerable are more affected by soaring food prices [44]. It is possible that due to financial constraints, disadvantaged urban households may opt for energy-dense foods, which are perceived to be more satisfying and better value for money, compared to their low energy counterparts, such as fruits and vegetables. The Vietnamese traditional diet is mostly rice, fish, and vegetables, plus pork or chicken if affordable [45]. Fruits may be perceived as having low energy density in relation to price, and as such considered a luxury among low income households [46,47]. This may raise a public health concern because limited consumption of fruits may result in lower intakes of some micronutrients and is implicated in the development of many non-communicable diseases [48,49].

There were no associations between food insecurity and intakes of meats, take away or fast foods, soft drinks, and alcohol at either the bivariate or multivariate level in our sample. Lower income urban populations are relatively 'conservative' with respect to the consumption of Western-style foods and potentially more "faithful" to traditional foods, contributing to very low consumption proportions of the Western-style foods [50]. In addition, these foods, for poor households in Vietnam, are considered luxury items [50]. This is consistent with tenets of the nutrition transition where these foods are more likely to be consumed by those with higher incomes in these countries [51,52].

A lack of association between food insecurity and consumption of take away or fast foods and soft drinks is consistent with the early stage of the nutrition transition when the costs of these foods are still high, and as such, less affordable for the lower income households. Furthermore, at the time of the data collection, there was still little penetration of Western-style foods into the Vietnamese market [53]. However, it should be noted that as the nutrition transition continues, these foods will be much more prevalent in the domestic market, and therefore the price of these foods will go down and they will become more affordable for disadvantaged households. Together with other factors, such as physical inactivity, this is likely to exacerbate obesity rates. Thus, we suggest that nutrition surveys should assess the consumption of take away or fast foods and sugar sweetened beverages regularly in order to establish appropriate plans and strategies to prevent obesity, in a timely fashion.

Interestingly, the present study found not only a high prevalence of food insecurity (34%), but also a high proportion of overweight/obesity among adults (42%). Although a statistically significant association between food insecurity and overweight/ obesity was not evident, trends existed whereby a higher proportion of those from food insecure households were overweight or obese compared to their food secure counterparts. This supports previous evidence which suggests that food insecurity and obesity coexist in the disadvantaged households in urban areas in developing countries [14,54-56]. In fact, as the Vietnamese economy continues to be integrated with international trading markets, the costs of processed foods will become less expensive. Cheaper prices may lead to increased consumption of these foods which when accompanied with lower levels of physical activity may contribute to the food insecurity – obesity paradox in urbanized areas. Thus, we suggest further research to explore this complex issue.

Our findings also suggest a higher rate of underweight among adults from food insecure households (compared to those from food secure households), however these results did not reach statistical significance. Given that self-reported weight and height tends to underestimate weight status the relationship between weight and food security in urban areas, in countries undergoing the nutrition transition warrants further investigation [57]. Food insecurity may still predict underweight among socio-economically disadvantaged populations undergoing the nutrition transition [58]. The traditional energy deficits associated with food insecurity in countries experiencing the nutrition transition is likely to change. Households will potentially move away from small amounts of traditional foods, and corresponding underweight/malnutrition, to a situation in which food insecurity is associated with a surfeit of high fat, high sugar foods and overweight/malnutrition. Regardless, both of these forms of food insecurity are characterized by a household's reduced ability to access affordable foods needed for health.

Consistent with previous studies, we did not identify a significant association between food insecurity and child weight status. In addition, the estimates of thinness, overweight, and obesity among children in previous studies [29,58] were higher than our findings. Research among low-income mothers in Canada has revealed that parents often 'protect' their children from food insecurity by compromising their own intakes first [59]. As such, it is possible that until more severe forms of food insecurity are reached, children will not experience any changes to their food intake, and consequently no changes to their weight status. Alternatively, our null finding could be due to a sole focus on the poor urban population, rather than a more socio-economically diverse sample, resulting in a homogenous sample in regards to weight status. Furthermore, it is possible that overweight and obesity among children may be underestimated as our study relied on parental proxy report of weight and height for children. Previous studies have suggested that the use of such self-reported data often results in an underestimation of weight and overestimation of height, resulting overall in an underestimation of BMI among children and subsequently an underestimation of the association between overweight and obesity and food insecurity [60-62]. If feasible, future investigations should use more objective methods to measure the weights and heights of children more accurately.

The results of the current study should be interpreted within the context of several limitations. The cross-sectional design makes it impossible to investigate the temporality of the associations identified and as such a causal relationship cannot be established. We relied on self-reported data and therefore response bias is a potential issue. Previous studies have suggested that the use of such self-reported data often results in an underestimation of weight and overestimation of height, resulting overall in an underestimation of BMI among both adults and children [60-62]. In particular, this may have resulted in an underestimation of the true association between food insecurity and overweight and obesity in the current sample. Where possible, studies should seek to collect objective measurements of these variables to more accurately determine whether associations between food security and weight status exist.

Finally, information regarding the specific types of public assistance program participation was not collected. As a result, the survey could have overestimated food insecurity if the respondents had expectations that the answers would influence their access to government support.

CONCLUSIONS

This research is the first to assess household food insecurity using the ELCSA in Vietnam. Although poverty may be deeper and more widespread in rural and ethnic minority groups, our findings suggest that a focus on household food insecurity in urban settings is warranted. Public health nutrition programs should work with local social welfare programs to discuss resolutions to improve the affordability of core and healthy foods in general, and for fruits in particular to prevent unexpected health-related consequences for food insecure households.

DECLARATIONS

Acknowledgements

This research was undertaken in partial fulfillment of the Masters in Public Health. The authors thank all members of the People's

Committees and the Youth Union of D8 as well as all those who supported us to conduct this research.

Competing interests

The authors declare that they have no competing interests.

Authors' contributions

TNV, DG and RR conceptualized the research design. TNV collected and coordinated data collected and undertook all data analyses and wrote the manuscript. DG, RR reviewed the analyses and contributed to the writing of the manuscript. All authors read and approved the final manuscript.

REFERENCES

1. Basic definitions: Food insecurity. [http://www.fao.org/hunger/en/] [cited 3 April 2012]

2. Ramsey R, Giskes K, Turrell G, Gallegos D. Food insecurity among adults residing in disadvantaged urban areas: potential health and dietary consequences. Public Health Nutr. 2011;15(2):227–37.

3. Holben DH, Pheley AM. Obesity, diabetes, and blood pressure are greater in food insecure households in rural Appalachian Ohio. J Prev Chronic Dis. 2006;3(3):A82–91.

4. Eicher-Miller HA, Mason AC, Weaver CM, McCabe GP, Boushey CJ. Food insecurity is associated with iron deficiency anemia in US adolescents. Am J Clin Nutr. 2009;90(5):1358–71.

5. Kirkpatrick SI, Tarasuk V. Food insecurity is associated with nutrient inadequacies among Canadian adults and adolescents. J Nutr. 2008;138(3):604–12.

6. Stuff JE, Casey PH, Szeto KL, Gossett JM, Robbins JM, Simpson PM, et al. Household food insecurity is associated with adult health status. J Nutr. 2004;134(9):2330–5.

7. Popkin BM. The nutrition transition in low-income countries: an emerging crisis. Nutr Rev. 2009;52(9):285–98.

8. Nhat TTH. Tackling household food insecurity: the experience of Vietnam. Asian J Agric Dev. 2010;5(2):41–56.

9. Mishra V, Ray R. Dietary diversity, food security and undernourishment: the Vietnamese evidence. Asian Econ J. 2009;23(2):225–47

10. Suryanarayana MH, Silva D. Is targeting the poor a penalty on the food insecure? Poverty and food insecurity in India. J Hum Dev. 2007;8(1):89–107

11. Hunger Statistics - Viet Nam. [http://www.fao.org/hunger/en/] [cited 3 April 2012]

12. Food insecurity and vulnerability in Vietnam: Profiles of four vulnerable groups. [www.fao.org/es/esa] [cited 4 April 2012]

13. Vietnam Government. Resolution 63 on national food security. Hanoi: Socialist Republic of Vietnam; 2009. p. 2–5

14. Cohen MJ, Garrett JL. The food price crisis and urban food (in)security. Environ Urban. 2010;22(2):467–82.

15. Ivanic M, Martin W. Implications of higher global food prices for poverty in low-income countries. Agric Econ. 2008;39(Suppl s1):405–16.

16. Tran MH. Food security and sustainable agriculture in Vietnam. In: Country Report: Vietnam. Hanoi: Viet Nam Institute of Agricultural Engineering and Post-harvest Technology (VIAEP); 2009. p. 3.

17. Thang NM, Popkin BM. Patterns of food consumption in Vietnam: effects on socioeconomic groups during an era of economic growth. Eur J Clin Nutr. 2004;58(1):145–53.

18. Melgar-Quinonez H, Hackett M. Measuring household food security: the global experience. Rev Nutr Campinas. 2008;21(Suppl0):27s–37.

19. Guide to measuring household food security. [www.fns.usda.gov/fsec/files/fsguide.pdf] [cited 5 September 2011]

20. Bermudez O, Palma De Fulladolsa P, Deman H, Melgar-Quinones H. Food insecurity is prevalent in rural communities of El Salvador, Guatemala, Honduras and Nicaragua. FASEB J. 2010;24(Suppls1):104–7

21. Pérez-Escamilla R, Paras P, Hromi-Fiedler A. Validity of the Latin American and Caribbean Household Food Security Scale (ELCSA) in Guanajuato, Mexico. J Fed Am Exp Biol. 2008;22 Suppl 1:871–2.

22. Pérez-Escamilla R. The Latin American Household Food Security Measurement Scale (ELCSA). In: International Congress of Nutrition. Bangkok, Thailand: International Union of Nutritional Sciences; 2009. p. 7.

23. Average population by districts. [http://www.pso.hochiminhcity.gov.vn/] [cited 15 October 2012].

24. District 8 moves households living near channels. [www.sggp.org.vn/chinhtri/tientoidhd/2010/7/231776/] [10 October 2011]

25. Donor bicycles for poor students in District 8. [http://www.congan.com.vn/?mod=detnews&catid=681&id=313036] [15 October 2011]

26. Sullivan LM. Power and sample size determination. In: Gartside M, editor. Essentials of Biostatistics in public health. 2nd ed. Sudbury, MA, USA: Jones & Bartlett Learning; 2008. p. 169–76.

27. Ballantine NM. Purchasing determinants of food insecurity conditions amongst shoppers in Klipplaat. PhD thesis. Nelson Mandela Metropolitan University, Faculty of Arts; 2007.

28. New poor and marginally poor household standard, period 2011–2015. [http://www.molisa.gov.vn/news/detail/tabid/75/newsid/52409/language/vi-VN/Default.aspx?seo=Chuan-ho-ngheo-can-

ngheo-moi-giai-doan-2011-%E2%80%93-2015] [15 October 2011]

29. Tang KH, Nguyen HHDT, Michael JD, David WS, Phan NTB, Tran TMH. Overweight and obesity are rapidly emerging among adolescents in Ho Chi Minh City, Vietnam, 2002–2004. Int J Pediatr Obes. 2007;2(4):194–201.

30. Acker T. Measuring food insecurity in Guatemala. PhD thesis. The Ohio State University, Department of Human Nutrition; 2011.

31. Rivera JA, Barquera S, González-Cossío T, Olaiz G, Sepúlveda J. Nutrition transition in Mexico and in other Latin American countries. Nutr Rev. 2004;62(7 Pt 2):S149–149.

32. Microfinance Poverty Assessment Tool. [http://www.cgap.org/gm/document-1.9.3004/TechnicalTool_05.pdf] [cited 11 June 2011]

33. Cuong T, Dibley M, Bowe S, Hanh T, Loan T. Obesity in adults: an emerging problem in urban areas of Ho Chi Minh City, Vietnam. Eur J Clin Nutr. 2007;61(5):673–81.

34. Dang CV, Day RS, Selwyn B, Maldonado YM, Nguyen KC, Le TD, et al. Initiating BMI prevalence studies in Vietnamese children: changes in a transitional economy. Asia Pac J Clin Nutr. 2010;19(2):209–16.

35. Kusama K, Le DSNT, Hanh TTM, Takahashi K, Hung NTK, Yoshiike N, et al. Reproducibility and validity of a food frequency questionnaire among Vietnamese in Ho Chi Minh City. J Am Coll Nutr. 2005;24(6):466–73.

36. Cole TJ, Bellizzi MC, Flegal KM, Dietz WH. Establishing a standard definition for child overweight and obesity worldwide: international survey. BMJ. 2000;320:1240–3.

37. Brittany GH, Ashley GM, Terry M, Tom H, Jodie LG. Prevalence and predictors of food Insecurity in migrant farmworkers in Georgia. Am J Public Health. 2011;1(5):831–3.

38. Gallegos D, Ellies P, Wright J. Still there's no food! Food insecurity in a refugee population in a refugee population in Perth, Western Australia. Nutr Diet. 2008;65(1):78–83.

39. Nolan M, Rikard-Bell G, Mohsin M, William M. Food insecurity in three socially disadvantaged localities in Sydney, Australia. Health Promot J Austr. 2006;17(3):247–54.

40. Gopichandran V, Claudius P, Baby LS, Felinda A, Mohan VR. Household food security in urban Tamil Nadu: a survey in Vellore. Natl Med J India. 2010;23(5):278–80.

41. Melgar-Quinonez HR, Zubieta AC, MkNelly B, Nteziyaremye A, Gerardo MFD, Dunford C. Household food insecurity and food expenditure in Bolivia, Burkina Faso, and the Philippines. J Nutr. 2006;136(5):1431S–7.

42. Ahmed AU, Hill RV, Smith LC, Wiesmann DM, Frankenberger T, Gulati K, et al. The world's most deprived: characteristics and causes of extreme poverty and hunger, 2020 vision for food. Washington DC: International Food Policy Research Institute (IFPRI); 2007.

43. Vietnam consumers struggle with rising food prices. [http://news.monstersandcritics.com/business/news/article_1635177.php/Vietnam-consumers-struggle-with-rising-food-prices] [cited 11 June 2011]

44. High food prices: Causes and possible actions. [www.ima.kth.se/utb/MJ1501/pdf/Engfeldt.pdf] [cited 11 July 2011]

45. Vietnamese cultural profile. [http://ethnomed.org/culture/vietnamese/vietnamese-cultural-profile] [cited 1 February 2012]

46. Scheier LM. What is the hunger-obesity paradox? J Am Diet Assoc. 2005;105(6):883–5.

47. Tanumihardjo SA, Anderson C, Kaufer-Horwitz M, Bode L, Emenaker NJ, Haqq AM, et al. Poverty, obesity, and malnutrition: an international perspective recognizing the paradox. J Am Diet Assoc. 2007;107(11):1966–72.

48. Increasing fruit and vegetable consumption becomes a global priority. [http://www.fao.org/english/newsroom/focus/2003/fruitveg1.htm] [27 September 2012]

49. Promoting fruit and vegetable consumption around the world. [http://www.who.int/dietphysicalactivity/fruit/en/] [cited 27 September 2012]

50. Le CQ. An empirical study of food demand in Vietnam. ASEAN Econ Bull. 2008;25(3):283–92.

51. Popkin BM. Urbanization, lifestyle changes and the nutrition transition. World Dev. 1999;27(11):1905–16.

52. Popkin BM. The nutrition transition and its health implications in lower-income countries. Public Health Nutr. 1998;1:5–21.

53. Business Monitor International. Vietnam Food & Drink Report Q4 2009. 2009:19–40.

54. Agneta Y, Barrie M, Roger H, Marilyn T. Food security - not just about rural communities in Africa and Asia. Public Health Nutr. 2009;12(11):1971–2.

55. Doak CM, Adair LS, Bentley M, Monteiro C, Popkin BM. The dual burden household and the nutrition transition paradox. Int J Obes. 2005;29(1):129–36.

56. Tran TMH, Komatsu T, Nguyen TKH, Nguyen VC, Yoshimura Y, Pham GT, et al. Nutritional status of middle-aged Vietnamese in Ho Chi Minh City. J Am Coll Nutr. 2001;20(6):616–22.

57. Nyholm M, Gullberg B, Merlo J, Lundqvist-Persson C, Rastam L, Lindblad U. The validity of obesity based on self-reported weight and height: Implications for population studies. Obesity. 2007;15(1):197–208.

58. Isanaka S, Mora-Plazas M, Lopez-Arana S, Baylin A, Villamor E. Food insecurity is highly prevalent and predicts underweight but not overweight in adults and school children from Bogota, Colombia. J Nutr. 2007;137(12):2747–55.

59. McIntyre L, Glanville NT, Officer S, Anderson B, Raine KD, Dayle JB. Food insecurity of low-income lone mothers and their children in Atlantic Canada. Can J Public Health. 2002;93(6):411–5.

60. Maynard LD, Galuska DA, et al. Maternal perceptions of weight status of children. Pediatrics. 2003;111(5 Pt2):1226–31.

61. Scholtens SB, Brunekreef B, et al. Reported versus measured body weight and height of 4-year-old children and the prevalence of overweight. Eur J Pub Health. 2007;17(4):369–74.

62. Wald E, Ewing L, et al. Parental perception of children's weight in a paediatric primary care setting. Child Care Health Dev. 2007;33(6):738–43.

4

FRUIT AND VEGETABLES CONSUMPTION AMONG CHILDREN AND ADOLESCENTS: DETERMINANTS OF CONSUMPTION AND POSSIBLE SOLUTIONS

Ahlam B El Shikeri

Taibah University, Al Madinah Al Munawarah, Saudi Arabia

ABSTRACT

Nutritional health during childhood and adolescency is important for supporting the growing body and for preventing future health problems. Fruits and vegetables are important components of a healthy **diet**. Their consumption varies considerably among and within countries. Large proportions of children do not fulfill the World Health Organization recommendation of eating fruit and vegetables per day. Reduced fruit and vegetables' consumption is linked to poor health, constipation and increased risk of non-communicable diseases including cancer. The dietary fibre available in the outer skin of these foods could help to lower blood pressure, and together with phytochemicals such as plant sterols, flavonoids and other **antioxidants** found in fruit and vegetables may be important in modulating **cholesterol**and other biological processes. In addition, obesity and overweight among this age group is being associated with low intake of fruit and vegetables. The determinants for high consumption levels of fruit and vegetable are found to be related to female gender, socioeconomic status, high preferences for fruit and vegetables, large parental intake of fruit and vegetables and high availability/accessibility of fruit and vegetables at home as well as peer influence. Possible solutions to improve fruit and vegetables' consumption include behavioural interventions and improvements in agricultural and food systems will be discussed.

Keywords: Fruit and vegetable consumption; Sudan; Children; Determinants of intake

INTRODUCTION

Nutritional health during childhood and adolescency is important for supporting the growing body and for preventing future health problems. Eating behaviour during this developmentally critical age period affects later life growth and disease prevention. Fruit and vegetables are important components of a healthy diet and their consumption is linked to improved health and reduced risk of various diseases including non-communicable diseases [1], certain types of cancers, as well as improving school performance and productivity [2]. In addition, specific components of fruit and vegetables known as phytochemicals such as plant sterols, flavonoids and other antioxidants may be important in modulating cholesterol and other biological processes thus protecting against chronic diseases such as hypertension [3]. They are also very high in water content, relatively high in carbohydrates, low in fat and proteins and are vital sources of vitamins such as vitamin C, thiamine, niacin, pyridoxine, folacin and many others.

Furthermore, **obesity** prevention from an early age has become a major public health priority. However, recent studies have linked obesity and overweight among this age group to low intake of fruit and **vegetables** [4,5]. Moreover, certain vegetables have been associated with reduced diarrhea-related deaths and **morbidity** probably due to their moderate amounts of α- and β-carotene [6]. In 2010, 6.7 million deaths were related to inadequate fruit and vegetables consumption. Adequate intake is defined as 400 to 500 grams per day (g/d) or 5 servings of fruit and/or vegetables [7]. The consumption of fruit and vegetables varies considerably among and within countries. For instance, in the United States, the per capita consumption of total vegetables among children aged 6-12 years decreased steeply from 386 in 2009 to 375 in 2014. Also, the per capita consumption of total fruit amongst those aged <6 years decreased from 474 in 2009 to 416 in 2014 [8].

Fruit and vegetable consumption amongst Sudanese children

Khartoum, the capital of Sudan, is one of the main areas for the production of fruit and vegetables in general and for their export in particular [9]. Our research team conducted a study on university students (n=121), aged 16-19 (mean 17.7 ± 0.5) years, aiming at determining their dietary pattern. Repeated 24 hour recall records (n= 3) were used. The findings indicated that fruits were only consumed as snacks. Students (60%; 43% boys compared to 68% girls) did not consume fruits and only 7% had whole fruit pieces whereas 33% had fruit juices (50% boys whereas 25% girls). Significant differences were found between boys and girls regarding their fruit **consumption** (P= 0.005). On the other hand, 90% of the children did not consume vegetables on a daily basis with only 7.5% having potato chips. No significant differences were reported between boys and girls in terms of their vegetable consumption.

In another study conducted in Khartoum, aiming at determining the fruit and vegetables consumptions amongst children (n=150) aged 7-12 (mean 10 ± 1.7) years, a specifically designed food frequency questionnaire was used. Children (59.3%) did not consume vegetables at all compared to 28.6% for fruit. The main reason for this was their dislike to the taste (49%) whereas and the remaining children reported no consumption mainly due to high, unaffordable price as well as taste preferences. The servings consumed by fruit and vegetable consumers are shown on (**Table 1**). Similar reasons were reported elsewhere [2,8]. Interestingly, there was a significant correlation between the fathers' educational level and children's fruit and vegetable consumption (P= 0.02, r=0.2).

Moreover, our study team conducted another study including children (n=100), aged 6-9 years (mean 89.5 ± 15.7 months). The mean daily intake of fresh fruit and vegetables was 89 g and 180 g respectively. Parental consumption of these foods affected their children's consumption positively. Similar findings were reported elsewhere [5,10]. Other studies conducted in various countries found that the consumption of fruit and vegetables among children was determined by factors such as gender where boys' intake was lower than their counterparts [11], **socio-economic**status [12] and peers and/or teacher influence [2].

Table 1: Number of servings consumed by children from the vegetable and fruit groups: Number and percent are shown.

Number of servings	n (%)
Vegetable consumption	
Not eaten	89 (59.3)
1-2 servings	22 (14.7)
3-4 servings	39 (26)
Fruit consumption	
Not eaten	89 (28.6)
1-2 servings	43 (28.6)
3-4 servings	18 (12.0)

Possible solutions to improve fruit and vegetable consumption amongst children

According to the WHO recommendations, **behavioural interventions** and improvements in the agricultural and food systems play important roles in increasing fruit and vegetable consumption [1]. In a country such as Sudan, reducing the price of these **commodities** might help improve children's intake. One study found that a school cooking and tasting intervention helped in increasing the preferences for a variety of vegetables [13]. Other interventions used school gardening as a tool as well as nutritional education [1,14]. School gardening was very successful in the past in Sudan; however, it is no longer available. Nutrition education should not just target children but also their parents who, as stated earlier, could influence their children's intake. Moreover, education could explain the future health implications of not consuming fruit and vegetables. From personal experiences, having many children around the same table make feeding and eating situations more interesting and encouraging.

Similar solution was stated previously [15]. Others suggested that by letting children select vegetables themselves, this might have a positive significant effect on vegetable intake [10]. Preparing meals with children may also improve the intake of the children, enabling a positive experience with vegetables and fruits (from personal experience).

REFERENCES

1. World Health Organization (2014) Increasing fruit and vegetable consumption to reduce the risk of non-communicable diseases. WHO technical staff report.

2. Krølner R, Rasmussen M, Brug J, Klepp KI, Wind M, et al. (2011) Determinants of fruit and vegetable consumption among children and adolescents: a review of the literature. Int J BehavNutriPhy Act 8: 112.

3. Amir SM, Abumweis SS, Jones PJ (2013) Cholesterol-lowering efficacy of plant sterols/stanols provided in capsule and tablet formats: results of a systematic review and meta-analysis. J AcadNutri Diet 113: 1494-1503.

4. Rolls BJ, Roe LS, Meengs JS (2004) Salad and satiety. Energy density and portion size of a first-course salad affect energy intake at lunch. J Americ Diet Asso 104: 1570-1576.

5. Horne PJ, Greenhalgh J, Erjavec M, Lowe CF, Viktor S, et al. (2011) Increasing pre-school children's consumption of fruit and vegetables. A model RewInterven App 56: 375-385

6. Fawzi W, Herrera MG, Nestel P (2000) Tomato intake in relation to mortality and morbidity among Sudanese children. J Nutr 130: 2537-2542.

7. WHO (2014) Promoting a Healthy diet for the WHO Eastern Mediterranean region. WHO, Geneva, Switzerland.

8. State of the Plate (2015) Study on America's Consumption of Fruits & Vegetables.

9. Dhour MMK (2004) Economics of vegetables and fruits production oriented for export in Khartoum state. Sudan University of Science and Technology, Sudan.

10. Shim JE, Kim J, Lee Y (2016) Fruit and vegetable intakes of preschool children are associated with feeding practices facilitating internalization of extrinsic motivation. J NutrEducBehav 48: 311-317.

11. Rasmussen M, Krølner R, Klepp K, Lytle L, Brug J, et al. (2006) Determinants of fruit and vegetable consumption among children and adolescents: a review of the literature. Part I: quantitative studies. Int J BehavNutri Physic Act 3: 1-19.

12. Feeney EL, O'Brien SA, Scannell AG, Markey A, Gibney ER, et al. (2014) Genetic and environmental influences on liking and reported intakes of vegetables in Irish children. Food QualPref 32: 253-263.

13. Cunningham-Sabo L, Lohse B (2013) Cooking with kids positively affects fourth graders' vegetable preferences and attitudes and self-efficacy for food and cooking. Child Obes 9: 549-556

14. Jaenke RL, Collins CE, Morgan PJ, Lubans DR, Saunders KL, et al. (2012) The impact of a school garden and cooking program on boys' and girls' fruit and vegetable preferences, taste rating, and intake. Health Education & Behavior: The Official Publication of the Society for Public Health Education 39: 131-141.

15. Lehto E, Ray C, Haukkala A, Yngve A, Thorsdottir I, et al. (2015) Predicting gender differences in liking for vegetables and preference for a variety of vegetables among 11-year-old children. Appetite 95: 285-292.

5

ASSESSING COMMUNITY READINESS TO REDUCE CHILDHOOD DIARRHEAL DISEASE AND IMPROVE FOOD SECURITY IN DIORO, MALI

Erica C. Borresen [1], Cordelia Stone [1], Abdoulaye Boré [2], Alima Cissoko [3], Ababacar Maiga [3], Ousmane A. Koita [3,*] and Elizabeth P. Ryan [1]

[1]Department of Environmental and Radiological Health Sciences, Colorado State University, Fort Collins, CO 80523, USA

[2]Faculté des Sciences Humaines et des Sciences de l'Education, University of Letters and Human Sciences of Bamako, Bamako, BP 2191, Mali

[3]Laboratoire of Biologie Moléculaire Appliquée, University of the Sciences, Techniques and Technologies of Bamako, Bamako, BP 1805, Mali

ABSTRACT

Diarrhea and malnutrition represent leading causes of death for children in Mali. Understanding a community's needs and ideas are critical to ensure the success of prevention and treatment interventions for diarrheal disease, as well as to improve food security to help reduce malnutrition. The objective of this study was to incorporate the Community Readiness Model (CRM) for the issues of childhood diarrheal disease and food security in Mali to measure baseline community readiness prior to any program implementation. Thirteen key respondents residing in Dioro, Mali were selected based on varied social roles and demographics and completed two questionnaires on these public health issues. The overall readiness score to reduce childhood diarrheal disease was 5.75 ± 1.0 standard deviation (preparation stage). The overall readiness score to improve food security was 5.5 ± 0.5 standard deviation (preparation stage). The preparation stage indicates that at least some of the community have basic knowledge regarding these issues, and want to act locally to reduce childhood diarrhea and improve food security and nutrition. Proposed activities to increase community readiness on these issues are provided and are broad enough to allow opportunities to implement community- and culturally-specific activities by the Dioro community.

Keywords: community readiness; childhood diarrhea; food security; community interventions; Mali

1. INTRODUCTION

Mali, located in the Sahel of West Africa, covers approximately 475,000 square miles and has a population of 15 million. It shares borders with seven countries. Current country health statistics indicate that 38% of children under five are stunted, 13% are wasted, and 82% are anemic [1]. The long-term effects of food insecurity, particularly in children, lead to malnutrition, stunting, and impaired cognition [2]. These outcomes share complex relationships with diarrheal diseases, and may involve a subclinical gut inflammation and altered gastrointestinal structure, referred to as environmental enteric dysfunction (EED) [3]. These global public health issues merit sustainable solutions that are acceptable to the community and require engaged collaborations from multiple stakeholders across biomedical, agriculture, nutrition, public health, toxicology, engineering, and maternal and child health sectors [4]. Furthermore, a World Bank study estimated that Mali loses over $235 million in gross domestic product annually to vitamin and mineral deficiencies warranting immediate attention with sustainable solutions [5]. Current community perceptions and behaviors to address diarrheal disease and food security are essential to consider prior to any program implementation. Health behavior change at the community level and identification of existing community resources and national nutrition program policies will incite co-creation of programs that are socio-culturally motivated and engage positive health promotion behaviors [6]. The Community Readiness Model (CRM) is a tool that integrates social and cultural contexts to understand how an issue is perceived by the community and what types of strategies can be developed at the community level. The model was developed at the Tri-Ethnic Center for Prevention Research at Colorado State University (Fort Collins, CO, USA) to assess the level of readiness to engage in prevention activities targeting a particular issue [7]. A systematic review of CRM from the scientific literature demonstrated applications including, but not limited to facilitating community-based change, creating interventions that are community- and culturally-specific, and building cooperation among systems and individuals [8].

The objective of this study was to determine baseline community readiness scores for Dioro (a rice-producing community in Mali) on the public health issues of childhood diarrheal disease and food security, as both of these community issues are related and integrated with regards to child health. It is important to note that while this CRM assessment focused on the issue of food security as a means to reduce malnutrition, metrics for nutrition security are emerging to address the complexity of malnutrition, such that nutritious food is not only available and accessible, but also appropriately utilized by everyone, especially children [9]. Findings from the community readiness analysis will aid our translational research and development team to co-create an environment for participatory-driven strategies that promote healthy behaviors that are aimed to prevent or treat diarrheal disease in children, as well as to improve food security throughout the community.

2. MATERIALS AND METHODS

2.1. The Community Readiness Model (CRM)

Figure 1 provides an overview of the 6-step CRM assessment and application process. The assessment phase has four steps: (1) identify the issue; (2) define the community with respect to the issue; (3) conduct interviews with key respondents; and (4) score the interview responses. The second phase of community readiness is the application phase, and it has the final steps: (5) develop community-specific strategies based on the stage of readiness as determined in the assessment phase and (6) implement those strategies.

Figure 1. Step-by step process of community readiness. The first phase of community readiness (assessment) includes steps 1–4. Step 4 (scoring the interviews) determines the readiness level (1–9) of a community. The second phase (application) includes steps 5–6 and involves the community to develop and implement strategies based on the stage of readiness.

To conceptualize a community's readiness, nine stages are defined as part of the CRM and include: (1) No Awareness: the community accepts the behavior as normative; (2) Denial: belief that the problem does not exist within the community; (3) Vague Awareness: recognition of the issue, however no plans to take action; (4–5) Awareness of the issue and Preparing to take action; (6) Initiation: indicates a program is being implemented; and (7–9) Full awareness/implementation of programs, including effective training and evaluation that leads to a high level of community ownership (Figure 2). It is the scoring of the interview responses (Step 4) that determines which of the nine stages best describes the readiness level of the community. These stages are similar to the transtheoretical model with a focus on community behavior change rather than individual behavior change [7].

9. Community Ownership
Program(s) are an important part of the community.

8. Confirmation/ Expansion
Effective training and evaluation in place

7. Stabilization
Full awareness/implementation of program(s)

6. Initiation:
A program is being implemented

5. Preparation:
Preparing to take action on the issue

4. Preplanning:
Awareness of the issue

3. Vague awareness:
Recognition of the issue, however no plans to take action

2. Denial:
Belief that the problem does not exist within the community

1. No Awareness:
The community accepts the behavior as normative

Figure 2. Nine stages of community readiness, as determined through the scoring process.

This article provides results on the first four steps as an appropriate baseline before an intervention is developed in the community, as well as indicates proposed activities to begin the 5th step of developing community-specific strategies [8].

2.2. Community, Study Population, and Interview Process

Thirteen key respondents living and working in Dioro, Mali (located 275 km from the capital of Bamako) were selected to be interviewed for the CRM assessment using two questionnaires developed to assess childhood diarrheal disease and food security as they pertain to the Dioro community. These individuals were chosen based on their social role within the community—particularly when it came to knowledge about childhood health, agricultural production, involvement in community and government organizations, as well as representing Dioro's eight districts. The questions were developed to determine the level of readiness for each of the following dimensions: (1) Knowledge of efforts; (2) Leadership; (3) Community climate; (4)

Knowledge of issue; and (5) Resources. Additional questions pertaining to health and food behaviors of the Dioro community were included, but were not part of the CRM assessment. The responses to these additional questions provide important community information to be used during the development and implementation of community-specific strategies (Application Phase). The protocol for the study and the questionnaires (written in English first, and then translated to French and Bambara languages) were reviewed and approved by the Colorado State University Research Integrity and Compliance Review Office in Fort Collins, CO USA and the Institut National de Recherche en Santé Publique in Bamako, Mali (protocol #15-5727H). All interviews were conducted between June and July 2015 and questions were asked via an audio recording of a well-known individual in the village to maintain consistency in how the questions were provided and to ensure the questions were asked in the correct Bambara dialect from Dioro. Verbal consent was obtained prior to conducting the interviews and participants were reimbursed $2 (USD) for their time. Key respondent interviews were completed at a central facility at the Dioro clinic and were audio recorded. These recordings were translated from French or Bambara into English for scoring purposes.

2.3. CRM Scores and Analysis

Each completed interview received five readiness scores, one for each dimension, using dimension-specific rating scales. The scores were then averaged by dimension across all key respondents to provide a profile of dimension readiness scores for the Dioro community. Each dimension score corresponded to a stage of readiness, along with an overall average readiness score that was calculated from the five dimension scores. All scores were confirmed between two trained CRM scorers and there were no major deviations to the scoring protocol. The two questionnaires are included as supplementary data (Supplementary Materials). The additional health and food behavior questions used in the interview (but not part of the readiness scoring) are also included.

3. RESULTS

3.1. Participant Characteristics

Thirteen key respondents completed two CRM questionnaires on the issues of childhood diarrhea and food security. Four respondents were female (31%) and nine were male (69%). All lived in various neighborhoods of Dioro and ranged in age from 25 to 65 years old. These individuals were chosen to be key respondents based on their various areas of expertise. They ranged from a well-known radio spokesperson to a teacher to a health worker to a rice farmer. Table 1 illustrates the key respondent characteristics. Although thirteen key respondents were interviewed, a few interviews were not included in the final scoring due to lack of appropriate answers to the questions and the inability to provide a proper score. Ten respondents were used in the childhood diarrheal disease scoring and twelve respondents were used in the food security scoring.

Table 1. Key respondent characteristics (*n* = 13).

Characteristic	Number of Key Respondents (%)
Sex	
Male	9 (69%)
Female	4 (31%)
Age range	
25–34 y	2 (15%)
35–44 y	2 (15%)
45–54 y	1 (10%)
55–64 y	4 (30%)
65+ y	4 (30%)
Dioro neighborhood	
Bozola	3 (23%)
Darsalam	2 (15%)
Djeda	1 (8%)
Hamdalaye	2 (15%)
Mairie	2 (15%)
Médine	1 (8%)
Missira	1 (8%)
Tinti	1 (8%)

Characteristic	Number of Key Respondents (%)
Social roles/Professions	
CAFO [1]	2 (15%)
Community Health Worker	1 (8%)
Fisherman	1 (8%)
Merchant	2 (15%)
Neighborhood chief	2 (15%)
Radio director	1 (8%)
Rice farmer	2 (15%)
Teacher	2 (15%)

[1] CAFO = Coordination of Associations and NGOs of Women in Mali.

3.2. Community Readiness on Childhood Diarrheal Disease

The community readiness results assessing childhood diarrheal disease are provided in Table 2. The overall readiness score was 5.75 ± 1.0 standard deviation (SD), indicating that the community readiness level is at the preparation stage. In regards to specific readiness dimensions, Knowledge of Efforts received a score of 8.0 ± 0.5 SD, the confirmation stage. Leadership scored a 5.75 ± 1.75 SD, which falls into the preparation stage. Community Climate had a score of 5.75 ± 0.75 SD, again in the preparation stage. Knowledge of Issue also was in the preparation stage with a score of 5.5 ± 1.75 SD. Resources received a score of 4.75 ± 1.0 SD, the preplanning phase. Figure 3a illustrates the range of scores across each dimension based on all key respondents' answers.

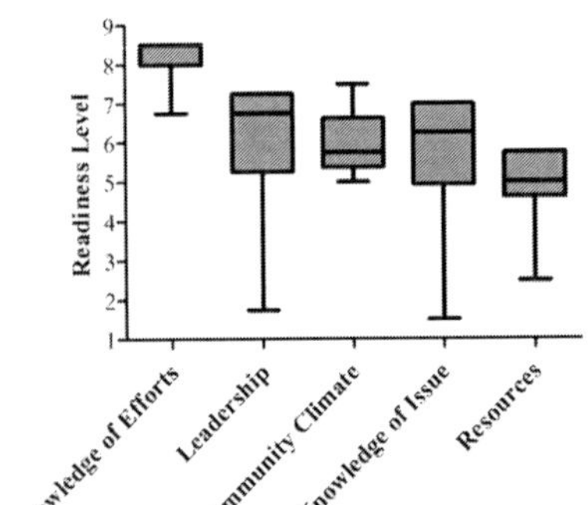

(a)

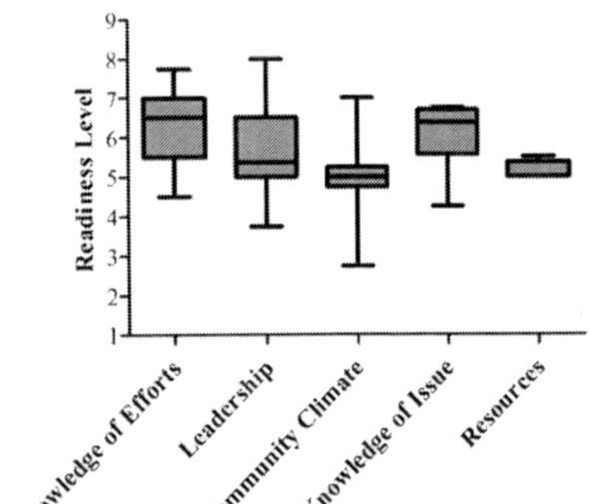

(b)

Figure 3. Community readiness results for (**a**) reducing childhood diarrheal diseases and (**b**) improving food security that show the full range of scores across each dimension (Median plus minimum and maximum scores).

Table 2. Community readiness scores following analysis of individual interviews, were averaged for each dimension and the overall readiness score for reducing childhood diarrheal diseases and improving food security [1].

Community Issue	Knowledge of Efforts	Leadership	Community Climate	Knowledge of Issue	Resources	Overall Readiness
Childhood diarrheal disease	8.0 ± 0.5 (Confirmation)	5.75 ± 1.75 (Preparation)	5.75 ± 0.75 (Preparation)	5.5 ± 1.75 (Preparation)	4.75 ± 1.0 (Preplanning)	5.75 ± 1.0 (Preparation)
Food security	6.25 ± 1.0 (Initiation)	5.5 ± 1.0 (Preparation)	5.0 ± 1.25 (Preparation)	5.75 ± 1.0 (Preparation)	5.0 ± 0.5 (Preparation)	5.5 ± 0.5 (Preparation)

[1] Values are reported as: Average Readiness Level ± Standard Deviation (Readiness Level).

3.3. Community Readiness on Food Security

The community readiness results assessing food security are provided in Table 2. The overall readiness score was 5.5 ± 0.5 SD, which is the preparation stage of readiness. For specific dimensions, Knowledge of Efforts scored a 6.25 ± 1.0 SD, the initiation stage. Leadership, Community Climate, Knowledge of Issue, and Resources all scored within the preparation stage with scores of 5.5 ± 1.0 SD, 5.0 ± 1.25 SD, 5.75 ± 1.0 SD, and 5.0 ± 0.5 SD, respectively. Figure 3b illustrates the range of scores across each dimension based on all key respondents' answers.

3.4. Collection of Health and Food Behaviors within the Community

In addition to asking questions based on the CRM, the interviewers were allowed to collect information to help develop community-driven strategies for implementing specific activities focused on both reducing childhood diarrheal diseases and improving food security. When asked what types of community leaders would need to be involved in these efforts, key respondents stated that the village chief, imams, community health workers, the Health Center Board, women and youth groups, the Coordination of Associations and NGOs of Women in Mali (CAFO), farmers, and rice millers should participate and be engaged.

In regards to current efforts occurring to improve these issues, key respondents provided information about programs that the community is familiar with and participates in, as resources are available. These efforts include educational programs to wash hands and clothes with soap and hygiene programs that include water, sanitation, and hygiene (WaSH). The local health center and its network of community health workers distribute zinc and oral rehydration salt solutions, as well as ready-to-use therapeutic foods for severe and moderately acute malnourished children, and monitor breastfeeding.

Additionally, an open-ended question was asked to get an idea on the major indications that influence reducing childhood diarrheal disease in Dioro. While WaSH strategies were mentioned, the key respondents also noted that safe and nutritious food was important, further indicative of an existing understanding of the complex connections between food systems and health.

3.5. Initial Proposed Activities to Improve Readiness

The CRM provides proposed activities to increase readiness to the next stage that are intended to keep the community on track for addressing the issue in a more culturally acceptable way. Table 3 and Table 4include a descriptive interpretation of the scores for each dimension, based on the readiness scores received from this study, as well as recommended activities to move the community to a higher stage of readiness. These proposed activities are broad enough to allow the community and invested groups of stakeholders the opportunity to determine and implement specific activities.

Table 3. Proposed activities to increase community readiness for reducing childhood diarrheal diseases according to each dimension (adapted from [10]).

Dimension	Score/Stage	Stage Definition	Goal to Maintain/Improve Stage	Activities to Increase Stage
Knowledge of Efforts	8.0/Confirmation	Most community members know a great deal about local efforts.	Conduct training and meetings to review progress and modify programs	Develop formal network Prepare community specific risk profile
Leadership	5.75/Preparation	Leadership is participating in developing and improving efforts. Some leaders are playing a key role.	Gather existing information to help plan strategies	Utilize community leaders to speak to groups and participate in local radio talk shows
Community Climate	5.75/Preparation	The community's attitude is concerned about this issue and wants to do something about it.	Gather existing information to help plan strategies	Conduct community surveys and public forums to develop strategies Sponsor a community event to initiate the effort
Knowledge of Issue	5.5/Preparation	The community members have basic knowledge about causes, consequences, signs and symptoms of childhood diarrheal diseases.	Gather existing information to help plan strategies	Conduct community surveys Present in-depth local information
Resources	4.75/Preplanning	There are limited resources currently available to address the issue.	Raise awareness with concrete ideas	Review existing efforts in community to determine who benefits and what the degree of success has been

Table 4. Proposed activities to increase community readiness for improving food security according to each dimension (adapted from [10]).

Dimension	Score/Stage	Stage Definition	Goal to Maintain/Improve Stage	Activities to Increase Stage
Knowledge of Efforts	6.25/Initiation	Most community members have at least basic knowledge of local efforts.	Provide community specific information	Plan publicity efforts associated with start-up of program/activity
Leadership	5.50/Preparation	Leadership is participating in developing and improving efforts. Some leaders are playing a key role.	Gather existing information to help plan strategies	Utilize key leaders and influential people to speak to groups and to participate in local radio shows
Community Climate	5.0/Preparation	The community's attitude is concerned about this issue and wants to do something about it.	Gather existing information to help plan strategies	Conduct community surveys and public forums to develop strategies Sponsor a community event to initiate the effort
Knowledge of Issue	5.75/Preparation	The community members have basic knowledge about causes and consequences regarding lack of food security.	Gather existing information to help plan strategies	Conduct community surveys Present in-depth local information.
Resources	5.0/Preparation	There are some resources identified that could be used to address the issue.	Gather existing information to help plan strategies	Conduct formal surveys with stakeholders to determine long-term plan of resources (both monetary and non-monetary)

4. DISCUSSION

The main purpose of this study was to conduct two CRM assessments in a rice growing community in Mali geared towards identifying strategies to address the issues of childhood diarrheal disease and food security to allow for future community-based projects. These baseline community readiness scores for the community of Dioro can be used as a starting point to organize activities that are specific to the community needs and ideas.

For both the issues of reducing childhood diarrheal diseases and improving food security, the community's overall readiness scores indicate that at least some members in the community have basic knowledge regarding these issues, are concerned, and want to do something locally about childhood diarrhea and food security. The assessments helped to collect important information on what community leaders and organizations should be involved in the planning, what resources are currently available that address these issues, and what can influence these issues the strongest. The purpose of using key respondents was to collect information from a wide range of people in the community, including community leaders, professionals in the field, and residents, all of whom have the knowledge and experience in the community as it relates to the issue being assessed.

Most of the community members of Dioro have a clear recognition that childhood diarrheal diseases and food security are a local problem, but given the absence of focused or detailed efforts (besides going to the health center for treatment), we confirmed that limited prevention efforts are in place. Results from the CRM assessment indicate that substantial additional initiatives are needed to expand benefits on a community level from these programs and include the degree of success to reduce childhood diarrheal diseases and food security. Given the breadth of community knowledge that our key respondents provided, these baseline scores should be considered representative of the current readiness of Dioro residents on these important issues.

The additional health and food behavior questions found that rice is a very important staple food in this community as it is easy to access since it is grown there and is part of the main meal. Key respondents noted that there was interest in the community to modify ingredients of traditional foods as long as it elevated taste, was convenient, was nutritious, able to improve health, and that the community is well-informed of what the modifications are. Having an overall score of 5.5 (Preparation) for community readiness in regards to improving food security, Dioro represents a promising community for implementation of novel food-focused projects. This community is aware of food security issues, but requires practical, concerted efforts to be put in place to address and improve the current situation, such as proper storage units to store food to be used during times of limited food access.

This study had limitations and important lessons learned when applying the CRM assessment to an international setting. One limitation was that the CRM assessment was developed in English and then translated into French and Bambara. The responses were also recorded in French and Bambara and translated into English for scoring and analysis. While some information may be lost in translation, our research group standardized the minimum number of translators based on fluency in all three languages. Also, while the CRM requires 4–6 key respondents within a community, this study utilized 10 key respondents for the issue of childhood diarrheal disease and 12 for the issue of food security. The additional number of individuals helped strengthen the responses to each question since each interview had to be translated for scoring purposes. This group of key respondents was a good representation of the Dioro community that incorporated a breadth of social roles and professions, especially by including women. Additionally, the questionnaire assessing food security was developed and translated prior to the availability of the expanded version of the CRM questionnaire. Since each key respondent had to complete two questionnaires in one sitting, it was decided to keep the food security questionnaire in its simplified form to reduce interviewer/interviewee fatigue. The different versions were scored following the same CRM scoring protocol.

Finally, Dioro was part of the Millennium Villages Project, an international nonprofit organization focused on accelerating the Millennium Development Goals that ended in 2015 [11]. This designation allowed for specific development initiatives (e.g., road construction, electricity, drinking water) to advance in this region of Mali, particularly infrastructure and accessibility to nutritional supplementations to treat severely and moderately acute malnourished children. Participation in the Millennium Villages Project is a major strength of the Dioro community's awareness to local public health issues and efforts, including childhood diarrheal disease, malnutrition, and food security, which may explain the high readiness scores, especially in the knowledge of efforts dimension.

5. CONCLUSIONS

Issues of childhood diarrheal diseases and food security have not previously been assessed through the CRM, and particularly in a rural, developing country setting. Due to the complexity of these global health issues and the high level of urgency to address childhood diarrhea and malnutrition in Mali, it is undoubtedly essential to integrate the community viewpoints and attitudes in these discussions and to verify how invested they are in resolving these issues [6].

This study provided baseline community readiness scores for a rice-producing community of Dioro in Mali on public health issues of childhood diarrheal diseases and food security. Next steps in this initiative will be for the Dioro community to develop and implement sustainable, community- and culturally-specific strategies based on these baseline readiness stages. In addition to a focus on reducing childhood diarrheal diseases and improving food security, future plans should also include a reassessment of readiness after community interventions take place. Moreover, continuous monitoring and evaluation of whether these public health issues begin to resolve locally will be an important outcome measure for the community.

SUPPLEMENTARY MATERIALS

The following are available online at www.mdpi.com/1660-4601/13/6/571/s1, Assessing community readiness to reduce childhood diarrheal disease questionnaire, Assessing community readiness to improve food security questionnaire.

ACKNOWLEDGMENTS

The authors would like to acknowledge support from the Bill and Melinda Gates Foundation Grand Challenges Explorations in Global Health award (OPP1043255). We wish to thank Fatoumata Cisse for her assistance in the Bambara translation of interviews and the Dioro Health Center Association in Mali for providing a private space to complete the interviews.

AUTHOR CONTRIBUTIONS

Elizabeth P. Ryan and Ousmane A. Koita are principal investigators for the CRM project in Dioro, Mali. Ababacar Maiga worked on the French translation of the questionnaires. Abdoulaye Boré and Alima Cissoko coordinated the interviews with the key respondents and helped with translations. Cordelia Stone scored the interviews and helped with translation. Erica C. Borresen developed the questionnaires, scored the interviews, and wrote the manuscript. All authors critically reviewed the manuscript and approved editorial comments for publication.

CONFLICTS OF INTEREST

The authors declare no conflict of interest.

REFERENCES

1. INFO-STAT. *Enquête Démographique et de Santé du Mali (EDSM-V) 2012–2013 Rapport Préliminaire*; Cellule de Planification et de Statistiques (CPS) & Institut National de la Statistique (INSTAT): Bamako, Mali; ICF International: Calverton, MD, USA, 2013.

2. FAO; IFAD; WFP. Meeting the 2015 international hunger targets: Taking stock of uneven progress. In *The State of Food Insecurity in the World 2015*; FAO: Rome, Italy, 2015.

3. Keusch, G.T.; Denno, D.M.; Black, R.E.; Duggan, C.; Guerrant, R.L.; Lavery, J.V.; Nataro, J.P.; Rosenberg, I.H.; Ryan, E.T.; Tarr, P.I.; *et al.* Environmental enteric dysfunction: Pathogenesis, diagnosis, and clinical consequences. *Clin. Res. Infect. Dis.* **2014**, *59*, S207–S212.

4. USAID; SPRING; GAIN. *Designing the Future of Nutrition Social and Behavior Change Communication: How to Achieve Impact at Scale*; USAID: Washington, DC, USA, 2014.

5. World Bank. World Development Indicators. 2015. Available online: http://data.worldbank.org/data-catalog/world-development-indicators (accessed on 2 March 2016).

6. Shekar, M.; Mattern, M.; Eozenou, P.; Eberwein, J.; Akoku, J.; Di Gropello, E.; Karamba, W. *Scaling Up Nutrition for A More Resilient Mali: Nutrition Diagnostics and Costed Plan for Scaling Up*; The International Bank for Reconstruction and Development/The World Bank: Washington, DC, USA, 2015.

7. Edwards, R.W.; Jumper-Thurman, P.; Plested, B.A.; Oetting, E.R.; Swanson, L. Community readiness: Research to practice. *J. Community Psychol.* **2000**, *28*, 291–307.

8. Kostadinov, I.; Daniel, M.; Stanley, L.; Gancia, A.; Cargo, M. A systematic review of community readiness tool applications: Implications for reporting. *Int. J. Environ. Res. Public Health* **2015**, *12*, 3453–3468.

9. Jones, A.D.; Ngure, F.M.; Pelto, G.; Young, S.L. What are we assessing when we measure food security? A compendium and review of current metrics. *Int. J. Environ. Res. Public Health* **2013**, *4*, 481–505.

10. Oetting, E.R.; Plested, B.A.; Edwards, R.W.; Thurman, K.; Kelly, J.; Beauvais, F.; Stanley, L. *Community Readiness for Community Change: Tri-Ethnic Center Community Readiness Handbook*; Tri-Ethnic Center for Prevention Research: Fort Collins, CO, USA, 2014.

6

INFLUENCE OF FOOD CULTURE AND PRACTICES ON HOUSEHOLD FOOD SECURITY IN NORTH CENTRAL NIGERIA

Mary Agada[1], Edwin Igbokwe[2]

[1]Department of Agricultural Extension and Communication, University of Agriculture, Makurdi, Nigeria

[2]Department of Agricultural Extension, University of Nigeria, Nsukka

ABSTRACT

The culture of a place and the cultural practices contribute directly or indirectly to the food security situation of a given society. This study assessed the influence of food culture and practices on household food security among Tiv, Igala and Eggon ethnic groups in North Central Nigeria in 2011. A sample of 120 Tiv, 108 Igala and 112 Eggon households was interviewed using a structured questionnaire and focus group discussion. The data were analyzed using descriptive statistics and a logistic regression procedure. Findings revealed that all households consumed carbohydrate based foods, men (93%) dominated agricultural decision making and undertake land preparation and ridging while women carried out weeding and food processing. All households practiced subsistence farming, 94.7% practiced mixed cropping, 93% acquired farmland through inheritance and 67 % sourced farm labour from the family. Males controlled household income (95%) and had preference in household food sharing (78%). Food culture and practices that significantly influenced household food security were control over household income (-1.056;

$p \leq 0.05$) and preference over household food sharing (0.834; $p \leq 0.05$). The study concluded that culture was a dominant factor in number of meals consumed per day, household food choices, agricultural decision making, cropping system, division of labour, land acquisition, control over household income, preference in household food sharing and hence food security. It is recommended that both male and female farmers should be encouraged to diversify their income sources and make more money accessible for food purchases. Also, both gender should be provided access to productive resources for increased agricultural production and productivity for food security. Furthermore, farmers should be encouraged to produce and consume food of increased quality and diversity for improved nutrition and food security and household food should be fairly distributed in order to take care of the nutritional needs of all family members.

Keywords: food, culture, practices, households, Nigeria

INTRODUCTION

Food security is physical and economic access to sufficient, safe and nutritious food to meet the dietary needs and food preferences by all people, at all times for an active and healthy life [1]. The major elements of food security are food availability, food access, food utilization and protection of access. Food availability for farm households in rural areas means assurance that they can access sufficient food through their own production or through purchase from markets, given sufficient purchasing power. Food access is ensured when households, and all individuals within them, have adequate resources to obtain appropriate foods for a nutritious diet. The key determinants of food access are economic, physical, political and socio-cultural factors [2]. Food utilization means ensuring nutritional outcome [3]. Stability of food supplies means that households do not risk losing access to food due to adverse weather conditions, political instability or economic factors such as unemployment or rising food prices [4].

Food security is a global challenge as reflected in the Millennium Development Goal (MDG) of eradicating extreme poverty and hunger. This includes reducing by half the proportion of people who suffer from hunger between 1990 and 2015. In 2010 an estimated 925 million people in the world were hungry, of which 907 million (98%)

were in developing countries [5, 6]. The food security situation in Nigeria has improved slightly recording only 6 percent level of undernourishment in 2006/2008. Both the number and proportion of undernourished individuals decreased from 16.3 million people in 1990/1992 to 9.4 million in 2006/2008 [7]. However, food availability does not necessarily ensure food accessibility at the household level.

Availability of food and access to food depend largely on the food culture and practices of a people among other factors. Culture is defined as the way of life of a particular society and it refers to the roles, uses, position and symbolism of individuals, ideas and objects such as food in all aspects of a society, including beliefs, values, norms, taboos, institutions, language, rituals and arts [8]. The culture of a place is intrinsically linked to the food consumed in the region as culture prescribes the interaction between people, between people and land, and between land and food [8, 9]. Culture impacts on food and nutrition security through the systems of crop production, distribution and utilization [8, 10, 11]. Ethnicity is also related to food security because the environments where people live and their ancestral origins influence food culture and practices with food and food cultures passed on from one generation to another [8]. Furthermore, the specific socio-cultural norms that govern control over income and household food allocation can influence access to food [12].

Studies on the cultural dimensions of food security in Nigeria are scanty. Some of the works that have been done in this area in Nigeria dwell mainly on listing traditional food taboos and their implications for food and nutrition security [13, 14]. However, the understanding of how food culture and practices influence household food security among ethnic groups is essential in order to take appropriate measures to ensure food security. This paper, therefore, examined the food culture and practices of the respondents and determined their effects on household food security in a study carried out in North Central Nigeria and provided this understanding.

METHODS

The data examined in this paper were part of a large survey of households' food security situation among selected ethnic groups in North Central Nigeria.A mixed methods approach was employed using a questionnaire and semi-structured interviews to collect quantitative and qualitative data.

2.1. Study Population and Setting

North Central Nigeria is known for its diversity of ethnic groups, including the Ibira, Nupe, Gwari, Eggon, Pyem, Goemai, Kofyar, Jukun, Igala, Idoma and Tiv who obtain their living from agricultural production. The study population comprised three of these ethnic groups and one village per ethnic group purposively selected based on differences in language and culture.

2.2. Quantitative Data Collection and Analysis

A random sample of 120 Tiv, 108 Igala and 112 Eggon households were interviewed using a structured questionnaire. Food security, which is the dependent variable, was measured as follows: Firstly, the household's calorie intake was obtained by requesting the person responsible for food preparation in the household to report the quantities of every food item consumed in the household in the past 24 hours. Secondly, the quantities were converted to grams and the calorie content was estimated using the available food consumption tables [15, 16]. Thirdly, per capita calorie intake was calculated by dividing the estimated total household calorie intake by the number of Adult Equivalent (AE) in the household using the consumption factor for age-sex categories [17]. Based on FAO criteria, the food security line for Nigeria was 2766 kcal [18]. Consequently, households whose daily per capita calorie supply per AE was greater than 2766 kcal were regarded as food secure and were assigned a value of 1 while households experiencing a calorie deficit were regarded as food insecure and were assigned a value of 0.

Five explanatory variables (cropping systems, land tenure systems, labour use, control over household income and preference in household food distribution), all measured as discrete variables, were identified to be major food culture and practices that influence household food security in this study. Except for control over household income and preference in household food distribution, the remaining three variables were a priori expected to have a positive impact on food security.

The Logit regression model was used to estimate the food security status of households as a function of a set of food culture and practices. The model has been widely used for binary dependent variables [19, 20]. The Logit regression model was used to determine the influence of food culture and practices on household food security is represented as:

$$Z = \ln \frac{p_i}{1-p_i}$$
$$= \ln Ya + b_1 x_1 + b_2 x_2 + b_3 x_3 + b_4 x_4$$
$$+ b_5 x_5 + b_6 x_6 + b_7 x_7$$

Where:

Z =probability of food security (1 = food secure; 0 = food insecure).

bs= coefficients of explanatory changes in z caused by change in the independent variables.

X1= Cropping systems (monocropping=1; Mixed cropping=0).

X2= Land tenure systems (inheritance=1; purchase=0)

X3= Labour use (family=1; hired, exchange=0).

X4= Control over household income (household head=1; wife=0)

X5 = Preference over household food sharing (husband/adult males=1; wife, children= 0).

2.3. Qualitative Data Collection and Analysis

Focus group discussions were held separately with groups of 10 men and 10 women in each village to elicit information on the cultural context of food and gender participation in agriculture.

RESULTS

3.1. Cultural Context of Food and Gender Involvement In Agriculture

3.1.1. Cultural context of Food

The focus group discussions revealed that among the three ethnic groups, food is taken for survival and consumption of 3 meals per day is customary. The foods consumed regularly by the households were yam, guinea corn and cassava by Tiv; cassava and maize by Igala and rice and beans by Eggon communities. At special events such as marriages and burials, pounded yam, cassava/corn food and rice are served by the Tiv, Igala and Eggon households respectively. In addition, the Eggon households serve local beans ('Ijeingbeckme') at traditional marriages and rice and beans at the naming of a new born child.

3.1.2. Traditional gender Involvement in Agriculture

Both the men and the women groups reported that household heads, who are usually men, took the decisions on agricultural production activities such as what fields to use, which crops to plant, who in the household should plant which crops and who should carry out what activity.

The group discussions further revealed that both men and women in Tiv farm households undertake the production of both food (yam, guinea corn and maize) and cash crops (beniseed, rice and groundnut). Gender disaggregation by agricultural activities in Tiv farm households is such that both men and women take part in planting, fertilizer application, seed storage and sale of produce. Men are responsible for land preparation, ridging, herbicide application and pest management while women carry out weeding, crop harvesting and processing.

Among the Igala ethnic group, men grow food crops such as cassava, yam and maize while women produce cassava, bambaranut and cocoyam. The cash crops for men include maize, yam and pigeon pea and those for the women are cassava, bambaranut and pepper. Both men and women undertake planting harvesting and storage of harvested crops. Men have the sole responsibility of land preparation, ridging, fertilizer application, pest management and seed storage while women undertake the tasks of weeding, crop processing and sale of produce.

Eggon men produce food crops such as rice, cassava, maize and guinea corn and the women grow cassava and rice. Both men and women grow cash crops such as rice, cassava, melon and beniseed. While the men are responsible for land preparation; ridging, fertilizer application, herbicide application and sale of produce the women carry out planting, weeding, seed storage and crop processing. Both men and women are involved in crop harvesting and storage.

3.2. Households' Food Culture and Practices

The results of household food culture and practices are summarized in Table 1.

3.2.1. Cropping System

Majority of the households practice mixed cropping (Tiv-91.7%, Igala-96.3%, Eggon-96.4%). In all, 94.7% of farmers in North Central Nigeria practice mixed cropping.

3.2.2. Land Tenure Systems

Findings revealed that majority (93%) of the households acquired farm lands through inheritance, although a small proportion (6.5%) cultivated lands they personally owned through outright purchase.

3.2.3. Labour Use

The types of labour used in agricultural production among the ethnic groups can be classified into three categories: family labour, hired labour and exchange labour. Of these, family labour was the main source of labour among the ethnic groups studied. Family labour accounted for 67.6% of total labour used in agricultural production whereas exchange labour contributed about 25% and hired labour 7%.

3.2.4. Control over Household Income

Majority of the households reported that husbands had control over household income (Tiv-92.5%, Igala-91.7%, Eggon-99.7).

3.2.5. Preference in Household Food Sharing

Majority of the households across the ethnic groups reported that husbands were served first in household food distribution (Tiv-70.4%, Igala-83.9%, Eggon-77.9). A small proportion of the households served children first (Tiv-9.2%, Igala-28.7%, Eggon-16.1%) while a minority served women and younger girls first (Anter-11.7%, Ikem-1 %.).

Table 1. Percentage distribution of food culture and practices among ethnic groups in North Central Nigeria

Food culture/practices	Tiv (n=120)	Igala (n=108)	Eggon (n=112)	Pooled (n=340)
Cropping systems				
Mixed cropping	91.7	94.4	95.3	94.7
Both monocropping and mixed cropping	8.3	5.6	4.5	5.3
Land tenure systems				
Inheritance	97.5	91.7	84.8	92.5
Purchase	2.5	8.3	15.2	6.5
Labour use				
Family labour	67.5	71.3	64.2	67.6
Hired labour	7.5	9.3	4.5	7.1
Labour exchange	25.0	19.4	31.2	25.3
Control over family income				
Husband	92.5	91.7	77.7	95.4
Wife	7.5	8.3	22.3	12.6
Preference in food sharing				
Husband/adult male	79.2	0.9	83.9	77.9
Women/children	20.9	57.4	0.0	22.0

Table 2. Logit estimation results of the effect of food culture and practices on household food security in North Central Nigeria

Food culture and practices	B	S.E	Wald	DF	Sig	(Exp (B)
Constant	-21.64	6674.51	.000	1	.997	.000
Cropping systems (X_1)	-1.29	.86	2.23	1	.135	.277
Labour use (X_2)	2.52	.295	72.99	1	.000	12.46
Land tenure system (X_3)	21.80	6674.51	.000	1	.997	29388026
Control over household income (X_4)	-1.06*	.48	4.829*	1	.028	.338
Preference over household food sharing (X_5)	.83*	.37	5.008*	1	.025	2.302

*Significant ($p \leq 0.05$).

3.3. Food Culture and Practices Influencing Household Food Security

The results of the logistic regression in Table 2 revealed that two out of the five variables on food culture and practices included in the model were significant in explaining the variations in the food security status of households in the study area. These variables are control over household income (-1.056; $p \leq 0.05$) and preference in household food sharing (0.834; $p \leq 0.05$). Control over household income was negative and significant at 5% level, implying that control over household income by husbands decreases the probability of food security. Preference over household food sharing was positive and significant at 5% level. This indicates that giving priority to husbands/adult males in household food distribution increases the probability of household food security.

DISCUSSION

The fact that the ethnic groups studied consumed mostly carbohydrate based foods the previous day suggests a low quality diet in North Central Nigeria. This may have far-reaching health and nutrition consequences in both the short and the long term. A diet too high in carbohydrate can upset the delicate balance of the body's blood sugar level, resulting in fluctuations in energy and mood that leave one feeling irritated and tired [21]. In addition, too much carbohydrate can lead to weight gain, obesity, diabetes and potentially other diet related diseases [22].

The domination of the household heads who are usually males in agricultural decision making may be attributed to the patriarchal nature of society and power relations as well as access to resources that has been structured in a way to favour men. This is despite the fact that women contribute about 70% of agricultural labour, 50% of animal husbandry related activities and 60% of food processing activities in Nigeria [23]. The exclusion of women from household decision-making could impact negatively on household food security.

The striking difference in the traditional gender division in agriculture among the three ethnic groups is that while women in Igala farm households undertake the sale of farm produce, men carry out the same task in Eggon farm households while in Tiv households both men and women are involved. Generally, the traditional division of agricultural activities among the three ethnic groups is such that men are responsible for heavy tasks of land preparation and ridging while women carry out the lighter tasks of weeding and crop processing. Increased agricultural productivity for farm households for food security, therefore, depends on increased access by both men and women to productive resources.

The practice of mixed cropping in the study area could have a positive influence on food security by providing security for farmers against pests, disease and unexpected climatic conditions. It may help small-scale farmers obtain higher yields, provides farming communities with a range of products with multiple uses and values as well as varieties of crops for immediate consumption and for long-term storage [24]. In the traditional mixed cropping system the diverse crop species usually grown together complement one another by using resources in different ways, scarce labour is sufficiently utilized, weeds and insects are suppressed, erosion is controlled, there is sequential harvesting and the risk of total crop loss is averted. In the light of this, being subsistence farmers, the practice of multiple cropping found to be dominant in the region should be encouraged while research and extension activities should focus on developing and promoting appropriate technologies, including use of inputs that can raise productivity in mixed cropping system.

The analysis of the method of land acquisition indicated that inheritance was the most important means of acquiring farm land in North Central Nigeria. Similar result was obtained in South West Nigeria [25]. However, it must be noted that the traditional land tenure system, including land inheritance, hinders large scale farming or cultivation. It also restricts the freeing of land to would be investors for socio-economic development, particularly in rural areas of Nigeria [26]. In view of the fact that the livelihoods of over 70% of the inhabitants of the area are linked to land and natural resource exploitation, access to land and provision of necessary inputs and incentives by governments in North Central Nigeria would increase agricultural production and productivity leading to food security and sustainable development in the region.

The importance of family labour in farm work and the lack of mechanization in agricultural production imply that the availability of family labour is a prerequisite for a household to increase farm size. In addition, the use of family labour reflects the subsistence nature of the farming system, which is mainly for family survival. Labour is a key asset for smallholder households in rural Nigeria. In the context of Nigeria's smallholder production where farm mechanization is virtually non-existent and all farm work is done manually, having access to necessary labour for agricultural production directly affects the levels of household farm income and hence food security.

The finding of this study on control over the household income by men concurs with the report of the United Nations that, in areas where men are in control of household income, less money is spent on food when compared to those where women have control over income [27] but contrasts the research in Bangladesh which showed that, increases in fathers' income share lead to increased spending on food [28]. However, numerous studies have found that increases in women's income share are associated with a variety of improved child outcomes or with spending on goods likely to benefit children. For instance, income in mother's control has been found to be associated with improvements in child health in Brazil [29] and increased spending on nutrients, health and housing in rural Mexico [30]. In Cote d'Ivoire, it was found that wife's income share had a positive effect on the budget allocated to food [31]. In addition, it has been reported that the income controlled by women has greater immediate benefits for the family's nutritional well-being than male-controlled income[32].It should be noted, however, that cultures assign responsibility for different household domains to women and men, and these gendered social arrangements influence how money is used. These differential impacts of male-and female-controlled income can have important implications for the design and evaluation of income-related projects or policies for improving food security. It is, therefore, suggested that more research be conducted on implications of male versus female controlled income for family members' food consumption and nutritional status in the region before any substantial resources are devoted to this issue in the policy arena.

The general practice in household food sharing in North Central Nigeria is for husbands to be served first. The finding of this study indicates that giving priority to husbands/adult males in household food distribution increases the probability of household food security. This is so because in the traditional division of labour in agricultural activities in North Central Nigeria, males undertake the heavy agricultural tasks while females carry out the lighter tasks. Besides, farm work is manually done in the study area. Therefore, the males may require more food in order to produce enough food for household consumption and for enhanced income, which could be used for purchases during food crisis. However, this could threaten the nutritional wellbeing of the vulnerable members of the family. The finding also agrees with other studies [33, 34, 35] which revealed that inequalities in food distribution within families in many countries have favoured men over women, among other variables. Furthermore, it has been found that, in Bangladesh women eat after men and children have eaten and what is left after all others have eaten [36]. However, giving priority to the head of the family and the income-earning members of the household in eating could result in mothers and young children receiving a smaller share of the family's food relative to their nutritional needs [37]even though a household may have enough food. There is, therefore, the need to create awareness among all family members and particularly fathers of the benefits of adequate nutritional intake for the nutritional well-being and productive capacities of all household members.

CONCLUSION

The study concluded that culture is a dominant factor in number of meals consumed per day, household food choices, agricultural decision making, cropping system, division of labour, land acquisition, control over household income, preference in household food sharing and hence food security. Food culture and practices that significantly influenced household food security were control over household income and preference over household food sharing.

Although decision making in agriculture is often seen as a male task, women's capacities should be built through training to use their bargaining power to negotiate their participation. Additionally, farmers should be encouraged to produce and consume food of increased quality and diversity for improved nutrition and food security, and household food should be fairly distributed in order to take care of the nutritional needs of all family members. Both male and female farmers should be encouraged to diversify their income sources and make more money accessible for food purchases. Furthermore, both male and female farmers should be provided access to productive resources for increased agricultural production and productivity for food security.

ACKNOWLEDGEMENT

The authors thank the farmers in Tiv, Eggon and Igala villages who generously gave their time to participate in the study. They are also especially grateful to their research assistants, Simon Ejembi and Francis Ukohol.

STATEMENT OF COMPETING INTERESTS

The authors have no competing interests.

FUNDING

This research was self-funded by the authors.

REFERENCES

1. FAO. United Nations Food and Agriculture Organization. Rome declaration on world food security and world food summit plan of action. FAO, Rome, 1996.

2. Kidane W, Maetz M and P Dardel Food security and agricultural development in sub-Saharan Africa. Building a case for more public support. Main Report. Policy Assistance Series 2, 2006: 1-7.

3. Cohen MJ, Tirado C, Aberman N and B Thompson Impact of Climate Change and Bioenergy on Nutrition. IFPPRI/FAO, Rome, 2008.Retrieved from ftp://ftp.fao.org/docrep/fao/010/ai799e/799e02.pdf.

4. FAO. United Nations Food and Agriculture Organization. Practical Guides: An Introduction to the Basic Concepts of Food Security. FAO, Rome, 2008.

5. FAO. United Nations Food and Agriculture Organization. The state of food insecurity in the world 2009.FAO, Rome, 2010.

6. Hunger Notes. World hunger and poverty facts and statistics. Washington D.C.World Hunger Education Service, 2011. Retrieved from http://www.worldhunger.org/learn/worldhungerfacts2002.htm.

7. FAO. United Nations Food and Agriculture Organization. Monitoring Progress towards Hunger Reduction Targets of the World Food Summit (WFS) and the Nigeria Millennium Development Goals (MDGs).Global Statistics Service-Food Security Indicators. FAO, Rome, 2011.

8. Byaruhanga YB and PM Opedum The Impact of Culture on Food Security in Uganda: A Study on How Paternal Society and TraditionsImpact on Food Security in Uganda. Global Knowledge, 1. Retrieved from Front-Page/Global-knowledge/issues/No-1-2008/.

9. Ashish C, Majeed CAF and C Sudhir A comparative study of food consumption pattern across selected Indian villages. Theme paper submitted to URAVU, BAIF, CCD and RACHANA, 2008: 6-8.

10. Villarreal M Culture, agriculture and rural development: A review from FAO's Population Programme Service. Sustainable Development Department Retrieved from. http://www.fao.org/ 2000.

11. Hagg D Arts, culture and food security in Southern African Development. Draft Report by the South African Department of Arts and Culture. Retrieved from 4195_Hagg_Artcultureandfoodsecurity (1) 2006.pdf.

12. World Bank Gender and food security. Retrieved from http://siteresources.worldbank.org/.

13. Nwajiuba CA and O Okechukwu Social status, Traditional Food Taboos and Food Security: A Study of Igbo Women in Imo State, Nigeria. Journal of Agriculture and Food Science 2006; 4 (2): 139-146.

14. Onuorah CI and IA Ayo Food Taboos and their Nutritional Implications for Developing Countries like Nigeria- a review 2003; 33 (5): 235-240.

15. Oguntona EB and IO Akinyele Nutrient Composition of Commonly Eaten Foods in Nigeria - Raw Processed and Prepared. Food Basket Foundation Series, Ibadan, 1995.

16. Smith IF The Case for Indigenous West African Food Culture. BREDA 9, UNESCO, Dakar.1995. Retrieved from unesdoc.unesco.org/images/0010/001055/105546E.pdf.

17. Falusi AO Socio-Economic Factors Influencing Food Nutrition Consumption of Urban and Rural Households: A Case Study of Ondo State of Nigeria. Nigerian Journal of Nutritional Sciences 1985; 6 (2): 52.

18. Swindale A and P Ohri-Vachaspati Measuring household food consumption: A technical guide. Food and Nutrition Technical Assistance Project (FANTA), Academy for Educational Development, Washington, DC.2005.

19. Bamire AS and O Olubode Socio-Economic Determinants of Land Degradation in Osun State. In: Agricultural Economics in

Nigeria. Proceedings of Association of Agricultural Economists. Nsukka, Nigeria, 2002: 212-217.

20. Oni OA, Omonona BT and AA Akinseinde Access to credit and food security status of farming households in Lagelu LGA of Oyo State, Nigeria. BOWEN Journal of Agriculture.I2004; (2):190-201.

21. Worden J Carbohydrates. www.netdoctor.co.uk>Diet and nutrition>Diet and nutrition facts.

22. Marie J What are the Dangers of Excessive Amounts of Carbohydrates? Healthyeating.sfgate.com? Nutrition>Nutrition in Foods.

23. FMWASD. Federal Ministry of Women Affairs and Social Development. National Gender Policy. Tonem Publicity and Publications Ltd, Abuja, Nigeria, 2007.

24. Boon EK Food Security in Africa: Challenges and Prospects. Regional Sustainable Review-Africa. UNESCO-EOLSS Sample Paper, Dakar, 2002.

25. Dayo P, Nkonya E, Pender J and OA Oni Constraints to Increasing Agricultural Productivity in Nigeria. International Food Policy Research InstituteBrief 2008; (4):1-3.

26. Ering SO Food Security, Land Rights and Land Reform In Nigeria: Implication for Socio-Economic Development. Sacha Journal of Human Rights 2011; 1(1): 37-49.

27. United Nations. Organic Agriculture and Food Security in Africa. UNEP-UNCTAD Capacity Building Task Force on Trade, Environment and Development, 2008.

28. Quisumbing A and B de la Briere Women's Assets and Intra-household Allocation in Rural Bangladesh: Testing Measures of Bargaining Power. FCND Discussion Paper 86. Washington, DC: IFPRI, 2000.

29. Thomas D Intra-household Resource Allocation: An inferential approach. Journal of Human Resources 1990; 25 (4):635-64.

30. Djebarri H The impact of nutrition of intra-household distribution of power. IZA Discussion paper 1701. Bonn, Germany: Institute for the Study of Labour, 2005.

31. Hodinott J and L Haddad Does Female Income Share Influence Household Expenditure? Evidence from Cote d Ivoire. Oxford Bulletin of Economics and Statistics 1995; 57 (1):77-96.

32. FAO. United Nations Food and Agriculture Organization. Agriculture, Food and Nutrition for Africa. A Resource Book for Teachers of Agriculture, FAO, Rome, 1997:12-242.

33. Behrman JR Intra-household Distribution and the Family. Unpublished draft. University of Pennsylvania, 1992.

34. Staatz JM, D'Agostino VC and S Sundberg Measuring Food Security in Africa: Conceptual, Empirical and Policy Issues. American Journal of Agricultural Economics 1990; 72 (5):1, 311-17.

35. Wise V Gender Issues in Food Security Research in the Sahel." Unpublished draft, 1992.

36. Rahman A On Measuring Intra-household Inequality in Food Distribution-Is Conventional Calories Intake Enough to Undertake Individual Wellbeing Within the Household? London: Department of Economics, University College, Mimeograph, 2002.

37. Basu A, Roy SK, Mukhopadhyay B, Bharati P, Grupta R and PP Majumder Sex bias in inter-household food distribution: Roles of ethnicity and socio-economic characteristics. Arthropod 1986; (27):536-539.

7

THE IMPACT OF FOOD INSECURITY ON THE HEALTH OF COLOMBIAN REFUGEES IN ECUADOR

Michele G. Shedlin[1,], Carlos U. Decena[2], Hugo Noboa[3], Oscar Betancourt[3], Stacia B. Birdsall[1], Kaitlyn M. Smith[4]

[1]College of Nursing, New York University, New York, USA

[2]School of Arts and Science, Rutgers State University of New Jersey, USA

[3]Fundacion Salud Ambiente y Desarrollo (FUNSAD), Quito, Ecuador

[4]Bucknell University, Lewisburg, USA

ABSTRACT

This paper illustrates the salience of the specific factors challenging the food security of a refugee population and the effects on their health and wellbeing. Data presented are part of an NIH/NIDA study that explored the health implications of the forced migration of Colombian refugees in Ecuador. The two-year investigation utilized a qualitative approach and methods including in-depth interviews with refugees (n=96), focus groups (n=5) and interviews with key informants (n=21), permitting the triangulation of data sources and methods. Ethnographic observations and media analysis of the refugee situation were carried out as well. Data were analyzed using Atlas.ti software. Food insecurity emerged as a primary factor affecting all aspects of refugee life, the result of a complex interplay of socio-political forces such as discrimination and high rates of unemployment. The results of the study suggest the need to develop grounded, informed, and situation-specific guidelines to address the burgeoning epidemic of food insecurity in Ecuador and among refugee communities.

Keywords: Colombian refugees, food insecurity, health, discrimination, Ecuador

INTRODUCTION

Food security is defined by the WHO as existing "when all people at all times have access to sufficient, safe, nutritious food to maintain a healthy and active life" [66]. Conversely, groups that experience food insecurity consume insufficient and/or poor quality food, and may engage in socially undesirable activities to obtain food. Food insecurity (FI) is a major cause of poor nutritional status in populations globally [15]. Serious short- and long-term health implications [18] include poor physical, mental, and social health [62]. FI can be chronic and persistent, generally caused by extreme poverty, or acute, which is transitory and often triggered by violent conflict or forced migration [27].

Refugees are particularly vulnerable to FI [14, 18, 23, 51, 52, 57], and the consequences of food insecurity often make the resettlement process more difficult [18]. It is important to understand the factors influencing forced migration and the development and prevalence of post-migratory FI among refugees. Although 75% of refugees worldwide relocate to neighboring, lower mid-income, non-OECD countries with 'similar ethnic, social, and cultural characteristics' [21, 26, 59], the existing literature has largely focused on refugees resettled in food-rich OECD nations such as Australia, the UK, and US [16, 18, 20, 34, 43, 44, 46, 49]. While acculturation variables such as English competency, time since resettlement, and adaptation to new shopping environments and budgeting practices are often cited as barriers to food security in these contexts [14, 23, 24, 51], refugees resettling in resource-poor countries likely face different barriers. The literature addressing this phenomenon in these countries is limited in scope, with the majority only briefly mentioning FI when discussing the benefits and burdens endured by host communities [1, 8, 36, 64]. This represents a significant gap in the literature.

This paper illustrates the context-specific factors challenging the food security of a refugee population and the effects on their health and wellbeing. The data presented were collected as part of an NIH/NIDA R21 study, completed in 2012, which explored the health implications of forced migration on Colombian refugees in Ecuador. The study addressed the need for a more complete understanding of the migration process and the vulnerabilities of refugees as they cross international borders, especially the understudied borders of South America. The study aims reflected the urgent need for research on specific health risks of populations in transition and how the nature and extent of disruption in their lives and environment affect voluntary and involuntary risk behaviors. Although not the primary focus of this study, food insecurity emerged as a major theme, impacting every aspect of daily life for refugees, including their struggles for safety and the health of their families. We present the context and data relating to food insecurity, as well as the salient factors of structural violence that interact with it including sending country drug-related violence, forced migration, and receiving-country stigma and discrimination.

Although FI among non-refugee populations in Latin America has been reliably measured using the Latin American and Caribbean Household Food Security Scale (ELCSA) [4, 41, 47], only limited data are available on the experience of FI among refugees in the region. Thus an exploratory, qualitative approach was used to elicit the 'rich detail about important elements of the household experience' often missed by quantitative scales [10]. Our study data add to a better understanding of the impact of forced migration on FI, and specifically identify factors that prevent the integration of Colombian refugees in Ecuador. The voices of the refugees themselves provide a deeper understanding of the nuances of FI in this population, and have relevance for food insecurity in migrant and refugee populations globally.

1.1. The Colombian Refugee Situation

Violent conflict between rival right-wing paramilitary groups and left-wing guerilla forces has been intensifying in Colombia since the 1970s [29], and has led to the internal and international displacement of over 10 percent of the Colombian population [30]. Military factions involved in Colombia's illegal drug trade, such as the Revolutionary Armed Forces of Colombia (FARC) and the National Liberation Army of Colombia (ELN), are known to target innocent civilians and engage in kidnapping, assassination, and extortion in the countryside [5]. Fearing for their lives, Colombian individuals and families are forced to flee to neighboring countries, often leaving behind relatives and personal possessions [59, 61]. The number of refugees leaving Colombia each year has increased significantly over the past decade [59]. By 2012, 374,000 people had left Colombia, ranking it 8th in the world among source countries of refugees [59]

In Latin America, no country receives more refugees than Ecuador, where 98 percent of the refugees are Colombian citizens fleeing violence in their home country [60]. It is estimated that more than 1,000 Colombian refugees enter Ecuador each month [60], and in 2012, the United Nations High Council on Refugees estimated that Ecuador was home to 123,000 refugees, of which only 54,600 were registered [59]. With little social or economic capital, these refugees are often unprepared to deal with the traumatic consequences of resettlement. They arrive in Ecuador lacking any valuable assets and are met with few employment opportunities, low wages, and limited social support, all of which compromise their food security [5]. In Ecuador, where more than 19 percent of the urban population suffers from chronic malnutrition [67], refugees are at even greater risk for food insecurity and its consequences [5]. In addition, refugees face discrimination, violence, inadequate health care and housing insecurity, all contributing to their health vulnerability [53]. The exacerbated vulnerability to FI facing refugees is the product of a unique interaction of variables [63] often characteristic of forced migration.

2. STUDY APPROACH AND METHODS

The major objective of this research was to collect descriptive data on the characteristics of recent refugees from the Colombian drug wars living in Ecuador, and the contextual and behavioral factors placing them at risk for substance abuse and sexually transmitted infections, including HIV. However, because the in-country collaborating agencies were concerned about the sensitivities associated with these topics, the bi-national research team expanded the focus to include general health-related issues into which the more sensitive topics were embedded. Modifications included the addition of the topic of food insecurity.

Grounded theory served as the rationale for methodological decisions regarding the qualitative approach and methods, and the emphasis on multiple perspectives [56]. Our two-year study involved in-depth interviews and focus groups. Inclusion criteria for refugee participants included: adult men and women 18 years of age or older; born in Colombia; minimum residency in Ecuador of three years; and migration due to violence and concerns for physical or emotional safety. Semi-structured individual interviews were conducted with 96 refugees. The refugee interviews utilized a questionnaire with open and closed-ended questions. This questionnaire was developed in Spanish by the international, interdisciplinary team of researchers and pre tested by the implementing NGO. Five focus groups (total n=41) were facilitated by the Principal Investigator or NGO investigators. These sessions took place with various sectors of the population: sex workers; drug users; male refugees; female refugees; and key informants. Interviews with key informants (n=21) contributed to the triangulation of data sources and methods. The key informant interview guides and the focus group moderator guide were developed to provide additional depth and detail to the survey data and to obtain additional perspectives from knowledgeable gatekeepers and refugees respectively. In addition, in-country researchers carried out ethnographic observations and a review of printed media coverage of the refugee situation during the period of data collection. The ethnographic component of the study provided important information on the context of health challenges for the refugee population. Observation guides were used to obtain some degree of comparability of observations in the community by NGO investigators. Thus four (4) separate instruments were developed for this study in order to better obtain multiple perspectives on the key research questions.

All data collection was carried out in Spanish and analyzed in Spanish using Atlas.ti.

3. ETHICS

The Institutional Review Boards (IRBs) of the University of Texas at El Paso (where the study was originally funded), New York University (where the study was transferred) and the Universidad Central de Ecuador approved the study. Informed Consent documents were written in Spanish, modified in-country and adjusted to ensure compliance with all regulations of the IRBs of the US and Ecuadorian universities involved. This protocol conforms to the stipulations within the Helsinki Declaration. Basic demographic information about participants was collected to inform an overall participant profile, but identifying personal information was not collected and no individual names were used. Numbers and codes were used to identify each tape and transcript.

4. RESULTS

4.1. Refugees' Environment

Multiple waves of migration to Quito over the last forty years have created a distribution of settlements in several sectors of the city. Most of these sectors are of modest economic condition, densely populated with working class residents and internal migrants from the countryside. Ethnographic observation confirmed that overcrowding and substandard construction was common, with dirt-floored one or two-roomed cinderblock structures often housing a dozen refugees. Notably, study observations also found that all of the areas studied had a wide variety of fresh foods available in municipal markets, government warehouses, and grocery stores, indicating that food insecurity in the study population did not stem from a lack of availability of food.

4.2. Disrupted Social Support Networks

Many refugees who fled Colombia because of paramilitary violence experienced the disruption of their social networks as they came alone without friends or family. Often they had no time to coordinate travel with other people leaving Colombia and were unable to find them once they arrived in Ecuador. All members of a family were not always able to leave together. Sending a mother with her children to escape an attack, or sending the man of the household first to find work and shelter, meant that refugees had to survive on their own for extended periods of time.

In reflecting on their displacement, many participants noted new obstacles that confronted them in Ecuador and shared how difficult resettlement was without the help of family and friends. One man described that it was much more difficult to survive in Ecuador than in Colombia because he was alone as never before:

Once I ate breakfast and did not eat until lunch the next day. And here it is more difficult because if you don't have money to buy food, you don't eat because you are alone, while in Colombia if you don't have [food], you go to your brother, your uncle, your grandmother, and they feed you.

Similarly, a 30-year-old mother came alone to Quito with her two children, leaving their father and her parents behind in Colombia for one year commented:

Well, my kids sometimes, sometimes did not eat enough, many times I went without eating...because I didn't have money, I didn't have a stable job, I didn't have access. Well, it's different when you're home [in Colombia], you go to your mom, even though you disguise it, 'Hi mom, how're you doing this morning?' And then they offer you lunch, [you can go to] your sister, [or] a friend. Here it's not like that, or it could be that we don't have family here and we don't have a close friend with whom you can pretend you don't know anything at lunchtime, and help wash the dishes so they feed you; there wasn't a way, so we endured [the hunger].

4.3. Economic Instability

Participants cited economic instability and lack of employment opportunities as the most significant impediments to accessing sufficient quantities of nutritious food. The majority of respondents reported surviving on limited incomes with little to no outside financial support. They often described living in poverty with their families and reported being forced to compromise on basic needs, most often limiting their food intake. Given the circumstances under which many were forced to flee Colombia, participants typically left most, if not all, valuable assets behind, and had few resources to rely upon during their initial displacement.

Many refugees were involved in informal economic activity such as the selling of CDs, clothing, and food and beverages, along with domestic work for women and construction work for men. The use of survival sex was another salient finding of the interviews. Many women reported having resorted to sex work as the only means of income. In fact, sex work was seen as one of the few stable jobs available to female refugees. As one of the women explained, "There are women who engage in prostitution so their children don't go hungry, and their husbands have to accept this because neither is working."

When employment opportunities were available, participants described them as short-term, informal, and unstable. Some participants who were able to find work reported discriminatory and abusive practices. It was not uncommon to complete a job and have the employer refuse to pay or pay less than the agreed-upon amount. Workers had little recourse, as employers could threaten to report undocumented refugees to Ecuadorian authorities. More commonly, the refugees interviewed described discrimination from potential employers. A common complaint was, "Here we can't find work, nobody wants to give us work because we are Colombian."

4.4. Discrimination

Discrimination was described as a fundamental issue affecting refugees. Study participants consistently reported experiencing stigma and discrimination in all aspects of their lives in Ecuador, including in jobs, schools, clinics, and social venues. Colombians, they said, were seen as a threat to Ecuadorian society. As a result, they experienced threats, verbal abuse, and violence, especially when seeking charitable assistance. One participant noted, for example, that his health was directly affected because of discrimination:

...a woman was giving me breakfast, but not anymore, and I wanted to see if I could go to the large supermarket to see if they would give me something but people always say bad things to me and I have to put up with it.

Another participant described facing both hunger and unkindness:

Sometimes I look purple when I wake up. I have gone three days without eating. I beg people but they tell me to work.

It is not surprising that when asked about the greatest needs of Colombian refugees in Ecuador, one participant stated, "food and good treatment."

4.5. Inadequate Government and Charitable Assistance

The conditions of displacement were compounded by differential access to state assistance and international aid to supplement refugees' access to work and income. Participants also reported few resources of governmental and charitable support, such as vouchers, for accessing food. Interestingly, food security was rarely a concern for Colombians prior to migration. Even amidst violence, many described governmental support and greater access to food in Colombia. One participant described the following:

When I was displaced, I went to Bogota and I received coupons for the supermarket from the international community [agency] and I was able to get everything [I needed]...dairy, fruits and everything, and outside of this they helped me get fresh vegetables and then my conditions were better.

4.6. Food Donations and Health Concerns

Without a steady income, participants reported having to rely on food donations from charitable sources. However, taking advantage of foods that were donated was seen as risky, since they were said to often be expired. Participants cited food borne illness as one of the major health problems facing them, blaming expired food donations. Multiple respondents specifically linked expired food donations to conditions within refugee shelters with outbreaks of illness among children and adults. As one respondent explained, "In the shelter they were sick a lot because the donations that come in are expired foods, preserved foods...the children had diarrhea and became pale." Participants also linked what they perceived as a high prevalence of intestinal parasites among children to their consumption of contaminated fruits and vegetables.

The questionable safety of food donations was thought to exacerbate the effects of already nutritionally poor diets. The incidence of food borne illness stemming from these donations by governmental and non-profit agencies was so troubling, one participant reported bringing it to the attention of authorities stating, "The prosecutor's office knows about this." As a strategy to stay healthy, many refugees, especially those with children, reported thoroughly washing and cooking any fruits and vegetables they received. Others stated that they did not accept donated fruits and vegetables because they appeared rotten.

4.7. The Centrality of Food Insecurity

Displacement posed numerous threats to the health and wellbeing of this population. Though having faced extreme violence and tragedy in Colombia, some participants said that life in Ecuador was worse for them. As one woman described:

In Colombia you were well. Here we are in terrible conditions, both [for] food, and where one lives, sleeping on the ground, many things, because imagine, to pay rent you have to eat less; it's very difficult.

Food insecurity was a nearly universal health concern. Access to stable and healthy food sources was reported to be one of the most urgent and unmet needs among study participants, often superseding discrimination, social isolation, and job security. Food was a consistent source of preoccupation for many. As one participant noted, “Always, every day, I start my day worried, because I am always thinking about food, I always wake up with a pain in my stomach.” One participant described hunger as a sickness that plagued the refugee population, saying that he viewed fellow Colombians as “dying of hunger.” It was not uncommon for participants to arrive at the interviews having not eaten for several days. They reported regularly experiencing hunger while resettling in Ecuador, and for many, dietary inadequacies persisted well beyond initial displacement. One mother reported being in Ecuador for six years before eating a consistent and regular diet, “Well actually, actually the lack [of food] for the children, I said hunger, they never endured hunger, but I could not feed them well for 6 years, not until I could stabilize myself.”

4.8. Rationing

Rationing was the most common strategy reported for coping with food insecurity. Most often this entailed adults eating less in order to provide sufficient food for their children. Participants largely described this method of rationing as a strategy to ensure sufficient childhood growth and development. However, many respondents suggested a deeper underlying context for this decision—ensuring that children had enough to eat, even if it meant the adults themselves went hungry, was seen as a mechanism by which children were protected from the hardships being faced. Women were seen as more likely to control how food was distributed among household members. One mother stated, “I have forgone eating several times in order to feed my children, so that they can wake up with a full stomach, because they don’t know that we are going through difficult times.”

However, participants often stated that every member of their family experienced the ramifications of food insecurity; “there wasn’t enough for anybody,” as one of them stated. Despite efforts to ration, the effects of food shortages trickled down to the youngest members of the refugee households. In these instances, it was common to skip or delay meals in order to make up for household food insufficiency. Since many participants lacked a steady income, rationing strategies were particularly used to cope with food insecurity during periods of unemployment.

4.9. Limited Food Choices

Along with rationing, participants also described eating only a limited range of foods, especially in the initial months of resettlement, which many refugees found to be extremely difficult. As one participant relayed:

I have a friend in Carapungo and he told me that things were hard the first few days. Because they did not give him work or anything, he had to sleep in cardboard boxes with his wife and daughter. He didn't sleep, didn't eat, didn't have money.

One woman who reported significant weight loss in her entire family during this period described how they only ate rice for the first four or five months after arriving in Ecuador. Also during this time, refugees commonly reported only having access to rice, bread, or lentils, and never fruit, vegetables, or meat.

Lack of employment was also seen to have an important role in limiting the range of foods that Colombian refugees could access:

We are five people, and food is a problem. The other day [we had] lentils, and I couldn't buy eggs because my husband doesn't have a stable job.

The lack of reliable employment and steady income forced household heads to make choices among competing needs, such as food, shelter, and health care. Participants commonly described having enough income only to pay their rent, with little left over to feed their families.

The small portion of household income participants had allocated to food was reported to be used to purchase inexpensive, nutritionally devoid foods. Although respondents described the importance of fruits and vegetables in a healthy diet, they found them to be cost-prohibitive. One participant, responding to questions about variety in their diet stated:

It's very little, and this relates to buying it, and sometimes we have so few earnings. Then you have to make enough for the rent, and then there is no opportunity left to buy small things, because the truth is that I am aware that fruits and vegetables are very good for better eating but I can't [afford them].

Many interviewees described having to subsist on rice and oatmeal for weeks at a time, rarely having traditional Colombian meals. Colombian foods were seen as either too expensive or largely unavailable in Ecuador.

4.10. Food-Related Health Beliefs and Concerns

Study participants were asked to describe what they did in their daily lives to maintain good health. While a small number of the respondents identified getting adequate rest and controlling anxiety as healthy practices, the overwhelming majority cited an adequate diet as the most essential component of physical wellbeing. Respondents used adjectives such as "basic" and "fundamental" to describe the relationship between nutrition and health. They affirmed that the consumption of nutritious foods was a means of maintaining health and preventing disease for all segments of the population. The refugees interviewed associated a well-balanced diet with improved immune health, longevity, higher energy levels, childhood growth and development, and overall physical wellbeing. Others made a connection between adequate nutrition and physical and mental wellbeing. "The basic thing for a person is food," one participant noted, "it is fundamental to good physical and emotional health."

Participants also demonstrated an understanding of the role certain foods and nutrients play in maintaining a healthy diet. One participant stated, for example, "Proteins are a source of strength." Certain foods were believed to have healing and protective powers as well. As one participant explained, "Above all, soup fortifies and protects against illness."

Underlying the association between nutrition and health was the assumption that food contributes to general wellbeing when it is both plentiful and nutritious. This, unfortunately, was rarely the case for most of the interviewees. Conversely, they frequently saw food insufficiency as contributing to the etiology of disease. As one participant noted, "When someone isn't eating well, bodily defenses are reduced." Participants saw malnutrition as leaving them weak and increasingly vulnerable to illness and poorer health, especially among children. Many refugees we interviewed associated poor performances at work or in school with hunger and malnutrition.

4.11. Impact on Children

Despite the willingness of parents to go hungry so their children could eat, children of Colombian refugees in Ecuador were extremely vulnerable to the negative consequences of food insecurity. Parents frequently reported that their entire households, including their children, were forced to go days without food. One respondent reported a four-month period in which he could not adequately provide his children with food, resulting in his daughter's malnourishment.

The health effects of malnutrition were perceived as being far more severe in children. The impact of food insufficiency on child health was not simply a function of parental perceptions. Children frequently complained of headaches, abdominal pain, nausea, and fatigue to their parents, and many parents stated that their pediatrician told them that their children's symptoms were a consequence of malnutrition. One of the most obvious signs of nutritional deficiencies at medical check-ups was their children's weight. Parents described visits to the pediatrician during which they were told their infant or toddler was dramatically underweight for their age. One parent stated, "The last time I took the child for a check-up, they told me he should be 24 (kg) and he is 18 kg."

Parents interviewed also described profound changes in the demeanor of their children, which they primarily attributed to insufficient food. One parent noted the increased physical and mental suffering of her daughter due to hunger and her diagnosis of anemia:

My daughter didn't have this, she didn't suffer from anything. Now she suffers a great deal, her bones hurt, she suffers from headaches, she is pale and weak. I will say, she suffers from nutrition, because a person can't live like this.

Another mother lamented that her sons were "not active like they were before [they moved from Colombia]: their hair, their nails, their skin, their spirit, they are so thin." Parents of school-aged children believed that malnutrition contributed to their children's lower level of academic achievement in Ecuador. Respondents associated skipped meals, unhealthy foods, and periods of hunger with poor performance in school and lower self-esteem among children.

4.12. Health Consequences

Food insecurity also negatively affected the self-assessed health status of the adult study participants. When asked to rate their health, they often reported poorer overall health as a result of limited food. They explained that the increased susceptibility to illness was the result of compromised immunity stemming from malnutrition. They also described the negative sequelae of malnutrition in terms of specific medical diagnoses or somatic manifestations. Most commonly reported medical diagnoses were gastritis, anemia, and tension headache. They also complained of fatigue, chronic body ache, sporadic fever, and generalized weakness, for which they routinely sought medical advice. One participant said, "I feel, as I have told you, like it is a grand weakness, and because of this I got such fevers and headaches, it is the result of hunger I think." They also reported a perception of poor control over cardio-metabolic diseases as a result of a poorly balanced diet. "Because of the economic situation you need to eat a lot of oatmeal, in the streets, for example, the thing they give us most is oatmeal, then it bloats you and your cholesterol and sugar go up." Participants also reported that chronic diseases had become worse as a result of limitations on food. Additionally, participants who experienced hunger and malnutrition were more likely to feel they needed medical attention. Perceptions of enhanced disease susceptibility and a deteriorating physical condition seemed to reflect a broader sense of not having control over their health.

The toll of displacement and food insufficiency was quantified in terms of perceived weight loss. Reports of weight loss ranged anywhere from 10 to 30 pounds and often occurred rapidly over a period of weeks. Some simply stated they had noticed their clothes were becoming too big. Precipitous drops in body weight were noted by several participants, while others focused their comments on establishing a connection between lack of food and fatigue and their mood. "I feel tired," said one participant, "I don't feel like working or doing anything with high spirits. I think [lack of food] influences this."

4.13. Mental Health

The refugees interviewed described numerous threats to their mental health stemming from displacement. Among these were: the traumatic nature of their displacement and violence in their sending-communities; discrimination and prejudice towards Colombian refugees; substance abuse; sexual violence; and most commonly, concern over their basic survival, which included access to food. Refugees reported feelings of sadness, stress, and worry, driven by concern over where their next meal would come from. They often used the terms 'depressed,' 'exhausted,' or 'helpless,' and described feeling more susceptible to depression as a consequence of FI.

One respondent stated, "[I feel] stress and sadness, I spend a lot of time thinking about the things that I don't have, and who I am going to ask for money for food." They commonly reported sleep disturbances and a sense of decreased morale as a result of their circumstances. One respondent stated, "Psychologically most everything is bad, I have low morale, physically also because I have to endure hunger and everything."

For many, FI was a manifestation of the social position refugees in Ecuador occupy, and reinforced their sense of powerlessness. It was a constant reminder of the lack of social support, the prejudicial attitudes of others, and the oppressive reality of displacement. Food insecurity was associated with negative feelings of anger, resentment, and weakness, all of which reflected the emotional instability among respondents.

5. DISCUSSION

Consistent with the literature on other refugee populations [2, 19], the results of this study indicate that the Colombian refugee community in Ecuador is vulnerable to severe and persistent FI. Additionally, the health risks and sequelae described by our respondents find echo in other food insecure populations globally. Among refugees resettled in developing world nations, food insecurity has been found to be associated outcomes ranging from decreased resilience [55] and poor mental health [37] to decreased antiretroviral adherence [42] . However, the particular circumstances in which FI develops, along with the demographics and sociocultural norms that influence the community's perception of and response to the experience, provide a lens through which to interpret the detailed accounts of the men and women interviewed. They also foster a more complete understanding of the complexity of the experience of FI, which can assist in the development of targeted aid and policy.

The context of forced migration varies among refugee populations and can be an important factor in the challenges of resettlement. The presence of family and social support is critical to the health and wellbeing of refugees [35, 54]. However, Colombians fleeing violence often migrate alone and arrive in Ecuador without a support network. As many respondents described, this lack of social support makes it harder to cope with and recover from the acute post-migratory food insecurity often characteristic of initial resettlement. This is an aspect of the FI experience unique to displaced populations. The single most important predictor of being able to recoup the losses incurred during displacement is 'belonging to a spatially bound community or geo-political entity,' as belonging is essential to accessing basic needs [32]. Unlike most developing host countries, Ecuador does not place refugees in camps [65]. This leaves Colombian refugees on their own to seek assistance or file for benefits upon arrival. The enactment of a new refugee decree (no. 1182) in 2012, required asylum requests to be made within 15 days of arrival in Ecuador [60]. As a result, the number of applicants achieving asylum status drastically declined [60], from 45% in 2009 to 13% in 2012 [61]. Without documentation and legal working papers, 70% of refugees are forced to rely on low-wage irregular and short-term employment [68].

Another key element of the context of forced migration is the proximity of the receiving country, Ecuador, to the four decades of violent conflict in Colombia. This complex geopolitical situation influences the factors associated with the persistence of FI. Pre-existing animosities existing between cultural or ethnic groups may exacerbate tensions and discrimination when these populations are forced to coexist due to a refugee situation [21]. The familiarity of the Ecuadorian host communities with the longstanding violence in Colombia has significant implications for host-refugee relations and refugee integration. This familiarity also gives specificity and grounded nuances to discrimination in how Ecuadorians perceive and interact with Colombian refugees. The literature on the effects of refugee resettlement in neighboring countries sparse; however studies from Tanzania, a nation that since its independence has hosted refugees from a dozen nearby African countries [9], highlight both potential adverse effects on receiving communities [3, 40] and the experience of significant discrimination for refugees [38].

Food insecurity is located within a continuum of structural violence, beginning with sending country drug-related violence from which individuals and families flee, into an economically stressed receiving environment where fears of drugs and violence, as well as competition for scarce resources, shape the discrimination faced by those forcibly displaced. Such discrimination appears to be a major factor in the transition from the acute food insecurity faced by refugees in the initial resettlement period, to the chronic food insecurity described by our respondents, all of who have resided in Ecuador for at least 3 years. This discrimination affects options and opportunities for the refugees, especially employment, and thus the economic stability needed for addressing the basic needs of housing and food. With little money and no support system, refugees must often resort to negative coping and adaptive strategies. These findings are consistent with those in other refugee populations demonstrating that post-resettlement traumas and stressors may continue to negatively affect the lives of refugees even after they have escaped violence and trauma in their home countries [33, 31].

Women can be most vulnerable to the negative coping mechanisms and risk behaviors of food insecurity. They are often in control of the food distribution in their homes, and female respondents described rationing as maternal shielding to protect their children from the harsh realities of the circumstances. Similar patterns of household food allocation have been found in other refugee populations [45]. These coping strategies represent an immediate response to FI, which tend to indicate a worsening of conditions [13, 39].

The qualitative approach employed in this study provided insight into the perceptions of this refugee population, which shape their behaviors [46]. The ways in which our respondents adapted long-term food procurement practices, such as resorting to troubling methods to earn a living, can serve as indicators of vulnerability and food insecurity [39, 50]. The composition of the displaced Colombian population in Ecuador is significant as nearly 50 percent of registered refugees are females, many of whom are young heads of household [7, 58]. Among Colombian women in Ecuador, sex work was seen as socially unacceptable, but often necessary for survival. This is not uncommon, as indicated by Hamelin and colleagues [25], whose results suggested that eventually, the search for food takes precedence over previously held values of socially or culturally acceptable ways to provide for one's family.

6. CONCLUSION

In Ecuador, discrimination and exclusion weigh heavily on refugees, impeding their integration into the host community and their ability to establish sustainable livelihoods, all of which contribute to FI and health vulnerability. The stigma and discrimination faced by refugees was the most salient finding of this study, impacting all aspects of their daily lives despite the efforts of Ecuadorian governmental agencies and refugee-serving NGOs to support these populations. Discrimination experienced by refugee groups in host communities is a predictor of social exclusion, which in itself has significant implications for poor health outcomes [11]. It is important to appreciate that one consequence of the experience of discrimination is a refugee's inability to afford a balanced diet and that humanitarian efforts to provide nutritional provisions could benefit from stricter controls to ensure that the donated foods meet standards of nutrition, hygiene, and safety.

It is often incorrectly assumed that refugees crossing international borders in search of safety successfully resettle with dignity in the host community [32]. National and local governments, responsible for ensuring food security for vulnerable populations, including displaced populations and refugees, need policies directed at assuring that these populations achieve sustainable work, fair pay, and the elimination of discrimination [17]. Hidrobo et al. [28] compared the varying efficacies of different forms of short-term assistance such as cash, food, and vouchers to Colombian refugees who had been in Ecuador for 6 months. However, the chronic food insecurity affecting this population calls for a more sustainable solution to address the specific factors that influence its persistence. Despite the best intentions of the Ecuadorian government, work that specifically engages Ecuadorian society is also clearly needed to achieve their desire to support the refugee population. Public campaigns to help sensitize the Ecuadorian population about the refugees might go a long way towards reducing quotidian expressions of stigma and discrimination.

The majority of Colombians living in Ecuador intend to settle there permanently, with less than 7% wishing to return to their country of origin [58]. Therefore, there is an urgent need to understand and address the health implications for long-term refugees. In order to do so, the risk factors that contribute to health vulnerability, such as those associated with chronic food insecurity, must be well understood [48].

The data in this study support an increase in ongoing efforts to educate Ecuadorians and Colombians about each other's circumstances and the need for efforts to diffuse tensions and increase understanding in a difficult situation for all involved. Promoting the inclusion of refugees via economic participation and reducing discrimination can have benefits for both the displaced and host populations [12]. For example, it may help reduce food insecurity prevalence in general, which may limit the future healthcare costs needed to treat long-term health consequences of poor nutrition within these populations [52]. Although refugees are often presented as burdens on developing host countries, they can be social agents [22] with positive economic impacts [6] in developing countries as they are in developed countries. Consideration should be paid to the knowledge brought to light by previous studies, such as Whitaker [64] in Tanzania, which noted that benefits and burdens can be unequally distributed across a host community, with wealthier, empowered members reaping benefits of a stimulated economy and affordable labor, and poorer members facing resource and job competition.

The experience of seeking safety in a neighboring nation is shared among many refugee populations. As illustrated by our respondents, the proximity of the sending and receiving countries is significant in conflict-driven migration. Our findings offer an opportunity to better appreciate challenges to food security for populations resettling in neighboring, economically unstable nations in the Global South. As similar patterns of forced population movements between neighboring countries unfortunately increase around the world, the findings discussed in this article will have resonance beyond the specific conditions and contexts negotiated by this refugee group.

7. LIMITATIONS

Caution is necessary when interpreting the results of this study. Participants recruited for this study collaborated with us through outreach carried out by peers and trusted sources. The convenience sample is not representative of all Colombian refugees in Ecuador since participants were recruited only in urban Quito, and the sample size does not permit generalization. Data obtained also do not capture the perspectives of refugees not connected with the partner advocates and providers in Ecuador. Finally, the perspectives shared by the women and men in this study need to be situated in the larger context of how the Ecuadorian government and society have grappled with a complicated humanitarian issue despite the economic limitations of their country and the additional demands on scarce resources with the continuing increase of the refugee population.

ACKNOWLEDGEMENTS

This research was funded by the NIH National Institute on Drug Abuse (NIDA), (5R21DA024706). The content is solely the responsibility of the authors and does not necessarily represent the official views of NIDA or the National Institutes of Health. We are grateful to the US and Ecuadorian organizations and governmental and non-governmental institutions that contributed to the development and implementation of this research. We especially thank Michelle Baez and Sebastián Betancourt of the Fundación Salud, Ambiente y Desarrollo and Juan Villalobos and Paola Moreno of the ServicioJesuita a Refugiados y Migrantes in Quito for their key roles as in-country co-investigators. We also recognize Ruth Álvarez and Omar Ocoro for their valuable assistance with the interviews and ethnographic observations. We acknowledge the contributions of Mary Margaret

Weigel and Rodrigo Armijos who suggested the importance of this inquiry and participated as co-investigators during the initial stage of research. We also acknowledge Tina Sadarangani for her work on an earlier draft and Chris Hilliard for his tireless assistance in the preparation of the manuscript. Special thanks are due to Peter Hartsock, our NIDA Project Officer, who understands not only research, but also the commitment necessary to address inequities and inform change. And to the Colombian study participants who represented their displaced community of people needing international protection, we are sincerely grateful for their generosity in sharing their time and lives with us.

REFERENCES

1. Alix-Garcia, J. and Saah, D. (2010) 'The Effect of Refugee Inflows on Host Communities'. World Bank Economic Review 24(1), 148-170.

2. Abdollahi, M., Abdollahi, Z., Sheikholeslam, R., Kalantari, N., Kavehi, Z., & Neyestani, T. R. (2015). High occurrence of food insecurity among urban Afghan refugees in Pakdasht, Iran 2008: a cross-sectional study. Ecology of Food and Nutrition, 54(3), 187-199.

3. Anderson, S.A. (1990) 'Core Indicators of Nutritional Status for Difficult-to-Sample Populations'. The Journal of Nutrition 120(Suppl.), 1559-1600.

4. Baez, J. E. (2011). Civil wars beyond their borders: The human capital and health consequences of hosting refugees. Journal of Development Economics, 96, 391-408.

5. Bermudez, O.L., Palma De Fulladolsa, P., Deman, H., and Melgar-Quinonez, H. (2010) 'Food Insecurity is Prevalent in Rural Communities of El Salvador, Guatemala, Honduras and Nicaragua'. The FASEB Journal 24(104.7).

6. Bilsborrow, R.E. and CEPAR. (2006) The Living Conditions of Refugees, Asylumseekers, and Other Colombians in Ecuador: Millennium Development Indicators and Coping Behaviour. NIDI: The Netherlands.

7. Brees, I. (2010) 'Burden or Boon: The Impact of Burmese Refugees on Thailand'. The Whitehead Journal of Diplomacy and International Relations: 35-47.

8. Capurro, M. (2014) 'The Dilemma that Faces Some Female Colombian Refugees: Telling the Human Story'. UNHCR: Esmeraldas, Ecuador. Available at: http://www.unhcr.org/53738c839.html (Accessed: 21 February 2015).

9. Chambers, R. (1986) 'Hidden Losers? The Impact of Rural Refugees on Poorer Hosts'. International Migration Review 20(2), 245-263.

10. Chaulia, S. S. (2003). Politics of Refugee Hosting in Tanzania: From Open Door to Unsustainability, Insecurity and Receding Receptivity, The [article]. Journal of Refugee Studies, (2), 147.

11. Coates, J., Frongillo, E.A., Rogers, B.L., Webb, P., Wilde, P.E., and Houser, R. (2006) 'Commonalities in the Experience of Household Food Insecurity across Cultures: What Are Measures Missing?'. The Journal of Nutrition 136(Suppl.), 1438S-1448S.

12. Correa-Velez, I., Gifford, S.M., and Barnett, A.G. (2010) 'Longing to Belong: Social Inclusion and Wellbeing Among Youth with Refugee Backgrounds in the First Three Years in Melbourne, Australia'. Social Science & Medicine 71(8), 1399-1408.

13. Correa-Velez, I., Spaaij, R., and C, S. (2012) "We Are Not Here to Claim Better Services Than Any Other': Social Exclusion among Men from Refugee Backgrounds in Urban and Regional Australia'. Journal of Refugee Studies 26(2), 163-186.

14. Davies, S. (1993) 'Are Coping Strategies a Cop Out? IDS Bulletin 24(4), 60-72.

15. De Vriese, M. (2006) 'Refugee Livelihoods: A Review of the Evidence'. Evaluation and Policy Analysis Unit. UNHCR: Geneva.

16. Dharod, J.M., Croom, J.E., and Sady, C.G. (2013) 'Food Insecurity: Its Relationship to Dietary Intake and Body Weight among Somali Refugee Women in the United States'. Journal of Nutrition Education and Behavior 45(1), 47-53.

17. FAO, IFAD, and WFP. (2013) The State of Food Insecurity in the World 2013. The Multiple Dimensions of Food Security. Rome, FAO.

18. Foley, W., Ward, P., Carter, P., Coveney, J., Tsourtos, G., and Taylor, A. (2010) 'An Ecological Analysis of Factors Associated with Food Insecurity in South Australia, 2002-7'. Public Health Nutrition 13(2), 215-221.

19. Food and Agriculture Organization Of The United Nations (FAO). (1996) Rome Declaration on World Food Security and World Food Summit Plan of Action. FAO: Rome.

20. Gallegos, D., Ellies, P., and Wright, J. (2008) 'Still There's No Food! Food Insecurity in a Refugee Population in Perth, Western Australia'. Nutrition & Dietetics 65: 78-83.

21. Ghattas, H., Sassine, A. J., Seyfert, K., Nord, M., & Sahyoun, N. R. (2015). Prevalence and Correlates of Food Insecurity among Palestinian Refugees in Lebanon: Data from a Household Survey. PLoS ONE, 10(6).

22. Gillam, L., and Clapham, M. (2009) 'The Relationship Between Food Insecurity and Practical Food Issues amongst a Sample of Refugees in Edinburgh'. Journal of Human Nutrition and Dietetics 22(3), 258-259.

23. Gomez, M.P. and Christensen, A. (2011) World Development Report 2011: The Impacts of Refugees on Neighboring Countries: A Development Challenge. World Bank: Washington, DC.

24. Grabska, K. (2006) 'Marginalization in Urban Spaces of the Global South: Urban Refugees in Cairo'. Journal of Refugee Studies 19(3), 287-307.

25. Hacket, M., Zubieta, A.C., Hernandez, K., and Melgar-Quinonez, H. (2007) 'Food Insecurity and Household Food Supplies in Rural Ecuador'. Archivos Latinoamericanos de Nutrición 57(1), 10-7.

26. Hadley, C., and Sellen, D. (2006) 'Food Security and Child Hunger among Recently Resettled Liberian Refugees and Asylum Seekers: A Pilot Study'. The Journal of Immigrant and Minority Health 8(4), 369-375.

27. Hadley, C., Zodhiates, A., and Sellen, D.W. (2007) 'Acculturation, Economics and Food Insecurity among Refugees Resettled in the USA: A Case Study of West African Refugees'. Public Health Nutrition 10(4), 405-412.

28. Hamelin, A., Habicht, J., and Beaudry, M. (1999) 'Food Insecurity: Consequences for the Household and Broader Social Implications'. Journal of Nutrition 129(2), 525S-528S.

29. Hatton, T.J., and Williamson, J.G. (2003) 'Demographics and Economic Pressure on Emigration out of Africa'. Scandinavian Journal of Economics 105(3), 465-486.

30. Hendrix, C.S., and Brinkman, H. (2013) 'Food Insecurity and Conflict Dynamics: Causal Linkages and Complex Feedbacks'. Stability: International Journal of Security and Development 2(2:26), 1-18.

31. Hidrobo, M., Hoddinott, J., Peterman, A., Margolies, A., and Moreria, V. (2012) Cash, Food, or Vouchers? Evidence from a Randomized Experiment in Northern Ecuador. Discussion Paper 01234. Washington, DC: International Food Policy Research Institute.

32. Ibánez, A.M., and Vélez, C.E. (2008) 'Civil Conflict and Forced Migration: The Micro Determinants and Welfare Losses of Displacement in Colombia'. World Development (36)4: 659-676.

33. Ibánez, A.M., and Moya, A. (2010) 'Vulnerability of Victims of Civil Conflicts: Empirical Evidence for the Displaced Population in Colombia'. World Development 38(4), 667-663.

34. Idemudia, E. S., Williams, J. K., & Wyatt, G. E. (2013). Migration challenges among Zimbabwean refugees before, during and post arrival in South Africa. Journal of Injury and Violence Research, 5(1), 17-27.

35. Kibreab, G. (2003) 'Displacement, Host Governments' Policies, and Constrainsts on the Cosntruction of Sustainable Livelihoods'. International Social Science Journal 55(175), 57-67.

36. Kim, I. (2015). Beyond Trauma: Post-resettlement Factors and Mental Health Outcomes Among Latino and Asian Refugees in the United States. Journal of Immigrant and Minority Health / Center for Minority Public Health.

37. iptiness, C. and Dharod, J. (2011) 'Bhutanese Refugees in the US: Their Dietary Habits and Food Shopping Practices Upon Resettlement'. Journal of Hunger and Environmental Nutrition 6(1), 1-11.

38. Lamkaddem, M., Essink-Bot, M.-L., Devillé, W., Gerritsen, A., & Stronks, K. (2015). Health changes of refugees from Afghanistan, Iran and Somalia: the role of residence status and experienced living difficulties in the resettlement process. European Journal of Public Health, 25(6), 917-922.

39. Lavik, N.J., Hauff, E., Skrondal, A., and Solberg, O. (1996) 'Mental Disorder among Refugees and the Impact of Persecution and Exile: Some Findings from an Out-Patient Population'. British Journal of Psychiatry 169(6), 726-732.

40. Mabiso, A., Maystadt, J., Vandercasteelan, J., and Hirvonen, K. (2014) 'Refugees, Food Security, and Resilience in Host Communities: Transitioning from Humanitarian Assistance to Development in Protracted Refugee Situations'. 2020 Resilience Conference Paper 2: Building Resilience for Food & Nutrition Security, May 15-17, 2014, Addis Ababa, Ethiopia. International Food Policy Research Institute: Washington, D.C.

41. Maharaj, V., Tomita, A., Thela, L., Mhlongo, M., & Burns, J. K. (2016). Food Insecurity and Risk of Depression Among Refugees and Immigrants in South Africa. Journal of Immigrant and Minority Health / Center for Minority Public Health.

42. Mann, G. (2012). On Being Despised: Growing up a Congolese Refugee in Dar es Salaam. In J. Boyden & M. Bourdillon (Eds.), Childhood Poverty (pp. 185-199). Palgrave Macmillan UK. Retrieved from http://link.springer.com/chapter/10.1057/9780230362796_12.

43. Maxwell, D. (1996) 'Measuring Food Insecurity: The Frequency and Severity of "Coping Strategies"'. Food Policy 21(3), 291-303.

44. Maystadt, J.-F., & Verwimp, P. (2014). Winners and Losers among a Refugee-Hosting Population. Economic Development & Cultural Change, 62(4), 769-809.

45. Melgar-Quinonez, H.R., Zubieta, A.C., Mknelly, B., Nteziyaremye, A., Gerardo, M.F., and Dunford, C.J. (2006) 'Household Food Insecurity and Food Expenditure in Bolivia, Burkina Faso, and the Philippines'. The Journal of Nutrition 136(5), 1431S-1437S.

46. Melgar-Quinonez, H., Alvarez Uribe, M.C., Paras, P., and Pérez-Escamilla, R. (2010) 'Assessing Differences in the Psychometric Characteristics of the Latin American and Caribbean Food

Security Scale in Colombia and Mexico'. The FASEB Journal 24(104.8).

47. Mendelsohn, J. B., Rhodes, T., Spiegel, P., Schilperoord, M., Burton, J. W., Balasundaram, S., ... Ross, D. A. (2014). Bounded agency in humanitarian settings: A qualitative study of adherence to antiretroviral therapy among refugees situated in Kenya and Malaysia. Social Science & Medicine, 120, 387-395.

48. Patil, C.L., Hadley, C., and Nahayo, P.D. (2009) 'Unpacking Dietary Acculturation among New Americans: Results from Formative Research with American Refugees'. The Journal of Immigrant and Minority Health 11(5), 342-358.

49. Patil, C.L., Mcgown, M., Nahayo, P.D., and Hadley, C. (2010) 'Forced Migration: Complexities in Food and Health for Refugees Resettled in the United States'. NAPA Bulletin 34: 141-160.

50. Paul, A., Doocy, S., Tappis, H., & Funna Evelyn, S. (2014). Preventing malnutrition in post-conflict, food insecure settings: a case study from South Sudan. PLoS Currents, 6.

51. Pelletier, D.L., Olson, C.M., and Frongillo, E.A. (2012) 'Food Insecurity, Hunger, and Undernutrition'. In Erdman Jr., J.W., Macdonald, I.A., and Zeisel, S.H. (eds) Present Knowledge in Nutrition, Tenth Edition. Iowa, USA: John Wiley & Sons, pp. 1165-1181.

52. Pérez-Escamilla, R., Segall-Corréa, A.M., Kurdian Maranha, L., Sampaio Md. Mde. F., Marín-León, L., and Panogasso, G. (2004) 'An Adapted Version of the U.S. Department of Agriculture Food Insecurity Module is a Valid Tool for Assessing Household Food Insecurity in Campinas, Brazil'. The Journal of Nutrition 134(8), 1923-8.

53. Pérez-Escamilla, R., Melgar-Quinonez, H.R., Nord, M., Alvarez, M.C., and Segall-Corréa, A.M. (2007) 'The Latin American and Caribbean Food Security Scale (Escala Latinoamericana y Caribeña de Seguridad Alimentaria (ELCSA)), Proceedings of the 1st Latin American Conference on Household Food Security Measurement'. Perspectivas en Nutrición Humana (supplement), 117-134.

54. Peterman, J.N., Wilde, P.E., Silka, L., Bermudez, O.I, and Rogers, B.L. (2013) 'Food Insecurity Among Cambodian Refugee Women

Two Decades Post Resettlement'. Journal of Immigrant and Minority Health 15(2), 372-380.

55. Piwowarczyk, L., Keane, T.M., and Lincoln, A. (2008) 'Hunger: The Silent Epidemic among Asylum Seekers and Resettled Refugees'. International Migration 46(1), 59-77.

56. Radimer, K.L., Olson, C.M., Greene, J.C., Campbell, C.C., and Habicht, JP. (1992) 'Understanding Hunger and Developing Indicators to Assess It in Women and Children'. The Journal of Nutrition Education and Behavior 24(1), 36S-45S.

57. Sellen, D.W., and Tedstone, A. (2000) 'Nutritional Needs of Refugee Children in the UK'. Journal of the Royal Society of Medicine 93: 360-364.

58. Sellen, D.W., Tedstone, A.E., and Frize, J. (2002) 'Food Insecurity among Refugee Families in East London: Results of a Pilot Assessment'. Public Health Nutrition 5(5), 637-644.

59. Shedlin, M.G., Decena, C.U., Noboa, H., and Betancourt, Ó. (2014) 'Sending-Country Violence and Receiving-Country Discrimination: Effects on the Health of Colombian Refugees in Ecuador'. Journal of Immigrant and Minority Health 16(1), 119-124.

60. Simich, L., Beiser, M., & Mawani, F. N. (2003). Social Support and the Significance of Shared Experience in Refugee Migration and Resettlement. Western Journal of Nursing Research, 25(7), 872-891.

61. Siriwardhana, C., Abas, M., Siribaddana, S., Sumathipala, A., & Stewart, R. (2015). Dynamics of resilience in forced migration: a 1-year follow-up study of longitudinal associations with mental health in a conflict-affected, ethnic Muslim population. BMJ Open, 5(2).

62. Strauss, A. and Corbin, J. (1994) 'Grounded Theory Methodology: An Overview'. In Denzin, N.K. and Lincoln, Y.S. (eds) Handbook of Qualitative Research. London: Thousand Oaks: Sage, pp. 273-285.

63. Tusiime, H.A., Renard, R., and Smets, L. (2013) 'Food Aid and Household Food Security in a Conflict Situation: Empirical Evidence from Northern Uganda'. Food Policy 43: 14-22.

64. UNHCR (UNITED NATIONS HIGH COMMISSIONER FOR REFUGEES). (2012a) Ecuador: 2012 Global Report. UNHCR: Geneva.

65. UNHCR (United Nations High Commissioner for Refugees). (2012b) Statistical Yearbook 2012. UNHCR: Geneva.

66. UNHCR (UNITED NATIONS HIGH COMMISSIONER FOR REFUGEES). (2013) UNHCR Global Appeal 2014-2015 – Ecuador. UNHCR: Geneva.

67. UNHCR, Joint Idp Profiling Service (JIPS), and Feinstein International Center, Tufts University (FIC). (2014) Urban Profiles of the Colombian Population in Quito: Refugees, Asylum Seekers, and Other Migrants, Main Results and Recommendations. UNHCR: Geneva.

68. Vozoris, N., and Tarasuk, V. (2003) 'Household Food Insufficiency is Associated with Poorer Health'. Journal of Nutrition 133: 120-126.

69. Webb, P., and Harinarayan, A. (1999) 'A Measure of Uncertainty: The Nature of Vulnerability and Its Relationship to Malnutrition'. Disasters 23(4), 292-305.

70. Whitaker, B.E. (2002) 'Refugees in Western Tanzania: The Distribution of Burdens and Benefits among Local Hosts'. Journal of Refugee Studies 15(4), 339-358.

71. Women's Refugee Commission. (2006) Caught in the Crossfire: Displaced Colombians at Risk of Trafficking. Available at: http://www.refworld.org/pdfid/48aa82ea0.pdf (Accessed 22 February 2015).

72. WORLD HEALTH ORGANIZATION (WHO). (2016) Food Security. Available at: http://www.who.int/trade/ glossary/ story028/en/.

73. World Health Organization (WHO). (2013) Ecuador: Country Cooperation Strategy at a Glance. Available at: http://www.who.int/countryfocus/cooperation_strategy/ccsbrief_ecu_en.pdf (Accessed: 27 March 2015).

74. WFP. (2014) Terms of Reference End of Term Operations Evaluation: Ecuador – PRRO – 200275 – Assistance to Refugees and Persons Affected by the Conflict in Colombia (2011-2014). WFP Office of Evaluation: Evaluation Quality Assurance System. Available at: http://documents.wfp.org/stellent/groups/public/documents/tor/wfp269209.pdf (Accessed 9 March 2015).

8

OCCURRENCE OF AFLATOXINS IN FOOD

Ayhan Filazi[1] and Ufuk Tansel Sireli[2]

[1] Department of Pharmacology and Toxicology, Faculty of Veterinary Medicine, Ankara University, Turkey

[2] Department of Food Hygiene and Technology, Faculty of Veterinary Medicine, Ankara University, Turkey

1. INTRODUCTION

Mycotoxins are natural contaminants in raw materials, food and feeds [1]. Aflatoxins are toxic metabolites produced by different species of toxigenic fungi, called mycotoxins. The discovery of aflatoxins dates back to the year 1961 following the severe outbreak of turkey "X" disease, in the England, which resulted in the deaths of more than 100.000 turkeys and other farm animals. The cause of the disease was attributed to a feed using thin-layer chromatography (TLC) revealed that a series of fluorescent compounds, later termed aflatoxins, were responsible for the outbreak. The disease was linked to a peanut meal, incorporated in the diet, contaminated with a toxin produced by the filamentous fungus *Aspergillus flavus.* Hence, the name aflatoxins, an acronym, has been formed from the following combination: the first letter, "A" for the genus *Aspergillus,* the next set of three letters, "FLA", for the species *flavus,* and the noun "TOXIN" meaning poison [2].

Aflatoxins (AFs) are difuranocoumarins produced primarily by two species of *Aspergillus* fungus which are especially found in areas with hot, humid climates. *A. flavus* is ubiquitous, favouring the aerial parts of plants (leaves, flowers) and produces B aflatoxins. *A. parasiticus* produces both B and G aflatoxins, is more adapted to a soil environment and has more limited distribution [3]. *A. bombysis,A. ochraceoroseus, A. nomius*, and *A. pseudotamari* are also AFs-producing species, but are encountered less frequently. From the mycological perspective, there are qualitative and quantitative differences in the toxigenic abilities displayed by different strains within each aflatoxigenic species. For example, only about half of *A. flavus* strains produce AFs-producing species more than 10^6 μg kg^{-1} [4].

Among the 18 different types of aflatoxins identified, the major members are aflatoxin B1 (AFB1), B2 (AFB2), G1 (AFG1), G2 (AFG2), M1 (AFM1) and M2 (AFM2). AFB1 is normally predominant in amount in cultures as well as in food products. Pure AFB1 is pale-white to yellow crystalline, odorless solid. AFs are soluble in methanol, chloroform, acetone, acetonitrile. *A. flavus* typically produces AFB1 and AFB2, whereas *A. parasiticus* produce AFG1 and AFG2 as well as AFB1 and AFB2. Four other aflatoxins M1, M2, B2A, G2A which may be produced in minor amounts were subsequently isolated from cultures of *A. flavus* and *A. parasiticus.* A number of closely related compounds namely aflatoxin GM1, parasiticol and aflatoxicol are also produced by *A. flavus.* The order of acute and chronic toxicity is AFB1 > AFG1 > AFB2 > AFG2, reflecting the role played by epoxidation of the 8,9-double bond and also the greater potency associated with the cyclopentenone ring of the B series, when compared with the six-membered lactone ring of the G series. AFM1 and AFM2 are hydroxylated forms of AFB1 and AFB2 [5]. AFM1 and AFM2 are major metabolites of AFB1 and AFB2 in humans and animals and may be present in milk from animals fed on AFB1 and AFB2 contaminated feed [6, 7]. AFM1 may be also present in egg [8], corn [9] and peanut [10, 11].

AFs interact with the basic metabolic pathways of the cell disrupting key enzyme processes including carbohydrate and lipid metabolism and protein synthesis [12]. The health effects of aflatoxins have been reviewed by a number of expert groups. Aflatoxins are among the most potent carcinogenic, teratogenic and mutagenic compounds in nature [13]. The International Agency for Research on Cancer (IARC) has concluded that naturally occurring aflatoxins are carcinogenic to humans (group 1), with a role in etiology of liver cancer, notably among subjects who are carriers of hepatitis B virus surface antigens. In experimental animals there was sufficient evidence for carcinogenicity of naturally occurring mixtures of aflatoxins and of AFB1, AFG1 and AFM1, limited evidence for AFB2 and inadequate evidence for AFG2.

The principal tumors were in the liver, although tumors were also found at other sites including the kidney and colon. AFB1 is consistently genotoxic in vitro and in vivo [3].

The Joint Food and Agriculture Organization of the United Nations (FAO)/World Health Organization (WHO) Expert Committee on Food Additives (JECFA) estimated potency values for AFB1 from the epidemiological data. These corresponded to 0.3 cancers/year per 100,000 population per ng aflatoxin/kg body weight (b.w). per day (uncertainty range: 0.05-0.5) in hepatitis B virus antigen positive individuals and 0.01 cancers/year per 100,000 population per ng aflatoxin/kg b.w. per day (uncertainty range: 0.002-0.03) in hepatitis B virus antigen negative individuals. AFM1 has been evaluated separately from AFB1 by the JECFA, because of its potential to be present in milk and milk products of livestock fed on aflatoxins contaminated feed [14]. The JECFA concluded that AFM1 should be presumed to induce liver cancer in rodents by a similar mechanism to AFB1, and that estimates of the potency of AFB1 can be used for determining the risk due to intake of AFM1, including those for populations with a high prevalence of carriers of hepatitis B virus. The carcinogenic potency of AFM1 was estimated to be one-tenth that of AFB1, based on a comparative study in the Fischer rat conducted by Cullen et al. [15].

Humans can be exposed to aflatoxins by the periodic consumption of contaminated food, contributing to an increase in nutritional deficiencies, immunosuppression and hepatocellular carcinoma. AFs have a wide occurrence in different kind of matrices, such as spices, cereals, oils, fruits, vegetables, milk, meat, etc. [5]. About 4.5 billion people, mostly in developing countries, are at risk of chronic exposure to aflatoxins from contaminated food crops [16]. Therefore, in order to avoid the toxicity, the levels of aflatoxins and similar toxic compounds in foodstuffs have to be monitored closely, and to be kept under control continuously. Otherwise, related health effects like acute and chronic intoxications, and even deaths, will still be an issue [17].

In this review, we are presenting a report on the situation of aflatoxin contamination in food and foodstuffs such as oilseeds (peanuts, almonds, pistachios and other tree nuts), cereals (wheat, barley, rice, corn, etc), spices, milk and dairy products and other foods of animal origin (meat, offal, eggs etc) in world. Incidence of contamination will classified as country and type of food and discussed. Also, we are reviewing the scientific literature on aflatoxins in foods and how they affect animal and human health.

2. OCCURRENCE OF AFLATOXIN IN OILSEEDS

Oilseed crops are primarily soybeans, sunflower seed, canola, rapeseed, safflower, flaxseed, mustard seed, peanuts and cottonseed, used for the production of cooking oils, protein meals for livestock, and industrial uses. These specific oilseeds are eligible for nonrecourse loans. Other oilseed crops include castor beans and sesame. After extraction of the oil the residue is a valuable source of protein, especially for animal feeding stuffs, as in oil-seed cake or press cake. Oilseeds and their products are mainly consumed as snacks as well as part of the ingredients of certain dishes in human daily diet [18].

According to many reports (Table 1), peanuts are the main susceptible products for aflatoxin contamination [19-21]. Tree nuts such as almonds, walnuts, and pistachios may be contaminated with aflatoxin, though at lower levels than for cottonseed and corn; however, the problem is very significant to producers because: (1) the crop has a high unit value, and (2) much of the crop is sold to European markets that enforce limits significantly lower than those in some countries [22].

For over all sanitary precaution, the European Union has enacted in 1998, very severe aflatoxin tolerance standards of 2 $\mu g\ kg^{-1}$ AFB1 and 4 $\mu g\ kg^{-1}$ total aflatoxins for nuts and cereals for human consumption and this has come into effect from January, 2001. Consumers in the developed world are well aware of the carcinogenic effect of aflatoxins and will thus stay away from a product that has aflatoxin beyond the acceptance level. Exports of agricultural products particularly groundnuts and other oilseeds from developing countries have dropped considerately in recent years resulting in major economic losses to producing countries as a result of this restriction. According to the World Bank estimate, the policy change by the European Union will reduce by 64%, imports of cereals, dried fruits, oil seeds and nuts from nine African countries namely Chad, Egypt, Gambia, Mali, Nigeria, Senegal, South Africa, Sudan and Zimbabwe and this will cost African countries about US $670 million in trade per year. However, the new rule of the EU has been criticized as being too stringent. There is the need for mycotoxin surveillance because of its wide occurrence in contaminated commodities [23].

Aflatoxin contamination of peanut, resulting from invasion by *A. flavus* or *A. parasiticus*, is a major problem in semi-arid tropical regions where plants are primarily rain-fed. Light sandy soils, where peanut is typically cultivated, favor these fungi. While *A. flavus* infection of peanuts does not affect yield, the fungus can produce high levels of aflatoxin in infected nuts, and these toxins can pose serious health risks to humans and animals [24]. The environmental conditions required to induce pre-harvest aflatoxin contamination of peanuts were studied. In the study, peanuts did not become contaminated with aflatoxins in the absence of severe and prolonged drought stress even when the frequency of infection by *A. flavus* and *A. parasiticus* was up to 80%. Also, larger, more mature peanut kernels required considerably more drought stress to become contaminated than did smaller, immature kernels [25]. Peanuts become infected with aflatoxigenic fungus when seed pods come into direct contact with aflatoxigenic fungus in soil. These fungi can invade and produce toxins in peanut kernels before harvest, during drying, and in storage [26].

Dried fruits can be contaminated with aflatoxins. Maximum permitted levels for total aflatoxins in the European Union are 4 μg kg^{-1} in dried fruit intended for direct human consumption. AFB1 was the most common mycotoxin encountered as a natural contaminant in stored samples [25].

Table 1. Aflatoxins in oilseeds.

Food Type	Country	Contaminated/ Total examined	Aflatoxin	Concentration (ppb)	Method	Reference
Peanut	Argentina	2/50	AFB1 AFG1	435-625 for AFB1 83-625 for AFG1	TLC	[19]
Peanut	Botswana	94/120	Total[a]	12-329	ELISA	[20]
Peanut	China	2/16	AFB1+AFB2	1.96 (mean)	UHPLC	[21]
Peanut	Malaysia	11/13	AFB1	1.47-15.33	ELISA	[27]
Peanut	China	15/65	Total[a]	0.03-28.39	HPLC	[28]
Fresh Peanuts	China	14/35	Total[a]	0.3-7.4	UHPLC-MS/MS	[10]
Musty Peanuts	China	5/5	Total[b]	1.2-1482	UHPLC-MS/MS	[10]
Peanut and products	Trinidad	0/186	AFB1	ND[c]	Charm II	[29]
Peanut and products	Brazil	41/80	Total[a]	43-1099	TLC	[30]
Peanut butter	China	41/50	AFB1	<LOD[d]-68.51	HPLC	[31]

Peanut butter	Sudan	120/120	AFB1	17-170	Fluorometer	[32]
Peanut butters	China	31/33	Total[e]	0.7-96	UHPLC-MS/MS	[10]
Pistachio	Turkey	48/95	Total[a]	0.007-7.72	HPLC	[33]
Pistachio	Iran	3699/10068	AFB1	5.9 ± 41.7 (Mean)	HPLC	[34]
Hazelnut	Egypt	18/20	Total[a]	25-175	TLC	[35]
Walnut	Egypt	15/20	Total[a]	15-25	TLC	[35]
Walnut	China	31/48	Total[a]	0.02-1.20	HPLC	[28]
Hazelnut	Turkey	43/51	Total[a]	<0.625-10	ELISA	[36]
Cacao hazelnut cream	Turkey	38/40	Total[a]	<0.625-10	ELISA	[36]
Unsorted, in-shell almonds	California, USA	10/74	Total[a]	1-107	TLC	[37]
Diced almonds	California, USA	13/27	Total[a]	<LOD-119	TLC	[37]
Sesame	Malaysia	7/8	AFB1	0.54-1.82	ELISA	[27]
Sesame paste	China	37/100	AFB1	<LOD-20.45	HPLC	[31]
Sunflower	Malaysia	6/7	AFB1	1.14-5.33	ELISA	[27]
Nuts	Malaysia	2/7	AFB1	0.66-1.09	ELISA	[27]
Pine nut	China	2/12	Total[a]	0.19-0.25	HPLC	[28]
Dried apricot	Iran	9/30	AFB1	"/0.2	HPLC	[38]
Prune	Iran	2/15	AFB1	"/0.2	HPLC	[38]

a. Total: AFB1+ AFB2+ AFG1+ AFG2

b. Total AFs including AFM1 (ND-64.7 ppb) and AFM2 (ND-3.6 ppb)

c. ND: Not detected

d. LOD: Limit of detection

e. Total AFs including AFM1 (ND-4.2 ppb) and AFM2 (ND-1.8)

3. OCCURRENCE OF AFLATOXIN IN CEREALS

Cereals and its products are the main foods for human consumption throughout the world. The cereal grains belong to corn, rice, barley, wheat and sorghum are found susceptible to AFs accumulation by aflatoxigenic fungus. The problem of aflatoxins occurring naturally in cereals, especially in rice and corn, has become troublesome because of changing agricultural technology. The aflatoxin problem in cereals is not restricted to any geographic or climatic region. Toxins are produced on cereals, both in the field and in storage; they involve both the grain and the whole plant [39].

Our results showed that rice was significantly more heavily colonized by aflatoxin-producing*Aspergillus* spp. than other cereals, with overall aflatoxin levels being correspondingly higher. But this may be caused by the variations in cultivars used. Additionally, corn is the second susceptible after rice for aflatoxin accumulation by *A. fungus* (Table 2).

Rice and sorghum are the most important staple food crops in many countries. In these countries, the majority of rice is grown in the rainy season. During the rainy season, sun drying of rice, which is practiced by most farmers, may not reduce the moisture content of grains sufficiently to prevent growth of fungi. As a result, rice grains with a moisture content higher than the desired level (>14%) may enter the storage system. The harmful effects of such fungal invasion are discoloration of the grain and/ or husk, loss in viability, loss of quality, and toxin contamination. Sorghum is grown in harsh environments where other crops do not grow well. Improvements in production, availability, storage, utilization, and consumption of this food crop will significantly contribute to the household food security and nutrition of the inhabitants of these areas. Sorghum is typically harvested as early as possible so that fields can quickly be planted with another crop. Sometimes the sorghum harvest coincides with heavy rainfall, hurricanes, and floods, all of which promote infection by mycotoxin-producing fungi [25].

As it is known, the consumption of large amounts of AFs contaminated food by starving people can cause toxic hepatitis (jaundice) and death. Aflatoxin epidemics were reported from India, in 1975 among the Bhils (the largest and most widely distributed tribal group in India), who had consumed corn heavily contaminated with *A. flavus*. The epidemic was characterized by jaundice, rapidly developing ascites, and portal hypertension. Approximately 400 persons were affected by the epidemic [40].

Table 2. Aflatoxins in cereals.

Food Type	Country	Contaminated/ Total examined	Aflatoxin	Concentration (ppb)	Method	Reference
Rice	India	814/1200	AFB1	0.1-308	ELISA	[25]
Rice	India	581/1511	AFB1	[n]/5	HPTLC	[41]
Rice	Iran	59/71	Total[a]	2.097-10.94	HPLC	[42]
Rice	Canada	99/199	AFB1	<0.002-7.1	HPLC	[43]
Rice	Sweden	57/99	Total[a]	0.1-50.7	HPLC	[44]
Rice	China	23/74	Total[a]	0.15-3.88	HPLC	[28]
Rice	Japan	0/48	Total[a]	ND[b]	HPLC	[45]
Rice	Nigeria	21/21	Total[a]	27.7-371.9	HPLC	[46]
Rice	Turkey	56/100	Total[a]	0.05-21.4	ELISA	[47]
Rice	Tunisia	2/16	Total[a]	2.0-7.5	ELISA	[48]
Rice	Tunisia	0/11	Total[a]	ND[b]	HPLC	[49]
Rice	Malaysia	9/13	AFB1	0.68-3.79	ELISA	[27]
Corn	Tunisia	1/17	Total[a]	0.42	HPLC	[49]
Corn	Malaysia	6/8	AFB1	1.75-8.95	ELISA	[27]
Corn	Brazilian	82/214	AFB1	0.2-129	ELISA	[50]
Corn	China	4/18	Total[a]	5.67 (mean)	UHPLC	[21]
Corn	China	52/84	Total[a]	0.02-1098	HPLC	[28]
Corn	Tunisia	9/21	Total[a]	2.9-12.5	ELISA	[48]
Corn flour	Morocco	16/20	AFB1	0.23-11.2	HPLC	[51]
Wheat	Ethiopia	5/120	AFB1	<1.0-12.3	HPLC	[52]
Wheat	Tunisia	15/51	Total[a]	4.0-12.9	ELISA	[48]
Wheat	Tunisia	10/46	Total[a]	0.15-18.6	HPLC	[49]
Wheat	Malaysia	9/14	AFB1	0.55-5.07	ELISA	[27]
Wheat	India	663/1646	AFB1	[n]/5	ELISA	[41]

Wheat flour	Morocco	3/17	AFB1	0.03-0.15	HPLC	[51]
Sorghum	Tunisia	36/49	Total[a]	0.4-25.8	HPLC	[49]
Sorghum	Ethiopia	5/82	AFB1	<1.0-25.9	HPLC	[52]
Sorghum	India	1173/1606	AFB1	0.01-263.98	ELISA	[53]
Sorghum	Tunisia	13/17	Total[a]	1.7-67.0	ELISA	[48]
Barley	Tunisia	2/46	Total	0.6-0.8	HPLC	[49]
Barley	Ethiopia	13/115	AFB1	<1.0-11.7	HPLC	[52]
Barley	Tunisia	11/25	Total	3.5-11.5	ELISA	[48]
Oat	Malaysia	5/10	AFB1	0.65-2.85	ELISA	[27]
Cereals	Ethiopia	31/352	AFB1	<LOD-26	HPLC	[52]

a. Total: AFB1+ AFB2+ AFG1+ AFG2

b. ND: Not detected

4. OCCURRENCE OF AFLATOXIN IN SPICES

The popularity of hot peppers (*Capsicum annuum* L.), also known as chili peppers, as spices or vegetables and for other uses increases every year. Powdered red pepper is one of the favorite spices in South Asia and is commonly used for flavoring, seasoning, and imparting aroma or coloring to foods. Hot peppers are the principal component of curry and chili powder and can be used to make pepper sauce, red pepper, and paprika [54].

Spices are often contaminated with mycotoxins (Table 3). The climatic conditions prevailing in the tropics are especially favorable for mold contamination and mycotoxin production. Of the different mycotoxins, aflatoxin is the commonest contaminant in spices [55].

Peppers are very susceptible to aflatoxin contamination, which is affected by atmospheric temperature, humidity, insects, and drying and processing conditions. Mold contamination can occur in the field during crop production and during storage when conditions are favorable. Sun drying is a common postharvest practice in some countries, which involves spreading peppers on soil in a single layer. Because of the drying processes are on the soil, some peppers are contaminated with fungus [54, 56].

Substantial aflatoxin contamination of ground red pepper has been reported from Ethiopia, where eight of 60 samples collected from markets, shops and storage facilities were contaminated with AFB1 in concentrations of 250-525 μg kg^{-1} [57]. In Turkey, 24% and 13% of samples of different pepper types contained 7.5-200 [58] and 1.1-97.5 μg kg^{-1} [56] total aflatoxins, respectively. Elshafie et al. [59] were surveyed one hundred and five samples of seven spices (cumin, cinnamon, clove, black pepper, cardamom, ginger, and coriander) for the mycoflora and AFs in the Sultanate of Oman. Twenty fungal species were isolated in which *A. flavus, A. niger. Penicillium, Rhizopus,* and *Syncephalastrum racemosum* were the most dominant. Of the seven spices studied, clove was found to be the least contaminated, while cumin was the most contaminated. None of the 15 selected samples of the spices contaminated by *A. flavus* were found to contain AFs [59]. Cooking revealed that the aflatoxin content of spices did not decrease [60].

Although the mold *A. flavus* grows well on the spices, the production of AFs is lower than in cereals. This indicates that spices are not an ideal substrate for AF formation. It has been shown that essential oils extracted from spices, e.g. cloves, can inhibit mold growth and AF production completely. According to some reports, fungal growth was weak on curcumin, black pepper and white pepper and no AF was detected in black or white pepper after 10 days at 25 °C. According Martins et al. [61], the results of the survey indicate that there is little evidence for significant AF contamination in spices. The majority of samples contained AFs at low levels and others were negative (cardamom, cloves, ginger and mustard). In the meat industry (sausage, dry cured ham, luncheon meat) and in confection of ethnic dishes, AF contamination of spices is probably not relevant as a direct health hazard [61].

5. OCCURRENCE OF AFLATOXIN IN MILK AND DAIRY PRODUCTS

Most of AFB1 and AFB2 ingested by mammals are eliminated through urine and faeces, however a fraction is biotransformed in the liver and excreted together with milk in the form of AFM1 and AFM2, respectively. AFM1 could be detected in milk 12-24 h after the first AFB1 ingestion, reaching a high level after a few days. The ratio between AFB1 ingested and AFM1 excreted has been estimated to be 1-3% [5].

Table 3. Aflatoxins in spices.

Food Type	Country	Contaminated/ Total examined	Aflatoxin	Concentration (ppb)	Method	Reference
Pepper	Turkey	12/90	Total[a]	1.1-97.5	TLC	[56]
Pepper	Turkey	12/49	Total[a]	7.5-200	TLC	[58]
Pepper	Malaysia	4/4	AFB1	0.65-2.1	ELISA	[27]
Ground red pepper	Turkey	33/164	Total[a]	"/5	HPLC	[33]
Ground red pepper	Ethiopia	8/60	AFB1	250-525	ELISA	[57]
Paprika	Spain	8/17	Total[a]	1.8-50.4	HPLC	[62]
Smoked Paprika	Spain	4/4	Total[a]	22.3-83.7	HPLC	[62]
Chilli	Malaysia	8/8	AFB1	0.58-3.5	ELISA	[27]
Chilli	Spain	6/11	Total[a]	1.9-65.7	HPLC	[62]
Cumin	Malaysia	2/3	AFB1	1.89-4.64	ELISA	[27]
Spices	Hungary	23/91	AFB1	0.14-15.7	HPLC	[55]
Spices	Portuqual	34/79	AFB1	1.0-59.0	HPLC	[61]

a. Total: AFB1+ AFB2+ AFG1+ AFG2

The system responsible for the biotransformation of AFB1 basically has five mechanisms, represented by reactions of reduction, hydration, epoxidation, hydroxylation and ortho-demethylation. The aflatoxicol is produced by reduction of AFB1 by an NADPH-dependent cytoplasmic enzyme present in the soluble fraction of the liver. The toxicity of aflatoxicol is apparently much smaller than AFB1, but the conversion is reversible and the aflatoxicol can serve as a reservoir toxicity of AFB1 in the intracellular space, it can be converted in this mycotoxin by microsomal dehydrogenase. The aflatoxicol can also be metabolized to AFM1 and AFH1. The hydration process results in a metabolite AFB2a. This compound has the main action the inhibition of enzymes, in the liver and other tissues, causing a reduction in proteic synthesis AFM1 and AFQ1 are results of hydroxylation reaction of AFB1. These compounds have a hydroxyl group, allowing their conjugation with glucuronic acid, sulfate and glutathione, making them very water-soluble substances that can be excreted in the bile, urine and milk. Most of the aflatoxins are excreted between 72 to 96 h after the exposure, with the liver and the kidney retaining the waste for a longer period compare to other tissues [63].

A tolerable daily intake of 0.2 ng kg^{-1} b.w. for AFM1 was calculated by Kuiper-Goodman [64] and this toxin has been categorized by the International Agency for Research on Cancer (IARC) as a class 2B toxin, a possible human carcinogen. In the assessment of cancer risk, the infants are more exposed to the risk because the milk is a major constituent of their diet. It must be also considered that young animals have been found to be more susceptible to AFB1 (and so probably AFM1) than adults. Therefore the presence of AFM1 in milk and milk products is considered to be undesirable [65].

The carcinogenicity of AFM1 may be influenced by the duration and level of exposure. Exposure is most likely to occur through the frequent consumption of milk and milk by-products (infant milk, cheese, butter, yoghurt). Several studies in different countries have reported high or low contamination levels of AFM1 in different categories of milk and dairy samples. These significantly variable AFM1 levels may be due to several influencing factors such as cheese manufacturing procedures and storage, types of cheese, conditions of cheese ripening, analytical methods and finally the geographical and seasonal effects [6].

The concentration of AFM1 is relatively increased in cheese samples because of its affinity to proteins. During cheese making, AFM1 can be decreased in cheese by increasing renneting temperature from 30 to 40°C, decreasing cutting size of curd and increasing press time from 1 to 2 h, which causes more loss of AFM1 in the whey [66]. On a weight basis, however, AFM1 concentration in cheese actually increases. In soft cheese, it becomes 2.5 to 3.3 times higher and in hard cheese, 3.9 to 5.8 times higher than in the milk from which the cheeses were made. Converting milk that may contain aflatoxin into a cheese, such as feta cheese, reduces the exposure of the consumer to this toxin. During pasteurization of milk, about 90% or more of the AFM1 is retained in the milk but during cheese manufacturing, there is a partitioning of AFM1 between the cheese, whey, and brine. During cheese manufacturing, results on the distribution of AFM1 between curd and whey can be variable. This variability has been associated with the type of cheese, the particular cheese-making process applied, the type and degree of milk contamination, and the analytical method employed. Lopez et al. [67] manufactured cheese using artificially AFM1 contaminated milk and found that the greatest proportion of toxin (60%) was in whey, while 40% AFM1 remained in cheese. Some researchers also reported that the greatest proportion of AFM1 was in the curd ranging between 66-80% [68]. About 37% of the AFM1 in milk is lost from the cheese into the whey, and another 30% diffuses from the cheese into brining solution during storage. Thus, the amount that would be ingested in a 30 g serving of cheese made from milk containing 500 ng AFM1/L would be only 35 ng AFM1 compared to 125 ng AFM1 from a 250 g serving of fluid milk. Thus, consumers in a region where there are high aflatoxin levels in milk would be at less health risk if the milk is pasteurized and converted into a cheese such as feta or other white pickled cheese before it is delivered to the consumer [69]. Applebaum et al. [70] reported that AFM1 concentration in cheese was about four times higher than the cheese milk. The increase in AFM1 concentration in cheese has been explained by the affinity of AFM1 for casein.

The Commission of the European Communities established a limit for AFM1 of 50 ng kg^{-1} for milk and a variable limit for cheese, depending on concentration caused by drying process or processing. Milk containing AFM1 concentrations above the action level must be discarded, causing significant economic loss for the dairy producer. Similar regulations exist in most developed countries.

In this Regulation the Commission stated that "even if AFM1 is regarded as a less dangerous genotoxic carcinogenic substance than AFB1, it is necessary to prevent the presence in milk, and consequently in milk products, intended for human consumption and for young children in particular". The Commission has also set a limit for AFB1 of 5 μg kg^{-1} for supplementary feedstuffs for lactating dairy cattle. However this tolerance level is difficult to observe because the average daily individual intake in a herd should be limited to 40 μg AFB1 per cow, in order to produce milk with less than 50 ng AFM1 per kg [65].

Many factors may affect the formation of aflatoxins in animal feeds. Geographic and climate changes can affect the farm management practices and feed quality. These effects can lead to the wide variations in AFM1 levels in milk (Table 4). The preserved fodder such as silage and hay might have been contaminated by aflatoxin producing fungi and the improper storage led to aflatoxin production. The level of AFM1 in feed in rainy seasons is more than in dry seasons. It can be also probable to use higher amounts of contaminated concentrates in the cold months [71].

Table 4. Aflatoxins in milk and dairy products.

Food Type	Country	Contaminated/ Total examined	Aflatoxin	Concentration (ppb)	Method	Reference
Raw Milk[a]	Italy	125/161	AFM1	<0.023	HPLC	[72]
Raw Milk[a]	Greece	40/58	AFM1	0.005-0.055	HPLC	[73]
Raw Milk[a]	North African	35/49	AFM1	0.03-3.13	HPLC	[74]
Raw Milk[a]	Italy	?/310	AFM1	0.002-0.09	HPLC	[75]
Raw Milk[a]	Trinidad	13/212	AFM1	NM[a]	Charm II	[29]
Raw Milk[a]	Slovenia	0/60	AFM1	ND[b]	HPLC	[76]
Raw Milk[a]	Indonesia	65/113	AFM1	5-25	ELISA	[77]
Raw Milk[a]	China	12/12	AFM1	0.16-0.5	ELISA	[78]
Raw Milk[a]	Croatia	NM[a]/61 (one sample exceeded limit EU)	AFM1	0.0006-0.059	ELISA	[79]
Raw Milk[a]	Turkey	43/50	AFM1	<0.03	ELISA	[80]
Raw Milk[a]	Iran	60/60	AFM1	2.0-64.0	HPLC	[81]
Raw Milk[a]	Pakistan	177/232	AFM1	0.002-1.9	ELISA	[82]
Raw Milk[a]	Pakistan	63/120	AFM1	0.004-0.174	HPLC	[83]
Raw Milk[a]	Syria	70/74	AFM1	0.02-0.69	ELISA	[84]
Raw Milk[a]	South Korea	48/100	AFM1	0.002-0.08	HPLC	[85]
Raw Milk[a]	Portugal	25/31	AFM1	<0.005-0.05	HPLC	[86]
Raw Milk[a]	Iran	128/128	AFM1	0.031-0.113	ELISA	[87]
Raw Milk[a]	Iran	117/140	AFM1	<0.01-0.10	ELISA	[88]
Raw Milk[a]	Spain	3/92	AFM1	0.014-0.019	HPLC	[89]
Buffalo raw milk	Pakistan	153/360	AFM1	0.002-0.087	HPLC	[83]
Pasteurized milk[a]	Greece	113/136	AFM1	0.005-0.05	HPLC	[73]
Pasteurized milk[a]	Morrocco	47/54	AFM1	0.001-0.117	HPLC	[51]
Pasteurized milk[a]	Brazil	7/10	AFM1	0.01-0.02	HPLC	[90]

Pasteurized milk[a]	Iran	83/116	AFM1	0.006-0528	ELISA	[91]
Pasteurized milk[a]	Iran	624/624	AFM1	0.045-0.08	ELISA	[92]
Pasteurized milk[a]	Syria	10/10	AFM1	0.008-0.765	ELISA	[84]
Pasteurized milk[a]	Iran	48/48	AFM1	0.01-0.10	ELISA	[88]
Pasteurized milk[a]	Brazil	58/79	AFM1	0.05-0.24	HPLC	[93]
Milk[a] (Raw, pasteurized and powder)	Argentina	18/77	AFM1	0.01-0.03	ELISA	[94]
UHT Milk[a]	Greece	14/17	AFM1	0.005-0.05	HPLC	[73]
UHT Milk[a]	Turkey	75/129	AFM1	Max.0.54	ELISA	[95]
UHT Milk[a]	Turkey	67/100	AFM1	0.01-0.63	ELISA	[96]
UHT Milk[a]	Brazil	40/40	AFM1	0.010-0.5	HPLC	[90]
UHT Milk[a]	Turkey	50/50	AFM1	0.01-0.244	ELISA	[7]
UHT Milk[a]	Iran	116/210	AFM1	0.012-0.249	ELISA	[97]
UHT Milk[a]	Iran	68/109	AFM1	0.006-0.516	ELISA	[91]
UHT Milk[a]	Brazil	53/60	AFM1	0.015-0.5	HPLC	[93]
UHT Milk[a]	Iran	48/48	AFM1	0.01-0.10	ELISA	[88]
UHT Milk[a]	Turkey	14/24	AFM1	<0.01-0.05	HPLC	[98]
UHT-whole milk	Portugal	17/18	AFM1	<0.005-0.059	HPLC	[86]
UHT-semi skimmed milk	Portugal	20/22	AFM1	<0.005-0.061	HPLC	[86]
UHT-skimmed milk	Portugal	23/30	AFM1	<0.005-0.02	HPLC	[86]
UHT-Pasteurized milk	Japan	207/208	AFM1	0.001-0.029	HPLC	[99]
Ewe's milk	Greece	19/27	AFM1	0.005-0.055	HPLC	[73]
Ewe's milk	Greece	27/54	AFM1	<0.005-0.182	ELISA	[100]
Ewe's milk	Syria	13/23	AFM1	0.006-0.634	ELISA	[84]

Goat milk	Greece	12/20	AFM1	0.005-0.05	HPLC	[73]
Goat milk	Syria	7/11	AFM1	0.008-0.054	ELISA	[84]
Milk (ewe, goat and buffalo mix)	Italy	85/102	AFM1	0.05-0.25	ELISA	[101]
Infant milk food, Milk based cereal, weaning food, infant formula and liquid milk	India	76/87	AFM1	0.063-1.012	ELISA	[102]
Milk powder	Brazil	72/75	AFM1	0.01-0.5	HPLC	[90]
Milk powder	China	15/15	AFM1	Max 0.54	ELISA	[78]
Milk powder	Syria	1/8	AFM1	0.012	ELISA	[84]
Milk powder	South Korea	17/24	AFM1	0.083-0.342	HPLC	[103]
Cheese[b]	Iran	66/80	AFM1	0.15-2.41	TLC	[104]
Cheese[b]	China	4/4	AFM1	0.16-0.32	ELISA	[78]
Cheese[b]	Lebanon	75/111	AFM1	0.056-0.315	ELISA	[105]
Cheese[b]	Iran	30/50	AFM1	0.041-0.374	ELISA	[106]
Cheese[b]	Brazil	39/58	AFM1	0.01-0.304	IAC/LC	[107]
Cheese[b]	North African	15/20	AFM1	0.11-0.52	HPLC	[74]
Cheese[b]	Turkey	14/20	AFM1	<0.155	ELISA	[80]
Cheese[b]	Turkey	10/200	AFM1	0.1-0.6	ELISA	[108]
Cheese[b]	Iran	93/116	AFM1	0.052-0.745	ELISA	[109]
Cheese[b]	Turkey	82/100	AFM1	<0.05-0.8	ELISA	[110]
Cheese[b]	Turkey	36/127	AFM1	0.07-0.77	ELISA	[111]
White brined cheese[b]	Turkey	31/50	AFM1	0.1-5.2	Fluorometri	[112]
White brined cheese[b]	Turkey	159/193	AFM1	0.052-0.86	ELISA	[113]
Herby cheese[b]	Turkey	52/60	AFM1	0.16-7.26	Fluorometri	[112]

Cream cheese[b]	Turkey	44/49	AFM1	Max 0.25	ELISA	[36]
Cream cheese[b]	Turkey	8/200	AFM1	0.1-0.7	ELISA	[108]
Cream cheese[b]	Turkey	99/100	AFM1	0.01-4.1	ELISA	[114]
Cream cheese[b]	Iran	68/94	AFM1	58.3-785.4	ELISA	[109]
Kashar cheese[b]	Turkey	47/53	AFM1	[B]/0.25	ELISA	[36]
Kashar cheese[b]	Turkey	12/200	AFM1	0.12-0.8	ELISA	[108]
Kashar cheese	Turkey	8/28	AFM1	<0.37	ELISA	[80]
Kashar cheese[b]	Turkey	109/132	AFM1	0.05-0.69	ELISA	[96]
Kashar cheese[b]	Turkey	85/100	AFM1	0.05-0.80	ELISA	[110]
Tulum cheese[b]	Turkey	16/20	AFM1	<0.378	ELISA	[80]
Tulum cheese[b]	Turkey	81/100	AFM1	0.05-0.80	ELISA	[110]
Ewe's cheese	Turkey	14/50	AFM1	0.02-2.0	TLC	[6]
Dairy drinks	Brazil	10/12	AFM1	0.01-0.05	IAC/LC	[107]
Milk products	China	66/104	AFM1	Max 0.5	ELISA	[78]
Butter	Turkey	92/92	AFM1	0.01-7.0	ELISA	[114]
Butter	Turkey	25/27	AFM1	Max 0.1	ELISA	[36]
Butter	Turkey	66/80	AFM1	0.01-0.12	ELISA	[115]
Yoghurt	Brazil	49/65	AFM1	0.01-0.529	IAC/LC	[107]
Yoghurt	Italy	73/120	AFM1	<0.032	HPLC	[72]
Yoghurt	Turkey	68/104	AFM1	<0.1	ELISA	[116]
Yoghurt	South Korea	31/60	AFM1	0.017-0.124	HPLC	[103]
Yoghurt	Portugal	2/48	AFM1	0.043-0.045	HPLC	[117]
Fruit yoghurt	Portugal	16/48	AFM1	0.019-0.098	HPLC	[117]

Fruit yogurt	Turkey	7/21	AFM1	<0.1	ELISA	[115]
Strained yoghurt	Turkey	29/52	AFM1	<0.15	ELISA	[116]
Yogurt (whole fat)	Turkey	18/25	AFM1	<0.069	ELISA	[80]
Yoghurt (Semi fat)	Turkey	10/25	AFM1	<0.078	ELISA	[80]
Infant formula	South Korea	18/26	AFM1	0.032-0.132	HPLC	[103]
Infant formula	Iran	116/120	AFM1	0.001-0.014	ELISA	[87]
Dairy dessert	Turkey	26/50	AFM1	<0.08	ELISA	[80]

a.Cow milk, b. Cow cheese

6. OCCURRENCE OF AFLATOXIN IN OTHER FOODS OF ANIMAL ORIGIN

Meat refers to meat flesh, skeletal muscles, connective tissue or fat and others than meat flesh, including brain, heart, kidney, liver, pancreas, spleen, thymus, tongue and tripe that is used as food, excluding the bone and bone marrow and it contains high biological value protein and important micronutrients that are needed for good health throughout life. Residues of aflatoxins and their metabolites could be present in the meat, offal and eggs of animals receiving aflatoxin contaminated feeds (Table 5). In addition to the economic losses, aflatoxin in feeds could pose a risk to human health because of ingestion of aflatoxin containing foods derived from the animals fed the toxin-contaminated diet [118].

Cytochrome P450 enzymes (CYP) (including CYP1A2, CYP3A4 and CYP2A6) in the liver and other tissues convert AFB1 to epoxides (AFB1-8,9-exo-epoxide, and AFB1-8,9-endo-epoxide), and to AFM1, AFP1, AFQ1, and its reduced form aflatoxicol. Of the epoxides, the AFB1-8,9-exo-epoxide can form covalent bonds with DNA and serum albumin resulting in AFB1-N7-guanine and lysine adducts, respectively. Like AFB1, AFM1 can also be activated to form AFM1-8,9-epoxide that binds to DNA resulting in AFM1-N7-guanine adducts. These guanine and lysine adducts have been noted to appear in urine. The metabolites AFP1, AFQ1, and aflatoxicol are thought to be inactive and are excreted as such in urine, or in the form of glucuronyl conjugates from bile in feces [119].

When chicken exposed to AFB1 with contaminated rations, AFB1, AFM1, and aflatoxicol have been detected in liver, kidneys, and thigh muscles. Besides these, AFB2a has also been detected in livers of both broilers and layers on a ration contaminated with a mixture of aflatoxins [120]. In laying hens the effects of exposure to AF are a dose-dependent decrease in egg production and egg quality with increased susceptibility to salmonellosis, candidiasis, and coccidiosis. AFs and some of their metabolites can be carried over from feed to eggs in ratios ranging from 5,000:1 to 66,200:1 and even to 125,000:1, whereas in other trials no measurable residual AFB1 or its metabolites were found in eggs. These contrasting results may be ascribed to the administration of naturally contaminated feeds containing different AF with different levels of toxicity [8].

Wolzak et al. [121] have reported that tissue residues of aflatoxins were highest in kidney, gizzard, and liver (average concentration 3 μg kg^{-1} mass) when broilers were exposed for 4 weeks to a mixture of AFB1 and AFB2. After 7 days of removal of the contaminated feed, aflatoxin residues could not be detected in above tissues. Hussain et al. [120] also indicated that the elimination of AFB1 in chicken increased during longer exposure to AFB1. They fed broiler chicks on rations containing 0, 1.6, 3.2, and 6.4 μg AFB1/kg for 7, 14, or 28 day's age. After 2 to 3 days of exposure, AFB1 could be detected in livers of the birds exposed to 1.6 μg AFB1/kg and higher dietary levels of the toxin. After cessation of toxin feeding, AFB1 residues decreased in livers and muscles of all the chicks, with lower levels at 10 days post-cessation in the chicks exposed to higher toxin levels. They concluded that the residues of AFB1 in tissues increase with increase in dietary concentration of the toxin but decrease with increase in age (or after longer exposure) of broiler chicks. The elimination of AFB1 from tissues was rapid in older birds than in younger birds [120].

Poultry birds fed AF contaminated rations under experimental conditions resulted in the presence of AF residues in their edible tissues like liver and muscles. Residues of AFB1 in liver of broiler and layer birds have been reported to vary from no detection to 3.0 μg kg^{-1} by feeding 250-3310 μg kg^{-1}AFB1 for variable periods [118, 119]. The wide variations in the tissue AF residue concentration suggested that these levels might be influenced by different factors including dietary AF levels, duration of administration, age, type of the birds etc. However, effect of such factors upon concentration of AFB1 residues in poultry meat (liver and muscles) and clearance of AFB1 from the body tissues after withdrawal of dietary AF have not been adequately studied [120].

Dietary contamination of aflatoxins pose a big risk to human health including acute aflatoxicosis, Hepatocellular carcinoma, hepatitis B virus infection, growth impairment in different regions of the World particularly Asian and African countries [122]. European community and many other countries have imposed 2 μg kg^{-1} AFB1 as maximum tolerance level in human food products. Birds fed Afs, following ingestion are rapidly metabolized into nontoxic substances in the body. A rapid decrease in AFB1 residues below the tolerance limits from the muscles and liver within 3 and 7 days of withdrawal of dietary AFB1 and that it may not become a significant human health risk. However, in areas with no regulatory limits on AFB1 levels of poultry feed, the secondary exposure to aflatoxins through consumption of chicken liver and meat derived from the poultry fed AF contaminated feed may pose a risk to consumers health [123].

Table 5. Aflatoxins in other foods of animal origin.

Chicken Liver	Thailand	248/450	AFB1	Mean 0.6092	HPLC	[118]
Chicken Muscle	Thailand	96/450	AFB1	Mean 0.0451	HPLC	[118]
Meat	Jordan	12/50	Total[a]	0.15-8.32	HPLC	[124]
Fresh Fish	Egypt	10/30	Total[a]	22-70.5	Florometric	[125]
Salted fish	Egypt	12/30	Total[a]	18.5-50	Florometric	[125]
Smoked Fish	Egypt	8/30	Total[a]	32-96	Florometric	[125]
Egg	Jordan	5/40	Total[a]	0.01-6.15	HPLC	[124]
Processed egg	Saudi Arabia	0/25	Total[a]	ND[b]	ELISA	[126]
Unwashed egg	Saudi Arabia	3/25	Total[a]	0.61-1.19	ELISA	[126]

a. Total: AFB1+ AFB2+ AFG1+ AFG2

b. ND: Not detected

7. CONCLUSION

AFs are toxic secondary metabolites produced by *Aspergillus* fungus growing in susceptible agricultural commodities. They can result in major economic losses and can negatively affect animal and human health. This review has sought to summarize the possible AFs contamination in a wide array of agricultural commodities worldwide.

AFs contamination can occur both in temperate and tropical regions of the World. Major food commodities affected are cereals, nuts, dried fruit, spices, oil seeds, dried peas and beans and fruit. Regulations for major mycotoxins in commodities and food exist in at least 100 countries, most of which are for aflatoxins, maximum tolerated levels differ greatly among countries [27].

Frequent analytical surveillance program by food control agencies is highly recommended to control the incidence of aflatoxins contamination in food grains to ensure food safety and to protect consumer's health [27]. Some analytical techniques such as thin-layer chromatography (TLC), high performance liquid chromatography (HPLC), two-dimensional thin layer chromatography and enzyme-linked immunosorbent assay (ELISA) have been available for the qualitative and quantitative analysis of AFs. Poor separation, unsatisfied accuracy and low sensitivity limit the application of TLC. Although ELISA is a fast and sensitive method for AFs analysis is liquid chromatography combined with fluorescence detection, which has been extensively studied in various food matrices. However, conventional approach by HPLC in a gradient reversed phase mode typically using columns with 6 μm particles often costs a lot of time to get a complete separation of the target compounds and additionally, in order to improve detection limits of AFB1 and AFG1 a tedious pre- or post- column derivatization must be done [10].

The inability to control and at times even predict AF production makes it a unique challenge to food safety. To avoid aflatoxin problem in food grains, farmers should improve the practice of drying seeds to the required moisture content immediately after harvest. They must also develop proper storage structures by spraying fungicides or some other chemicals to reduce Aspergilli and subsequent toxin accumulation on food grains under storage conditions. Although prevention is the best control strategy, it is not always possible to prevent all mycotoxin contamination. Optimal postharvest storage conditions will minimize consumer exposure to AFs, but decontamination procedures may be needed in some cases. One approach to managing the risks associated with AF contamination is use of an integrated system based on the Hazard Analysis and Critical Control Point (HACCP) approach. This approach involves strategies for prevention, control, good manufacturing practices, and quality control at all stages of production, from the field to the final consumer [25]. Cheap and environmentally sustainable methods that can be applied pre or post-harvest to reduce the contamination of AFs are available. These methods include proper irrigation, choice of genetically resistant crop strains and bio-pesticide management which involves using a non-aflatoxigenic strain of *Aspergillus* that competitively excludes toxic strains. Other methods include sorting and disposal of visibly moldy or damaged seeds, reducing the bioavailability of aflatoxins using clay and chemo-protection [16].

REFERENCES

1. F. Bosco, C. Mollea, 2012 Mycotoxins in Food In: Valdez B. (ed) Food Industrial Processes- Methods and Equipment InTech 169 200 Available fromhttp://www.intechopen.com/books/food-industrial-processes-methods-and-equipment (accessed 13 May 2012)

2. I. Y. S. Rustom, 1997 Aflatoxin in food and feed:occurrence, legistlation and inactivation by physical methods Food Chemistry 59 1 57 67

3. European Food Safety Authority (EFSA). Opinion of the scientific panel on contaminants in the food chain on a request from the commission related to the potential increase of consumer health risk by a possible increase of the existing maksimum levels for aflatoxins in almonds, hazelnuts and pistachios and derived products The EFSA Journal 2007 446 1 127

4. N. W. Turner, S. Subrahmanyam, S. A. Piletsky, Analytical methods for determination of mycotoxins: A review Analytica Chimica Acta 2009 632 168 180

5. G. C. Dors, S. S. Caldas, V. Feddern, R. H. Bemvenuti, H. C. S. Hackbart, M. M. Souza, M. S. Oliveira, J. Garda-Buffon, E. G. Primel, E. Badiale-Furlong, 2011 Aflatoxins: Contamination, Analysis and Control In:. Guevara-González RG. (Ed) Aflatoxins-Biochemistry cand Molcecular Biology InTech 415 438 Available from http://cdn.intechopen.com/pdfs/20401/InTech-Aflatoxins_contamination_analysis_and_control.pdf (accessed 13 May 2012)

6. A. Filazi, S. Ince, F. Temamogullari, Survey of the occurrence of aflatoxin M1 in cheeses produced by dairy ewe's milk in Urfa city, Turkey Veterinary Journal of Ankara University 2010 57 3 197 199

7. U. Gundinc, A. Filazi, Detection of Aflatoxin M1 Concentrations in UHT Milk Consumed in Turkey markets by ELISA Pakistan Journal of Biological Sciences 2009 12 8 653 656

8. A. Zaghini, G. Martelli, P. Roncada, M. Simioli, L. Rizzi, Mannanoligosaccharides and Aflatoxin B1 in Feed for Laying Hens: Effects on Egg Quality, Aflatoxins B1 and M1 Residues in Eggs, and Aflatoxin B1 Levels in Liver Poultry Science 2005 84 6 825 832

9. O. L. Shotwell, M. L. Goulden, C. W. Hesseltine, 1976 Aflatoxin M1. Occurrence in stored and freshly harvested corn Journal of Agricultural and Food Chemistry 24 3 683 684

10. B. Huang, Z. Han, Z. Cai, Y. Wu, Y. Ren, Simultaneous determination of aflatoxins B1, B2, G1, G2, M1 and M2 in peanuts and their derivative products by ultra-high-performance liquid chromatography-tandem mass spectrometry Analytica Chimica Acta 2010 662 1 62 68

11. Y. Ren, Y. Zhang, S. Shao, Z. Cai, L. Feng, H. Pan, Z. Wang, Simultaneous determination of multi-component mycotoxin contaminants in foods and feeds by ultra-performance liquid chromatography tandem mass spectrometry Journal of Chromatography A 2007 1143 48 64

12. C. F. Quist, D. I. Bounous, J. V. Kilburn, V. F. Nettles, R. D. Wyatt, 2000 The Effect of dieteray aflatoxin on wild turkey poults Journal of Wildlife Diseases 36 3 436 444

13. L. S. Jackson, F. Al-Taher, Factors Affecting Mycotoxin Production in Fruits In: Barkai-Golan R, Paster N. (Ed) Mycotoxins in Fruits and Vegetables Academic Press is an imprint of Elsevier 2008 75 104

14. Food and Agriculture Organization of the United Nations/World Health Organization (FAO/WHO) Evaluation of certain veterinary drug residues in food Forty seventh report of the joint FAO/WHO Expert Committee on Food Additives (JECFA) World Health Organization Technical Report Series 1998 876 1 85

15. J. M. Cullen, B. H. Ruebner, L. S. Hsieh, D. M. Hyde, D. P. Hsieh, 1987 Carcinogenicity of Dietary Aflatoxin M1 in Male Fischer Rats Compared to Aflatoxin B1 Cancer Research 47 1913 1917

16. F. M. B. Shuaib, J. Ehiri, A. Abdullahi, J. H. Williams, P. E. Jolly, Reproductive health effects of aflatoxins: A review of the literature Reproductive Toxicology 2010 29 262 270

17. U. K. Becer, A. Filazi, 2010 Aflatoxins, Nitrates And Nitrites Analysis In The Commercial Cat And Dog Foods Fresenius Environmental Bulletin 18 11 2523 2527

18. L. H. Princen, 1983 New oilseed crops on the horizon Economic Botany 37 4 478 492

19. V. Fernandez Pinto, A. Patriarca, O. Locani, G. Vaamonde, Natural co-occurrence of aflatoxin and cyclopiazonic acid in peanuts grown in Argentina Food Additives and Contaminants 2001 18 11 1017 1020

20. F. A. Mphande, B. A. Siame, J. E. Taylor, 2004 Fungi, Aflatoxins, and Cyclopiazonic Acid Associated with Peanut Retailing in Botswana Journal of Food Protection 67 1 96 102

21. Z. Fu, X. Huang, S. Mina, Rapid determination of aflatoxins in corn and peanuts Journal of Chromatography A 2008 1209 271 274

22. G. S. Shephard, 2003 Aflatoxin and Food Safety: Recent African Perspectives Journal of Toxicology 22 2-3 267 286

23. A. Negedu, S. E. Atawodi, J. B. Ameh, V. J. Umoh, H. Y. Tanko, Economic and Health Perspectives of Mycotoxins: A Review Continental Journal of Biomedical Sciences 2011 5 1 5 26

24. K. V. K. Kumar, M. S. Basu, T. P. Rajendran, 2008 Mycotoxin research and mycoflora in some commercially important agricultural commodities Crop Protection 27 6 891 905

25. K. R. N. Reddy, H. K. Abbas, C. A. Abel, W. T. Shier, C. A. F. Oliveira, C. R. Raghavender, 2009 Mycotoxin contamination of commercially important agricultural commodities Toxin Reviews 28 2-3 154 168

26. B. W. Horn, R. L. Greene, J. W. Dorner, 1995 Effect of corn and peanut cultivation on soil populations of Aspergillus flavus and A. parasiticus in southwestern Georgia Applied and Environmental Microbiology 61 7 2472 2475

27. K. R. N. Reddy, C. R. Raghavender, B. Salleh, C. S. Reddy, B. N. Reddy, Potential of aflatoxin B1 production by Aspergillus

flavus strains on commercially important food grains International Journal of Food Science and Technology 2011 161 165

28. J. Wang, X. M. Liu, Contamination of aflatoxins in different kinds of foods in China Biomedical and Envirionmental Sciences 2007 20 6 483 487

29. N. Offiah, A. Adesiyun, Occurrence of Aflatoxins in Peanuts, Milk, and Animal Feed in Trinidad Journal of Food Protection 2007 70 3 771 775

30. V. P. S. Freitas, B. M. Brigido, 1998 Occurrence of aflatoxins B1, B2, G1, and G2 in peanuts and their products marketed in the region of Campinas, Brazil in 1995 and 1996 Food Additives and Contaminants 15 7 807 811

31. F. Q. Li, Y. W. Li, Y. R. Wang, X. Y. Luo, 2009 Natural occurrence of aflatoxins in Chinese peanut butter and sesame paste Journal of Agricultural and Food Chemistry 57 9 3519 3524

32. S. Z. B. Elshafie, A. El Mubarak, S. A. F. El -Nagerabi, A. E. Elshafie, 2011 Aflatoxin B1 Contamination of Traditionally Processed Peanuts Butter for Human Consumption in Sudan Mycopathologia 171 435 439

33. E. Set, O. Erkmen, The aflatoxin contamination of ground red pepper and pistachio nuts sold in Turkey Food and Chemical Toxicology 2010 48 2532 2537

34. A. M. Cheraghali, H. Yazdanpanah, N. Doraki, G. Abouhossain, M. Hassibi, S. Ali-abadi, M. Aliakbarpoor, M. Amirahmadi, A. Askarian, N. Fallah, T. Hashemi, M. Jalali, N. Kalantari, E. Khodadadi, B. Maddah, R. Mohit, M. Mohseny, Z. Phaghihy, A. Rahmani, L. Setoodeh, E. Soleimany, F. Zamanian, Incidence of aflatoxins in Iran pistachio nuts Food and Chemical Toxicology 2007 45 5 812 816

35. A. I. Abdel-Hafez, S. M. Saber, 1993 Mycoflora and mycotoxin of hazelnut (Corylus avellana L.) and walnut (Juglans regia L.) seeds in Egypt Zentralblatt für Mikrobiologie 148 2 137 147

36. H. Aycicek, A. Aksoy, S. Saygi, Determination of aflatoxin levels in some dairy and food products which consumed in Ankara, Turkey Food Control 2005 16 263 266

37. J. E. Schade, K. McGreevy, A. D. King, B. Mackey, G. Fuller, 1975 Incidence of Aflatoxin in California Almonds Applied and Environmental Microbiology 29 1 48 53

38. S. S. F. Janati, H. R. Beheshti, M. Asadi, S. Mihanparast, J. Feizy, Preliminary survey of Aflatoxins and Ochratoxin A in dried fruits from Iran Bulletin of Environmental Contamination and Toxicology 2012 88 3 391 395

39. C. W. Hesseltine, 1974 Natural occurrence of mycotoxin in cereals Mycopathologia 53 1-4 141 153

40. K. A. V. R. Krishnamachari, R. V. Bhat, V. Nagarajan, T. B. G. Tilak, Hepatitis due to aflatoxicosis: An outbreak in Western India Lancet 1975 1 1061 1063

41. G. S. Toteja, A. Mukheriee, S. Diwakar, P. Singh, B. N. Saxena, K. K. Sinha, A. K. Sinha, N. Kumar, K. V. Nagaraja, G. Baj, C. A. Krishna Prasad, S. Vanchinathan, R. Roy, S. Sarkar, 2006 Aflatoxin B(1) contamination of parboiled rice samples collected from different states of India: A multi-centre study Food Additive and Contaminant 23 4 411 414

42. M. Mazaheri, Determination of aflatoxins in imported rice to Iran Food and Chemical Toxicology 2009 47 8 2064 2066

43. J. Bansal, P. Pantazopoulos, J. Tam, P. Cavlovic, K. Kwong, A. M. Turcotte, B. P. Y. Lau, P. M. Scott, Surveys of rice sold in Canada for aflatoxins, ochratoxin A and fumonisins Food Additives and Contaminants: Part A 2011 28 6 767 774

44. E. Fredlund, A. M. Thim, A. Gidlund, S. Brostedt, M. Nyberg, M. Olsen, Moulds and mycotoxins in rice from the Swedish retail market Food Additives & Contaminants: Part A 2009 26 4 527 533

45. K. Tanaka, Y. Sago, Y. Zheng, H. Nakagawa, M. Kushiro, 2007 Mycotoxins in rice International Journal of Food Microbiology 119 1-2 59 66

46. H. A. Makun, M. F. Dutton, P. B. Njobeh, M. Mwanza, A. Y. Kabiru, Natural multi-occurrence of mycotoxins in rice from Niger State, Nigeria Mycotoxin Research 2011 27 97 104

47. A. Aydin, H. Aksu, U. Gunsen, Mycotoxin levels and incidence of mould in Turkish rice Environmental Monitoring and Assessment 2011 178 1-4 271 280

48. R. Ghali, K. H. Khlifa, H. Ghorbel, K. Maaroufi, A. Hedili, 2008 Incidence of aflatoxins, ochratoxin A and zearalenone in tunisian foods Food Control 19 9 921 924

49. R. Ghali, K. H. Khlifa, H. Ghorbel, K. Maaroufi, A. Hedili, Aflatoxin determination in commonly consumed foods in Tunisia Journal of the Science of Food and Agriculture 2010 90 14 2347 2351

50. E. A. Vargas, R. A. Preis, L. Castro, C. M. G. Silva, Co-occurrence of aflatoxins B1, B2, G1, G2, zearalenone and fumonisin B1 in Brazilian corn. Food Additives and Contaminants 2001 18 11 981 986

51. A. Zinedine, L. Gonzalez-Osnaya, J. M. Soriano, J. C. Molto, L. Idrissi, J. Manes, Presence of aflatoxin M1 in pasteurized milk from Morocco International Journal of Food Microbiology 2007 114 25 29

52. A. Ayalew, H. Fehrmann, J. Lepschy, R. Beck, D. Abate, Natural Occurrence of Mycotoxins in Staple Cereals from Ethiopia Mycopathologia 2006 162 1 57 63

53. C. V. Ratnavathi, V. V. Komala, B. S. V. Kumar, I. K. Das, J. V. Patil, 2012 Natural occurrence of aflatoxin B1 in sorghum grown in different geographical regions of India Journal of the Science of Food and Agricultural

54. Q. Iqbal, M. Amjad, M. R. Asi, A. Arino, Assessment of Hot Peppers for Aflatoxin and Mold Proliferation during Storage Journal of Food Protection 2011 74 5 830 835

55. B. Fazekas, A. Tar, M. Kovacs, Aflatoxin and ochratoxin A content of spices in Hungary Food Additives and Contaminants 2005 22 9 856 863

56. A. Erdogan, The aflatoxin contamination of some pepper types sold in Turkey Chemosphere 2004 56 321 325

57. H. Fufa, K. Urga, Screening of aflatoxins in Shiro and ground red pepper in Addis Ababa Ethiopian Medical Journal 1996 34 243 249

58. S. Demircioglu, A. Filazi, Detection of aflatoxin levels in red pepper produced in Turkey Journal of Veterinary Medical Association 2010 81 2 63 66

59. A. E. Elshafie, T. A. Al-Rashdi, S. N. Al-Bahry, C. S. Bakheit, 2002 Fungi and aflatoxins associated with spices in the Sultanate of Oman Mycopathologia 155 155 160

60. S. MacDonald, L. Castle, 1996 A UK retail survey of aflatoxins in herbs and spices and their fate during cooking Food Additives and Contaminants 13 121 128

61. M. L. Martins, H. M. Martins, F. Bernardo, Aflatoxins in spices marketed in Portugal Food Additives and Contaminants 2001 18 4 315 319

62. L. Santos, S. Marin, E. M. Mateo, J. Gil-Serna, F. M. Valle-Algarra, B. Patino, A. J. Ramos, Mycobiota and co-occurrence of mycotoxins in Capsicum powder International Journal of Food Microbiology 2011 151 270 276

63. R. Heidtmann-Bemvenuti, G. L. Mendes, P. T. Scaglioni, E. Badiale-Furlong, L. A. Souza-Soares, Biochemistry and metabolism of mycotoxins: A review African Journal of Food Science 2011 5 16 861 869

64. T. Kuiper-Goodman, Uncertainties in the risk assessment of three mycotoxins: aflatoxin, ochratoxin and zearalenone Canadian Journal of Physiology and Pharmacology 1990 68 1017 1024

65. A. Prandini, G. Tansini, S. Sigolo, L. Filippi, M. Laporta, G. Piva, On the occurrence of aflatoxin M1 in milk and dairy products Food and Chemical Toxicology 2009 47 984 991

66. H. Mohammadi, M. Alizadeh, M. Bari, A. Khosrowshahi, H. Tajik, 2008 Minimization of aflatoxinM1 content in Iranian white brine cheese International Journal of Dairy Technology 6 2 141 145

67. C. Lopez, L. Ramos, S. Ramadan, L. Bulacio, J. Perez, Distribution of aflatoxin M1 in cheese obtained from milk artificially contaminated International Journal of Food Microbiology 2001 211 5

68. I. Y. Sengun, D. B. Yaman, S. A. Gonul, 2008 Mycotoxins and mould contamination in cheese: a review World Mycotoxin Journal 1 3 291 298

69. M. M. Motawee, D. J. McMahon, 2009 Fate of AflatoxinM1 during Manufacture and Storage of Feta Cheese Journal of Food Science 74 5 42 45

70. R. S. Applebaum, R. E. Brackett, D. W. Wiseman, E. H. Marth, 1982 Aflatoxins: toxicity to dairy cattle and occurrence in milk and milk products Journal of Food Protection 45 752 777

71. A. Kamkar, G. R. J. Khaniki, S. A. Alavi, Occurrence of aflatoxin M1 in raw milk produced in Ardebil of Iran Iranian Journal of Environmental Health Science and Engineering 2011 8 2 123 128

72. F. Galvano, V. Galofaro, A. Ritieni, M. Bognanno, A. De Angelis, G. Galvano, Survey of the occurrence of aflatoxin M1 in dairy products marketed in Italy: second year of observation Food Additives and Contaminants 2001 18 7 644 646

73. V. Roussi, A. Govaris, A. Varagouli, N. A. Botsoglou, Occurrence of aflatoxin M1 in raw and market milk commercialized in Greece Food Additives and Contaminants 2002 19 9 863 868

74. A. M. Elgerbi, K. E. Aidoo, A. A. G. Candlish, R. F. Tester, 2004 Occurrence of aflatoxin M1 in randomly selected North African milk and cheese samples Food Additives and Contaminants 21 6 592 597

75. C. Nachtmann, S. Gallina, M. Rastelli, G. L. Ferro, L. Decastelli, Regional monitoring plan regarding the presence of aflatoxin M1 in pasteurized and UHT milk in Italy Food Control 2007 18 623 629

76. G. K. Torkar, A. Venust, The presence of yeast, moulds and aflatoxin M1 in raw milk and cheese in Slovenia Food Control 2008 19 570 577

77. N. Nuryono, A. Agus, S. Wedhastri, Y. B. Maryudani, F. M. C. Setyabudi, J. Böhm, E. Razzazi-Fazeli, 2009 Food Control 20 721 724

78. S. C. Pei, Y. Y. Zhang, S. A. Eremin, W. J. Lee, 2009 Detection of aflatoxin M1 in Milk products from China by ELISA using monoclonal antibodies Food Control 20 1080 1085

79. N. Bilandzic, I. Vernina, B. Solomun, 2010 Aflatoxin M1 in raw milk in Croatia Food Control 21 1279 1281

80. N. Ertas, Z. Gonulalan, Y. Yildirim, F. Karadal, 2011 A survey of concentration of aflatoxin M1 in dairy products marketed in Turkey Food Control 22 1956 1959

81. A. M. Sani, H. Nikpooyan, Determination of aflatoxin M1 in milk by high-performance liquid chromatography in Mashhad (North east of Iran) Toxicology and Industrial Health 2012

82. A. Sadia, M. A. Jabbar, Y. Deng, E. A. Hussain, S. Riffatd, S. Naveed, M. Arif, 2012 A survey of aflatoxin M1 in milk and sweets of Punjab, Pakistan Food Control 26 235 240

83. I. Hussain, J. Anwar, M. A. Munawar, M. R. Asi, Variation of levels of aflatoxin M1 in raw milk from different localities in the central areas of Punjab, Pakistan Food Control 2008 19 1126 1129

84. I. Ghanem, M. Orfi, 2009 Aflatoxin M1 in raw, pasteurized and powdered milk available in the Syrian market Food Control 20 603 605

85. J. E. Lee, B. M. Kwak, J. H. Ahn, T. H. Jeon, 2009 Occurrence of aflatoxin M1 in raw milk in South Korea using an immunoaffinity column and liquid chromatography Food Control 20 136 138

86. M. L. Martins, H. M. Martins, 2000 Aflatoxin M1 in raw and ultra-high temperature-treated milk commercialized in Portugal Food Additives and Contaminants 17 10 871 874

87. M. R. Oveisi, B. Jannat, N. Sadeghi, M. Hajimahmoodi, A. Nikzad, Presence of aflatoxin M1 in milk and infant milk products in Tehran, Iran Food Control 2007 18 1216 1218

88. E. Rahimi, A. Shakerian, M. Jafariyan, M. Ebrahimi, M. Riahi, Occurrence of aflatoxin M1 in raw, pasteurized and UHT milk commercialized in Esfahan and Shahr-e Kord, Iran Food Sec. 2009 1 317 320

89. M. L. R. Velasco, M. M. C. Delso, D. O. Escudero, 2003 ELISA and HPLC determination of the occurrence of aflatoxin M1 in raw cow's milk Food Additives and Contaminants 20 3 276 280

90. L. Shundo, S. A. Navas, L. C. A. Lamardo, V. Ruvieri, M. Sabino, Estimate of aflatoxin M1 exposure in milk and occurrence in Brazil Food Control 2009 2009 655 657

91. A. A. Fallah, 2010 Assessment of aflatoxin M1 contamination in pasteurized and UHT milk marketed in central part of Iran Food and Chemical Toxicology 48 988 991

92. S. Alborzi, B. Pourabbas, M. Rashidi, B. Astaneh, 2006 Aflatoxin M1 contamination in pasteurized milk in Shiraz (south of Iran) Food Control 17 582 584

93. N. S. Garrido, M. H. Iha, M. R. S. Ortolani, R. M. D. Favaro, 2003 Occurrence of aflatoxins M1 and M2 in milk commercialized in Ribeira˜ o Preto-SP Brazil Food Additives and Contaminants 20 1 70 73

94. C. E. Lopez, L. L. Ramos, S. S. Ramadan, L. C. Bulacio, 2003 Presence of aflatoxin M1 in milk for human consumption in Argentina Food Control 14 1 31 34

95. N. Unusan, Occurrence of aflatoxin M1 in UHT milk in Turkey Food and Chemical Toxicology 2006 44 1897 1900

96. K. K. Tekinsen, H. S. Eken, 2008 Aflatoxin M1 levels in UHT milk and kashar cheese consumed in Turkey Food and Chemical Toxicology 46 3287 3289

97. A. Heshmati, J. M. Milani, 2010 Contamination of UHT milk by aflatoxin M1 in Iran Food Control 21 19 22

98. A. Gurbay, S. Aydın, G. Girgin, A. B. Engin, G. Sahin, Assessment of aflatoxin M1 levels in milk in Ankara, Turkey Food Control 2006 17 1 4

99. M. Nakajima, S. Tabata, H. Akiyamax, Y. Itoh, T. Tanakak, H. Sunagawa, T. Tyonan, T. Yoshizawaxx, S. Kumaga, Occurrence of aflatoxin M1 in domestic milk in Japan during the winter season Food Additives and Contaminants 2004 21 5 472 478

100. I. K. Grigoriadou, A. Eleftheriadou, A. T. Mouratidou, P. Katikou, Determination of aflatoxin M1 in ewe's milk samples and the produced curd and Feta cheese Food Control 2005 16 257 261

101. L. Anfossi, C. Baggiani, C. Giovannoli, G. D'Arco, C. Passini, G. Giraudi, Occurrence of aflatoxin M1 in Italian cheese: Results of a survey conducted in 2010 and correlation with manufacturing, production season, milking animals, and maturation of cheese Food Control 2012 25 125 130

102. S. Rastogi, P. D. Dwivedi, S. K. Khanna, M. Das, Detection of aflatoxin M1 contamination in milk and infant milk products from Indian markets by ELISA Food Control 2004 15 287 290

103. E. K. Kim, D. H. Shon, D. Ryu, J. W. Park, H. J. Hwang, Y. B. Kim, Occurrence of aflotoxin M1 in Korean dairy products determined by ELISA and HPLC Food Additives and Contaminants 2000 17 1 59 64

104. A. Kamkar, 2006 A Study on the occurrence of aflatoxin M1 in Iranian Feta cheese Food Control 17 768 775

105. A. Elkak, O. Atat, M. Abbas, Occurrence of aflatoxin M1 in cheese processed and marketed in Lebanon Food Control 2012 25 140 143

106. H. R. Tavakoli, M. Riazipour, A. Kamkar, H. R. Shaldehi, A. S. M. Nejad, Occurrence of aflatoxin M1 in white cheese samples from Tehran, Iran Food Control 2012 23 293 295

107. M. H. Iha, C. B. Barbosa, I. A. Okada, M. W. Trucksess, Occurrence of aflatoxin M1 in dairy products in Brazil Food Control 2011 22 1971 1974

108. T. Yaroglu, H. H. Oruc, M. Tayar, 2005 Aflatoxin M1 levels in cheese samples from some provinces of Turkey Food Control 16 883 885

109. A. A. Fallah, T. Jafari, A. Fallah, M. Rahnama, Determination of aflatoxin M1 levels in Iranian white and cream cheese Food and Chemical Toxicology 2009 47 1872 1875

110. B. Sarımehmetoglu, O. Kuplulu, T. H. Celik, Detection of aflatoxin M1 in cheese samples by ELISA Food Control 2004 15 45 49

111. K. Kav, R. Col, K. K. Tekinsen, Detection of aflatoxin M1 levels by ELISA in white-brined Urfa cheese consumed in Turkey Food Control 2011 22 1883 1886

112. K. K. Tekinsen, O. C. Tekinsen, 2005 Aflatoxin M1 in white pickle and Van otlu (herb) cheeses consumed in southeastern Turkey Food Control 16 565 568

113. M. Ardic, Y. Karakaya, M. Atasever, G. Adiguzel, 2009 Aflatoxin M1 levels of Turkish white brined cheese Food Control 20 196 199

114. K. K. Tekinsen, U. Gurkan, 2008 Aflatoxin M1 levels in butter and cream cheese consumed in Turkey Food Control 19 27 30

115. Atasever. M. Aydemir, M. Atasever, K. Oztorun, S. Urcar, Determination of aflatoxin M1 level in butter samples consumed in Erzurum, Turkey The Journal of the Faculty of Veterinary Medicine, University of Kafkas 2010 16 Suppl-A 159 162

116. L. Akkaya, Y. O. Birdane, H. Oguz, M. Cemek, Occurrence of aflatoxın M1 in yogurt samples from Afyonkarahisar, Turkey Bulletin of the Veterinary Institute Pulawy 2006 50 517 519

117. M. L. Martins, H. Marin, 2004 Aflatoxin M1 in yoghurts in Portugal International Journal of Food Microbiology 91 315 317

118. A. Bintvihok, D. Davitiyananda, Aflatoxins and their metabolites residues in chicken tissues from 5 parts (10 provinces) of Thailand Thai Journal of Health Research 2002 16 1 37 50

119. A. W. Yunus, E. Razzazi-Fazeli, J. Bohm, 2011 Aflatoxin B1 in Affecting Broiler's Performance, Immunity, and Gastrointestinal Tract: A Review of History and Contemporary Issues Toxins 3 566 590

120. Z. Hussain, M. Z. Khan, A. Khan, I. Javed, M. K. Saleemi, S. Mahmood, M. R. Asi, Residues of aflatoxin B1 in broiler meat: Effect of age and dietary aflatoxin B1 levels Food and Chemical Toxicology 2010 48 3304 3307

121. A. Wolzak, A. M. Pearson, T. H. Coleman, Aflatoxin carryover and clearance from tissues of laying hens Food and Chemical Toxicology 1986 24 37 41

122. C. P. Wild, Y. Y. Gong, Mycotoxins and human disease: a largely ignored global health issue Carcinogenesis 2010 31 1 71 82

123. C. Micco, M. Miraglia, R. Onori, C. Brera, A. Mantovani, A. Ioppolo, D. Stasolla, Long-term administration of low doses of mycotoxins to poultry. 1. Residues of aflatoxin B1 and its metabolites in broilers and laying hens. Food Additive and Contaminant 1988 5 303 308

124. S. M. Herzallah, Determination of aflatoxins in eggs, milk, meat and meat products using HPLC fluorescent and UV detectors Food Chemistry 2009 114 1141 1146

125. A. A. Hassan, M. A. Hassan, H. M. El Shafei, R. M. H. S. El Ahl, R. H. A. El -Dayem, 2011 Detection of Aflatoxigenic Moulds Isolated From Fish and their Products and its Public Health Significance Nature and Science 9 9 106 114

126. A. A. S. Bahobail, S. A. Hassan, B. A. El -Deeb, 2012 Microbial quality and content aflatoxins of commercially available eggs in Taif, Saudi Arabia African Journal of Microbiology Research 6 13 3337 3342

9

FOOD SECURITY: A COMPARISON OF INDICATORS FOR THE UNITED STATES AND THE UNITED REPUBLIC OF TANZANIA

Carlisle Pemberton[1], Mary Mgonja[2], Afiya De Sormeaux[3], Hazel Patterson-Andrews[4], Esther Mwaisango[5]

[1]Department of Agricultural Economics and Extension, University of the West Indies, St Augustine, Trinidad and Tobago (Retired)

[2]Country Head – Tanzania, Alliance for a Green Revolution in Africa (AGRA)

[3]MPhil Student, SALISES, University of the West Indies, St Augustine, Trinidad and Tobago

[4]Department of Agricultural Economics and Extension, University of the West Indies, St Augustine, Trinidad and Tobago

[5]Senior Agricultural Officer, Ministry of Agriculture Food Security and Cooperatives (MAFC), Dar es Salaam, Tanzania

ABSTRACT

Developing nations have struggled with the problem of food insecurity thus one of the United Nations Millennium Development Goals (MDG) was to 'eradicate extreme poverty and hunger' with a target of halving between 1990 and 2015, the proportion of people who suffer from hunger. Progress has been made by developing countries in increasing their food security, however a question remains about their status as compared to developed countries; thus this paper sought to devise a methodology to compare the food security status of a food surplus developing country to a food surplus developed country utilizing the four pillars of food security; availability, access, utilization and stability. To test the methodology a comparison was made between the United Republic of Tanzania, a bright spot in the developing world and the United States utilizing indicators for the four pillars from the FAOSTAT Food Security data domain. The results suggest that Tanzania is still deficient with respect to most food security indicators, including the key indicator - the "prevalence of undernourishment". Tanzania's food security status also compares unfavorably to that of the United States, which remains among the leading nations in maintaining a high level of national food security. Finally the paper explores the critical areas needed for the improvement of the food security status of Tanzania.

Keywords: food security, Tanzania, United States, food security indicators, application of MANOVA

1. INTRODUCTION

1.1. Problem and Objective

The State of Food Insecurity in the World (SOFI), 2015 has stated that global hunger has continued to decline "to an estimated 795 million undernourished people, or a reduction of 167 million hungry people over the last ten years" and that this decline has been most pronounced in developing countries, "despite significant population growth" [9]. The Report also states that 2015 marks the end of the Millennium Development Goal (MDG) monitoring period and for the developing regions as a whole, the hunger target to reduce the proportion of the world's hungry by 50 percent by 2015 was missed by a small margin [9]. SOFI also reports that some regions (such as Latin America, the eastern and south-eastern regions of Asia, the Caucasus and Central Asia, and the northern and western regions of Africa) and as many as 72 developing countries out of 129 have reached the MDG hunger target, as they made fast progress in reducing undernourishment and overcoming the dire food shortages reported in 2008 [4, 9]. However SOFI reports that despite many success stories at country and sub-regional levels, the highest burden of hunger occurs in Southern Asia, where as many as 281 million people are undernourished and in sub-Saharan Africa, where one in every four people, or 23.2 percent of the population, are hungry [9].

Despite the progress made by the developing countries with respect to increasing food security a question still remains as to how their status compares to that of developed countries, thus the objective of this paper is to devise a methodological approach to carry out inter-country comparisons of food security. This approach is tested by a comparison of the food security status of a food surplus developing country, Tanzania, to a food surplus developed country, the United States, utilizing the four pillars of food security, with the specific aim of identifying the dimensions of food security where Tanzania may be deficient, in relation to the United States.

The conceptualization of food security has changed over the years. The current focus is in terms of the four pillars of: availability, access, utilization and stability, consistent with the 1996 World Food Summit (WFS) definition that: "Food security exists when all people, at all times, have physical and economic access to sufficient, safe and nutritious food to meet their dietary needs and food preferences for an active and healthy life" [6]. However this multi-dimensionality of food security may not always be reflected in the popular literature, with an emphasis often-times on the "availability" pillar of food security. For example, in addition to noting that there are serious problems with food utilization and associated factors leading to high malnutrition in the country, a World Food Program (WFP) overview of The United Republic of Tanzania (hereafter referred to as Tanzania) pronounces: "Although the country is self-sufficient in food, reliance on the rain and traditional farming techniques means households, districts and regions may suffer food shortages. While the liberalization of exports has turned Tanzania into a regional grain supplier, domestically, high rates of malnutrition persist". [26].

Tanzanian President, Jakaya Kikwete called for investment to increase Tanzania's food surplus storage and the need to seek additional markets for surplus food products in New York on March 30th 2015. [20] He also stated that for the last three years, Tanzania has enjoyed surplus food production, but the challenge is to increase storage [20].

On the other hand for the USA, recent data from the USDA suggest that "one out of six Americans doesn't have enough to eat," and that this may still conjure up a "depression-era image of the unemployed scavenging for food" [17]. Reference [17] however states that the face of hunger in rural, suburban, and urban America has changed. Despite the reports of food surpluses in Tanzania and hunger in the United States, this paper hypothesizes that the overall food security status of Tanzania is deficient as compared to the United States.

1.2. Overall Approach of the Paper

The paper proceeds as follows: First in the paper, there is a review of recent developments in the food security status of Tanzania and the United States. Attention then turns to methodological issues and in particular, a consideration of the merits and demerits of using composite or aggregate indicators for inter-state comparison of food security, versus the use of MANOVA (multivariate analysis of variance). MANOVA is then utilized as the procedure to compare the food security status of the two countries according to the pillars of food security. The new "Food Security" data domain of the FAO provides readily available data on the pillars of food security that can be used to provide a comprehensive range of indicators of national food security [9]. Hence the dependent variables in the MANOVA are a range of indicators that are used to represent the four pillars of food security, while the independent variable has two possible values: "Tanzania" and "the United States". Multivariate tests of significance (Pillai Trace etc.) are used to test for the overall difference between the USA and Tanzania for each pillar. Then a determination is made of whether significant differences exist between the two countries for individual indicators as individual dependent variables within the four pillars by Analysis of Variance (ANOVA) also referred to in this context as "Tests of Between-Subjects Effects" (utilizing F-tests). Finally the paper discusses recommendations for Tanzania based on the analyses conducted.

1.3. Tanzania's Recent Food Security Experience

According to [15] during the 1961-1966 period in Tanzania, food self-sufficiency was taken for granted as "Tanzania was the only independent African country achieving a growth trend in food production greater than that of its population". This situation continued until the two drought years, 1973-75; when food grain imports especially maize were necessary for relief during these crisis years [15]. A campaign dubbed "Kilimo cha Kufa na Kupona" ("Agriculture as a matter of life and death") was then started and coupled with the World Bank financed 'National Maize Program',

Tanzania was once again able to produce enough food and exported maize in 1978 [15].

Reference [15] states that drought and adverse economic conditions caused an unprecedented food crisis from 1981 to 1984 and during this period there was food rationing, characterized by long queues and the provision of 'vibalis' (permits for purchase of essential items). However good rains during 1984-85 and price incentives from structural policy reforms, resulted in a significant increase in food production [1]. As seen in Table 1, the national level food balance data for the period 1984/85 to 1989/90 show that in aggregate terms, Tanzania produced enough food to satisfy domestic food requirements [15]. Thus [15] concluded that for this period "the aggregate level food security was not in jeopardy because of insufficient food production". Even the severe drought of 1992, which affected the Eastern and Southern Africa from Ethiopia to South Africa, did not seriously affect Tanzania, which experienced only pockets of severe food insecurity which were cushioned by internal redistribution of food and modest food aid and imports [15].

Table 1. Annual Aggregate Food Balance, Tanzania Mainland, 1984/85 - 1989/90

Years	Total Production		Total Requirements[1]		Available[2] Balance (% of Requirements)	
	Food '000 mt	Energy m.kcal	Food '000 mt	Energy m.kcal	Food	Energy
1984/85	7,026	24,261	4,543	21,047	131	98
1985/86	6,972	24,100	4,670	21,637	127	95
1986/87	7,048	24,499	4,801	22,243	125	94
1987/88	6,780	23,598	4,935	22,865	117	88
1988/89	7,919	27,355	5,073	23,506	133	99
1989/90	7,819	27,010	5,073	23,506	131	98

[1] Based on Tanzania Food and Nutrition Centre (TFNC) calculations. 1989/90 figures based on 1989 population estimates

[2] Excludes seed and post-harvest losses of 15 percent.

Source: (Kavisha, 1993)

However there has always been concern about the situation of Tanzania with respect to other pillars of food security [7]. Reference [3] for example reviewed the situation in Africa for what he termed "selected indicators of food security" as provided in Table 2. This table shows that Tanzania fared worse than all regions of Africa, except Central Africa, with respect to the key indicators of "Prevalence of Undernourished (% of Population)" and Dietary Energy Supply (Kcal per person per day). It could also be noted that the percentage of the population undernourished actually increased from 1990-1992 (35.2%) to 1999-2001 (43.3%).

Table 2. Selected National and Regional Indicators of Food and Nutrition Security for Africa

Region/Country	Under-nourished	Under-nourished	Dietary Energy Supply	Under-5 Mortality
	1999 - 2001	1990 - 1992	1999 - 2001	2002
	Prevalence (%)	Prevalence (%)	Kcal per person per day	Deaths per 1,000 births
Africa	27.4	28.8	2,370	154
North Africa	4.3	4.7	3,210	42
Sub-Saharan Africa	32.9	34.9	2,180	168
Central Africa	58.3	35	1,810	193
East Africa	38.8	44.1	2,020	154
Tanzania	43.3	35.2	1,970	165
Southern Africa	41.3	48.2	2,050	156
West Africa	14.7	20.7	2,590	186
Developing world	16.9	20.2	NA	NA

Source: (Benson, 2004).

Recently quite a favourable picture has emerged about Tanzania's food situation. Headlines point to a grain surplus situation in that nation as indicated earlier. For example, during the month of December 2011, the Tanzanian Ministry of Agriculture Food Security and Cooperatives (MAFC) conducted a Final Food Crop Production Forecast Survey to ascertain the food crop harvest status for the 2010/2011 production season and the corresponding food availability for the year 2011/2012 [22]. The report by the MAFC estimated overall national food crop production to reach 12.972 million MT, comprising of 7.033 million MT of cereals and 5.939 million MT of non-cereals and the report further established the total food requirement for 2011/2012 to amount to 11.532 million MT [22]. A comparison of the estimated production in the 2010/11 with the 2011/2012 food requirement by the report indicated that the country should have attained a Food Self Sufficiency Ratio (SSR) of 112 percent, slightly above that of the 2010/2011 consumption year, which was 111 percent, indicating a general food surplus of about 1.440 million MT.

The 2013/14 Preliminary Food Crop Production Forecast for Tanzania predicted a SSR of 125% made up of cereals - 121% and non-cereals - 134%. This represented 3,247,359 tonnes surplus of total food, a cereal surplus of 1,679,933 tonnes and a non-cereal surplus amounting to 1,567,425 tonnes, with the commodities contributing to these surpluses predicted to be: bananas (56%), potatoes (33%), millets (28%) and rice (12%) while a decline was forecasted for wheat (16%) and pulses (10%) [23]. The expected increased production was attributed mainly to the timely onset and fairly good distribution of rainfall over the growing season [23].

The concern for the other pillars of food security in Tanzania has continued however. A nutrition country report states that consumption of micronutrient dense foods such as animal products and fruits and vegetables is infrequent and subsequently micronutrient deficiencies are widespread in the country [22]. The Report also claims the dietary energy supply does not meet average energy requirements of the population and close to 40% of the population live in "chronic food-deficit regions", where rainfall is scarce and irregular [22]. The report also claims that rural households spend up to 66% of their income on food; price volatility is a major concern and the dietary diversification index is very low, as starchy foods provide almost three quarters of the total energy supply, despite the wide variety of food produced in the country [22]. According to this report the primary causes of malnutrition and food insecurity are an inadequate dietary intake (operating at individual level); disease and inconsistent food availability and these are caused secondarily by climatic variability and poor infrastructure, inadequate attention paid to nutritional requirements of the population in terms of vitamins and minerals; limited accessibility to food among the population; limited diversification in the utilization of different varieties of food; widespread poverty; inadequate access to health services; and infant and young child feeding (IYCF) practices that are not optimal [22].

1.4. Food Security in the U.S.A.

A recent review of food security in the United States reported that during the early 1980s, the U.S. economy suffered from a severe recession that left many Americans unemployed and Federal budget cuts weakened many social support programs. These two events caused a dramatic rise in poverty and hunger in the country while homelessness became increasingly apparent in large cities. "America's poor turned to food banks, food pantries, soup kitchens and other charitable programs for help (and) ... the size and number of these emergency food programs multiplied over the course of just a few years" [13].

As seen in Figure 1, by 1995 the percentage of households in the United States that were food insecure was about 12% and the rate remained below this level until 2007 (11.1%) Food insecurity increased from 10.5 percent in 2000 to nearly 12 percent in 2004, declined to 11 percent in 2005-07, then increased in 2008 (14.6 percent), remaining essentially unchanged at that level in 2009 and 2010 [25]. Reference [25] reports that the prevalence rates of food insecurity showed a cumulative decline from 2011 (14.9 percent) to 2014 (14.0 percent), which was statistically significant. Reference [25] also states that prior to 2008, the prevalence of very low food security had increased from 3.1 percent in 2000 to 3.9 percent in 2004, and remained essentially unchanged through 2007.

*Prevalence rates for 1996 and 1997 were adjusted for the estimated effects of differences in data collection screening protocols used in those years.
Source: Calculated by USDA, Economic Research Service (ERS) based on Current Population Survey Food Security Supplement data.

Figure 1. Trends in Prevalence Rates of Food Insecurity and Very Low Food Security in U.S. Households, 1995-2014

This prevalence of very low food security was essentially unchanged from 2011 and 2012 (5.7 percent in both years) to 2013 and 2014 (5.6 percent in both years)". The prevalence of very low food security was also 5.7 percent in 2008 and 2009. In 2010, the prevalence of very low food security had declined to 5.4 percent [25].

The USDA has produced an analysis of the food security status of the United States for 2014 [25]. The overall picture for the country is presented in Figure 2 which shows that the percentage of the population that is food secure – that is "These households had access, at all times, to enough food for an active, healthy life for all household members" – was 86.0 percent (106.6 million), which was essentially unchanged from 85.7 percent in 2013 [25]. The "food insecure" in the United States therefore stood at 14.0 percent of the population (17.4 million of U.S. households) and was also essentially unchanged from 14.3 percent in 2013. These were households which at times during the year "were uncertain of having, or unable to acquire, enough food to meet the needs of all their members because they had insufficient money or other resources for food". This category consisted of both groups of households with "low food security" and "very low food security" [25].

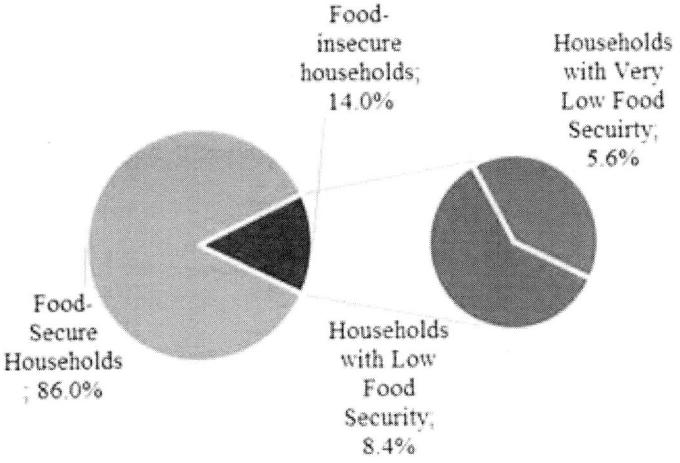

Source: Calculated by USDA, ERS using data from the December 2014 Current Population Survey Food Security Supplement.

Figure 2. US Households by Food Security Status (%), 2014

The "low food-secure" households obtained enough food to avoid substantially disrupting their eating patterns or reducing food intake by using a variety of coping strategies, such as eating less varied diets, participating in Federal food assistance programs, or getting emergency food from community food pantries and comprised 8.4 percent (10.5 million) and was also essentially un-changed from 8.7 percent in 2013 [25]. For the "very low food-secure" households, "normal eating patterns of one or more household members were disrupted and food intake was reduced at times during the year because they had insufficient money or other resources for food". These were 5.6 percent (6.9 million) of U.S. households, which was unchanged from 2013 [25].

2. MATERIALS AND METHODS

2.1. Aggregation versus Non-aggregation Approaches

As has been argued earlier the measurement of a multi-dimensional concept like food security requires the use of a number of indicators of the various dimensions of the concept. Inter-country comparisons of food security therefore require the comparison of the set of indicators for the respective countries. For such comparisons this paper considers the relative merits and demerits of using composite or aggregate indicators versus the use of multivariate analysis of variance (MANOVA) to determine whether significant differences exist among countries for the set of indicators.

Reference [19] has presented the following steps for devising an aggregate or composite indicator for a complex phenomenon like food security from a number of individual indicators:

1. The definition of the phenomenon under investigation.

2. Formulation of the different dimensions of the phenomenon. Such dimensions he states should "convey the different (and possibly unrelated) information" and should be (statistically) independent of each other.

3. Determination of the relative weights across different dimensions.

4. Selection of variables for the different dimensions. He states that obtaining variables of good quality is crucial for constructing composite indicators. Ideally, he states such "variables should be SMART: specific, measurable, accessible, relevant, and timely.

5. Selection of data. He states that this data can usually consist of "a set of heterogeneous indicators: quantitative (hard) data, qualitative (soft) data collected from surveys or policy reviews, or proxies aimed at conveying information on the phenomenon when specific variables are unavailable".

6. The imputation of missing data. This is required he states since most modern statistical techniques assume (or require) complete data, and because of deficiencies in the manner in which existing statistical packages deal with missing data.

7. Normalization of indicators by for example the computation of z-scores.

8. Weighting of the normalized indicators and other measures of the different dimensions.

9. Aggregation of indicators and dimensions using the weighting schemes of Step 3 and Step 8 to form the composite indicator via an aggregation method such as the popular linear aggregation or geometric aggregation.

However the derivation of these composite indicators has major problems [18]. One of these problems is the determination of the relative weights for the different dimensions and for the indicators within the dimensions as indicated in steps 3 and 8. These weights are usually subjectively determined which weakens the scientific nature of the aggregation exercise. Another problem with the aggregation is the interpretation of the values of the composite indicator, in other words what exactly do these numbers mean and does the aggregation actually present an accurate indication or measure of a multidimensional concept such as food security.

Using these composite indicators for comparisons (such as between the USA and Tanzania for food security as in this study) has an additional problem. The use of statistical methods such as tests of differences between the means or ANOVA may be precluded. The statistical properties, in particular the probability distribution, of the composite indicator may be unknown especially if the derivation involves non-linear transformations, such as involved in geometric aggregation, even if it is assumed that the individual indicators are normally distributed. If the numbers of observations of the composite indicators are small then recourse cannot even be made to the Central Limit theorem. Small sample sizes in fact usually characterize such comparisons. Recourse may then have to be made to more advanced statistical techniques such as bootstrapping which require no distributional assumptions.

2.2. Application of MANOVA

This paper proposes and utilizes an alternative approach of multivariate analysis of variance (in this case One-way MANOVA) to make inter-country comparisons of the food security. Here the dependent variables are a range of indicators that are used to represent the four pillars of food security as mentioned above and the independent variable is a "Country" variable with two possible values: "Tanzania" and "the United States", which two countries are usually termed "groups" in MANOVA.

MANOVA has several advantages in that it can test if differences exist for a dimension for the groups taking into consideration (simultaneously) all the indicators for that dimension, without the need to create an aggregate indicator for the dimension. Also, this method can indicate the confidence that can be placed in the test of differences between groups for a dimension via multivariate tests significance based on statistics such as the Wilks' lambda, Lawley-Hotelling trace, and Pillai's trace etc. using relevant tests based on the F statistic approximations to these statistics [12]. In addition if in MANOVA for a dimension differences exist for the groups taking into consideration (simultaneously) all the indicators for that dimension, further follow-up analyses can be conducted for each indicator to determine if differences exist between groups for each individual indicator of a dimension. These individual ANOVA tests for each indicator and the statistical confidence can be obtained from tests based on the F statistic [12].

Using MANOVA therefore, the comparison of the food security status of Tanzania and the United States was carried out in the following manner, within the general framework of [19]. With respect to steps 1 and 2 the concept of food security is well defined as noted above and the four pillars or dimensions of food security were used in the comparison: Availability, Access, Utilization and Stability. Then, given the use of MANOVA Step 3 was unnecessary. In step 4 the indicators that were chosen for each dimension were derived from the new FAOSTAT data dimension on Food Security. A detailed description of these indicators can be found at [8]. Reference [2] in discussing these indicators has stated that they possess the following desirable properties:

i. Valid in the conceptual representation of the underlying phenomenon they attempt to measure;
ii. Sensitive to change and unambiguous and easy to interpret;
iii. Robust and methodologically transparent in construction; and
iv. Timely – can be produced or updated on a regular basis.

In this application, all the indicators in the FAO data dimension for food security under the different pillars could not be used, since data was not available for some indicators for both countries. So the

MANOVA was limited to those indicators for which corresponding data existed for both countries at Step 5 of [19]. No figures are reported for the United States for the indicator "Prevalence of undernourishment (%) - 3 years average (2012-14)" in the FAOSTAT data base. For this important indicator of the "Access" pillar, the figure for Tanzania in the FAOSTAT data base was compared with the "Prevalence of food insecurity" figures reported by the USDA in Section 4 of this paper.

No imputation of missing data was carried out as suggested in Step 6 of [19] and Steps 7, 8 and 9 of[19] were unnecessary as instead MANOVA was carried out for each pillar or dimension of food security using the selected indicators. In the MANOVA, multivariate tests of significance were carried. However the results of the Pillai Trace alone are reported as all the alternative tests gave identical results.

One of the main assumptions of MANOVA is that the dependent variables come from group populations that are multivariate normal distributed [5, 11, 16, 21]. With respect to Type I error rate, MANOVA tends to be robust to minor violations of the multivariate normality assumption [12]. However Doornik-Hansen tests were performed to test for multivariate normality for the group (country) sample data for each pillar [5, 11].

Follow-up analyses were done for each MANOVA for the individual indicators, since all tests revealed significant differences between groups for all indicators for a dimension considered simultaneously. These individual univariate ANOVAs were used to determine whether there were significant differences between the two countries for each individual indicator using standard F-tests.

3.RESULTS

The results of the MANOVA carried out are presented in the Tables below. They are presented by the pillars of food security. For the results of the individual ANOVAs carried out, all but one of the F-tests were significant (with a p-value = 0.000) indicating that there were significant differences between the United States and Tanzania for the particular indicator. Hence the one case of non-significant difference is highlighted.

3.1. Availability Pillar

In Table 3 it is seen that the multivariate normality tests for the data for both the United States and Tanzania both fail to reject the null hypothesis of multivariate normality.

Table 3. Comparison of Tanzania and the United States - Availability Food Security Pillar

Availability*	Country	Average	Last Year	N
Average dietary energy supply adequacy (%) (3-year average)	USA	144.9	2014	20
	Tanzania	99.8	2014	20
Average value of food production (I$ per person) (3-year average)	USA	617.3	2012	22
	Tanzania	138.9	2012	13
Share of dietary energy supply derived from cereals, roots and tubers (%) (3-year average)	USA	25.2	2011	20
	Tanzania	64.9	2011	20
Average protein supply (g/capita/day) (3-year average)	USA	111.6	2011	22
	Tanzania	54.9	2011	13
Average supply of protein of animal origin (g/capita/day) (3-year average)	USA	71.9	2011	22
	Tanzania	10.6	2011	13

Tanzania: Doornik-Hansen $\chi 2$ (10) = 12.776; p-value = 0.2365
USA: Doornik-Hansen $\chi 2$ (10) = 12.614; p-value = 0.2461
Pillai's Trace = 0.9991; F (5, 34) = 7937.25; p-value = 0.0000
*All the p-values for the F-tests on the ANOVAs for the individual indicators = 0.0000

The Pillai's Trace test indicates that there is an overall significant difference in the availability pillar for the two countries. The individual ANOVA analyses carried out support the multivariate result, with all the p-values on the F-tests being approximately equal to zero. The results suggest that Tanzania should increase the production of fresh fruits and vegetables and reduce the share of dietary energy supply derived from cereals to a figure closer to that of the USA (25%). The high energy intake from cereals is matched by low protein per capita intake of Tanzania that is half that of the USA and per capita animal protein intake that is one-seventh that of the USA.

3.2. Access Pillar

In Table 4 it is seen that the Pillai's Trace test indicates that there is overall significant differences between the two countries with respect to the Access pillar. In Table 4 also, the multivariate normality test for the data for the United States fails to reject the null hypothesis of multivariate normality. However in the case of Tanzania the multivariate normality test for the data rejects the null hypothesis of multivariate normality. An examination of the data for Tanzania for "Rail-lines density (per 100 square km of land area)' and "Road density (per 100 square km of land area)" indicates that these variables display only a few fixed values in the data which suggests non-normal distributions. However these values are consistently very much less than the values for the United States giving support to the results of the Pillai's Trace. Again the individual ANOVA tests also support these results with all the p-values on the F-tests being approximately equal to zero.

Table 4. Comparison of Tanzania and the United States - Access Food Security Pillar

Access*	Country	Average	Last Year	N
Rail-lines density (per 100 square km of land area)	USA	2.0	2012	22
	Tanzania	0.5	2006	13
Road density (per 100 square km of land area)	USA	66.0	2011	22
	Tanzania	9.2	2005	13
Gross domestic product per capita, PPP (constant 2011 international $)	USA	45083.5	2013	24
	Tanzania	1185.0	2012	23

Tanzania: Doornik-Hansen; $\chi 2$ (6) = 50.948; p-value = 0.0000
USA: Doornik-Hansen; $\chi 2$ (6) = 6.893; p-value = 0.3309
Pillai's Trace = 0.9999; F(3, 31) = 87421.17; p-value = 0.0000
*All the p-values for the F-tests on the ANOVAs for the individual indicators = 0.0000

The results in Table 4 suggest that Tanzania's GDP/capita is 2.63% of the USA. Hence for the Tanzanian population to be able to access a greater and healthier household food consumption there is urgent need to increase the country's GDP/capita. A better road and rail network in the country will also help to improve the internal distribution of food in the country also enabling greater household access to food.

3.3. Utilization Pillar

In Table 5 it is seen that the Pillai's Trace test indicates that there is overall significant differences for the Utilization pillar for the two countries. In Table 5 also, the multivariate normality test for the data for Tanzania fails to reject the null hypothesis of multivariate normality. However in the case of the United States, the multivariate normality test for the data rejects the null hypothesis of multivariate normality. An examination of the data for the United States shows that the variables "Access to improved water sources (%)" and "Access to improved sanitation facilities (%)" remained at more or less the same values given in Table 5 over the entire data period which suggests non-normal distributions for these variables. However these values are consistently very much greater than the values for Tanzania, giving support to the results of the Pillai's Trace. Again the individual ANOVA tests also support these results with all the p-values on the F-tests being approximately equal to zero.

Table 5. Comparison of Tanzania and the United States - Utilization Food Security Pillar

Utilization	Country	Average	Last Year	N
Access to improved water sources (%)	USA	98.8	2012	20
	Tanzania	54.2	2012	20
Access to improved sanitation facilities (%)	USA	99.8	2012	20
	Tanzania	9.2	2012	20
Prevalence of anaemia among children under 5 years of age (%)	USA	7.4	2011	22
	Tanzania	72.0	2011	13
Prevalence of anaemia among pregnant women (%)	USA	14.8	2011	22
	Tanzania	54.9	2011	13
Tanzania: Doornik-Hansen $\chi 2$ (8) = 10.590; p-value = 0.2261 USA: Doornik-Hansen $\chi 2$ (8) = 24.453; p-value = 0.0019 Pillai's Trace = 1.00; F (4, 39) = 1.1e+06; p-value = 0.0000				

The results in Table 5 show that there an urgent need for Tanzania to improve the access of its population to sanitation facilities as these were available to less than 10 percent of the population. This compares quite un-favourably to the United States where almost all of the population has access to these facilities. There is also the need for Tanzania to reduce the prevalence of anaemia among pregnant women and children. Again Tanzania compares un-favourably to the United States in this regard since the prevalence of anaemia among children in Tanzania is 10 times greater than the prevalence among children in the USA.

3.4. Stability Pillar

In Table 6, it is seen that the Pillai's Trace test indicates that there is overall significant differences in the "Stability" pillar of food security for the two countries. In Table 6 also, the multivariate normality test for the data for the United States fails to reject the null hypothesis of multivariate normality. However in the case of Tanzania the multivariate normality test for the data rejects the null hypothesis of multivariate normality. An examination of the data for Tanzania does not lead to any straightforward reasons for this non-multivariate normality of the Tanzania data set. Again the individual ANOVA tests support the multivariate results as the means for four of the five indicators in this pillar were significantly different for the two countries with the p-values of the F-tests for these variables being approximately equal to zero. However for the indicator "Per capita food supply variability (kcal/capita/day)" there was no significant difference between the means for the two countries.

Table 6. Comparison of Tanzania and the United States – Stability Food Security Pillar

Stability	Country	Mean	Last Year	N
Cereal import dependency ratio (%) (3-year average)	USA	2.4	2011	20
	Tanzania	9.6	2011	20
Percentage of arable land equipped for irrigation (%) (3-year average)	USA	15.4	2012	20
	Tanzania	1.7	2012	20
Value of food imports over total merchandise exports (%) (3-year average)	USA	4.1	2011	20
	Tanzania	26.7	2011	20
Per capita food production variability (I$ per person constant 2004-06)	USA	18.0	2013	24
	Tanzania	6.3	2013	23
Per capita food supply variability (kcal/capita/day)	USA	36.3*	2014	24
	Tanzania	39.7*	2014	23

*No significant difference between the means. $F(1,45)=2.170$ p-value=0.148
Tanzania: Doornik-Hansen $\chi^2(10)=20.886$; p-value=0.0219
USA: Doornik-Hansen $\chi^2(10)=12.564$; p-value=0.2491
Pillai's Trace=0.9970; $F(5, 38)=2492.28$; p-value=0.0000

The results of the analysis for the "Stability" pillar therefore suggest that Tanzania needs to increase the percentage of arable land equipped for irrigation. The percentage of irrigated land in the USA (15.4%) is nine times greater than the percentage in Tanzania (1.7%). The small percentage of its land that is irrigated is a major risk factor affecting the stability of food security of Tanzania, as poor rainfall over one and especially over several seasons can lead to severe decreases in cereal production in the country and hence rapidly worsen its food security situation, since as noted previously approximately 65% of the dietary energy in the country comes from cereals.

4. CONCLUSION AND DISCUSSION

The study demonstrated the use of multivariate analysis of variance (MANOVA) as a viable technique for making inter-country comparisons of food security status based on the use of a range of indicators. The advantages of MANOVA were well demonstrated in the study, especially the avoidance of the subjective choices of weights for indicators and pillars as well as aggregation methods. However the problem of attaining the condition of multivariate normality of the data is one that has the possibility of limiting the applicability of the method especially with small samples. The results suggest that Tanzania's status with respect to the pillars of food security compares un-favourably with that of the United States.

The analysis performed in this study showed that Tanzania despite having its grain production exceeding its grain consumption in recent years still has problems with respect to the four pillars of food security. In particular, with respect to the key indicator chosen by the United Nations to measure the achievement of MDG Target 1.C (Indicator 1.9): "Proportion of population below minimum level of dietary energy consumption" measured as the "Prevalence of undernourishment (%) - 3 years average (2012-14)", the figure for Tanzania is 32.7% [10, 24]. In 1992 this indicator stood at 24.2% and rose to 37.7% in 2003. Thus Tanzania did not meet the "MDG 1: Eradicate extreme poverty and hunger, Target 1.C: Halve, between 1990 and 2015, the proportion of people who suffer from hunger" by reducing the proportion of its population's hungry by 50 percent by 2015"[24]. Tanzania's figure of 32.7% for the "Prevalence of undernourishment" also compares unfavorably with "Prevalence of food insecurity" figure for the United States in 2014 reported by the USDA of 14.0%.

With respect to the United States, in general, this country was seen to have very favorable food security pillars and indicators overall, but especially with respect to a low "Share of dietary energy supply derived from cereals, roots and tubers" (25%), a high "Average protein supply" (112g/capita/day) and "Percentage of arable land equipped for irrigation" (15.4%) and a low "Value of food imports over total merchandise exports" (4.1%). In addition, almost all of its population has access to improved water sources and improved sanitation facilities.

The study also highlighted the following areas that need urgent attention to raise the level of food security in Tanzania. In the first place Tanzania needs to increase the GDP/capita as Tanzania's GDP is 2.63% of the USA. Increasing GDP/capita appears to be the major long term solution to the country's chronic food insecurity. Also, Tanzania needs to increase its production and consumption of fresh fruit and vegetables to reduce the percentage of the dietary energy supplied by cereals. A holistic value chain approach may be needed to stimulate the production of fresh fruits and vegetables through enhancing productivity, the creation of markets at remunerative prices and by the establishment of enabling policy environments. Tanzania also needs to improve access to sanitation facilities and improved water sources. This is likely to be a major factor in improving health and wellness and reducing communicable diseases in this country. These improvements will lead to a reduction in the prevalence of malnourished persons. Finally, Tanzania needs to increase the percentage of arable land equipped for irrigation as this is a major risk factor affecting the stability of the country's food security with a lack of rainfall likely to quickly increase food insecurity.

REFERENCES

1. Amani, H.K.R.; Kapunda, S.M.; Lipumba, N.H.I. and Ndululu, B.J., "Effects of Market Liberalization on Food Security in Tanzania," In: Rukuni, M. and Bernsten, R.H. (eds.), Southern Africa: Food Security Policy Options. Proceedings of the Third Annual Conference on Food Security Research in Southern Africa. 1-5 November, 1987. 1988. Harare: University of Zimbabwe/Michigan State University Food Security Research Project, 65-101.

2. Aurino, E., Selecting a Core Set of Indicators for Monitoring Global Food Security A Methodological Proposal. Food and Agriculture Organization of the United Nations, Rome, 2014. Available: http://www.fao.org/3/a-i4095e.pdf. [Accessed Dec. 2, 2015].

3. Benson, T., "Africa's Food and Nutrition Situation: Where We Are and How Did We Get Here?," 2020 Discussion Paper No. 37, IFPRI, Washington DC. 2004. Available: http://www.ifpri.org/publication/africa%E2%80%99s-food-and-nutrition-security-situation. [Accessed Nov. 2, 2015].

4. Brown, L.R., "World Facing Huge New Challenge on Food Front. Business as Usual Not a Viable Option," Earth Policy Institute, Plan B Update; 2008. Available: http://www.earth-policy.org/plan_b_updates/2008/update72. [Accessed Nov. 15, 2015].

5. Doornik, J. A. and Hansen, H., "An Omnibus Test for Univariate and Multivariate Normality," Oxford Bulletin of Economics and Statistics, Vol. 70, Issue s1, 927-939, December 2008. Available: http://www.doornik.com/research/normal2.pdf. [Accessed Nov. 15, 2015].

6. FAO (Food and Agriculture Organization of the United Nations), Rome Declaration on World Food Security. World Food Summit, 13-17 November, 1996, Rome, Italy. Available: http://www.fao.org/docrep/003/w3613e/w3613e00.HTM. [Accessed Nov. 15, 2015].

7. FAO (Food and Agriculture Organization of the United Nations), Nutrition Country Paper – The United Republic of Tanzania, (Draft). CAADP Agriculture Nutrition Capacity Development Workshops, February 2013. Available: http://www.fao.org/fileadmin/user_upload/wa_workshop/EC Africa-caadp/TANZANIA_NUTRITION_COUNTRY_PAPER_ Mainland_and_Zanzibar__rwd_BTCR_v1.pdf. [Accessed Nov. 15, 2015].

8. FAO (Food and Agriculture Organization of the United Nations), Food Security Indicators. October 15, 2014. Available: http://www.fao.org/fileadmin/templates/ess/foodsecurity/Food_Security_Indicators.xlsx. [Accessed Dec. 20, 2015].

9. FAO (Food and Agriculture Organization of the United Nations), The State of Food Insecurity in the World 2015, 2015. Available: http://www.fao.org/hunger/en/ [Accessed Dec. 2, 2015].

10. FAOSTAT (Food and Agriculture Organization of the United Nations, Statistics Division), Food Security. 2015. Available: http://faostat3.fao.org/download/D/*/E. [Accessed Dec 12, 2015].

11. Farrell, P. J.; Salibian-Barrera, M. and Naczk, K., "On Tests for Multivariate Normality and Associated Simulation Studies," Journal of Statistical Computation & Simulation, January 2006, 1-14.

12. IDRE (Institute for Digital Research and Education). "One-way MANOVA," UCLA, 2015. Available: http://www.ats.ucla.edu /stat/spss/dae/manova1.htm.[Accessed Dec. 2, 2015].

13. Johns Hopkins Center for a Livable Future, "Teaching the Food System: Hunger and Food Security Background Reading," Available: http://www.jhsph.edu/research/centers-and-institutes/teaching-the-food-system/curriculum/_pdf/Hunger _and_Food_Security-Background.pdf [Accessed Dec. 2, 2015].

14. Kavishe, F.P., "The Origin and Spread of Maize and its Social and Nutritional Consequences of its Introduction into Tanzania," Essay, 1982, London School of Hygiene and Tropical Medicine, University of London.

15. Kavishe, F.P., Nutrition-Relevant Actions in Tanzania, Tanzania Food and Nutrition Centre, 20th Anniversary, 1973-1993, April 1993. Monograph Series No. 1. Available:

http://www.unsystem.org/scn/archives/tanzania/ch09.htm#bm7-National%20self%20foodsufficiency [Accessed Nov. 15, 2015].

16. Laerd Statistics. One-Way MANOVA. 2013. Available: https://statistics.laerd.com/spss-tutorials/one-way-manova-using-spss-statistics.php. [Accessed Nov. 15, 2015].

17. McMillan, T., The New Face of Hunger – Why are people malnourished in the richest country on Earth?, National Geographic Magazine, Food Features. Available: http://www.nationalgeographic.com/foodfeatures/hunger/. [Accessed Nov. 15, 2015].

18. Pemberton, C., Patterson-Andrews, H. and De Sormeaux, A., "Relative Vulnerability of Selected Caribbean States to Changes in Food Security Due to Tropical Storms and Hurricanes," International Journal of Food and Agricultural Economics, Vol. 4 No. 1, Special Issue, 2016, pp. 125-136.

19. Santeramo, F. G., "On the Composite Indicators for Food Security: Decisions Matter!," Food Reviews International, 31:1, 2015, 63-73.

20. Tanzania Invest, President Kikwete Calls for Food Surplus Storage Investment in Tanzania. Sunday, 12 April 2015. Available: http://www.tanzaniainvest.com/agriculture/tanzania-agriculture-news/1498-president-kikwete-calls-for-food-surplus-storage-investment-in-tanzania [Accessed Nov. 15, 2015].

21. The Pennsylvania State University, Lesson 13: Multivariate Analysis of Variance (MANOVA), 13.4 - Example: Pottery Data - Checking Model Assumptions. STAT 505 – Applied Multivariate Statistical Analysis, 2015. Available: https://onlinecourses.science.psu.edu/stat505/node/164. [Accessed Nov. 15, 2015].

22. The United Republic of Tanzania, Comprehensive Food Security and Nutrition Assessment Report of the April, 2012 Main (Masika) Season. Prepared by the Tanzania Food Security and Nutrition Analysis System - Muchali, Tanzania April 2012. Available: http://www.kilimo.go.tz/publications/english%20docs/FSNA%20Report%20April%202012.pdf.

23. The United Republic of Tanzania, Preliminary Food Crop Production Forecast of the Crop Monitoring and Early Warning Report. Ministry of Agriculture Food Security and Cooperatives (MAFC) 2013/14, 2014, pp. 22.

24. UNSD (United Nations Statistical Division), Millennium Development Goal Indicators: Official List of MDG Indicators, 2015. Available: http://mdgs.un.org/unsd/mdg/Host.aspx?Content=Indicators/OfficialList.htm. [Accessed Nov. 15, 2015].

25. USDA (United States Department of Agriculture, Economic Research Service), USDA Household Food Security in the United States in 2014, 2014. Available: http://www.ers.usda.gov/topics/food-nutrition-assistance/food-security-in-the-us/key-statistics-graphics.aspx. [Accessed Jan. 2, 2016].

26. WFP (World Food Programme), United Republic of Tanzania Current Issues and what the World Food Programme is Doing. 2016, Available: http://www.wfp.org/countries/tanzania. [Accessed August 20, 2016].

10

FOOD INSUFFICIENCY, VIOLENCE AND HIV RISK BEHAVIORS AMONG FEMALE SEX WORKERS IN INDIA

Sangram Kishor Patel[1], Madhusudana Battala[1], Rajatashuvra Adhikary[1]

[1]HIV and AIDS Program, Population Council, 142, Golf Links, New Delhi, India

ABSTRACT

Background: Food insufficiency is one of the important contributing factors among female sex workers (FSWs) to engage in risky sexual behaviors and cause of HIV infection in developing countries. Studies exploring linkages between food insufficiency and HIV risk behaviors among FSWs are limited despite having potential program and policy implications. This study attempts to assess the food insufficiency among FSWs and examine its relationship with HIV risk behaviors and violence in India. **Materials and Methods**: Data were drawn from the Avahan-III baseline evaluation survey- 2015, conducted among FSWs (n=4098) using a three-stage cluster sampling approach in four states of India. Multivariate logistic regression (with adjusted odds ratios (AOR) and their 95% confidence intervals (CI)), bivariate analysis and frequency were used to assess the relationships between food insufficiency, HIV risk behaviors and violence. **Results**: Nearly one-fifth of FSWs (17%) reported of facing food insufficiency in past 6 months. More than 35% of FSWs had entertained more clients to cope with the situation of food insufficiency followed by defaulted on loans (24%), borrowed money from informal sources (20%) and had sex without condoms (7%). The likelihood of consistent condom use with non-regular (67% vs. 77%; AOR: 0.6; 95% CI: 0.4-0.9) and regular partner (22% vs. 51%; AOR: 0.3; 95% CI: 0.2-0.4) were significantly lower among FSWs who reported food insufficiency than among those who did not. The likelihood of consistent condom use with occasional (90% vs. 95%; AOR: 0.5; 95% CI: 0.4-0.7) and regular clients (88% vs. 91%; AOR: 0.8; 95% CI: 0.6-0.9) were significantly lower among FSWs who reported food insufficiency compared to those who did not. FSWs who reported food insufficiency were also significantly more likely to report STI symptoms (28% vs. 13%; AOR: 2.7) and any violence (16% vs. 9%; AOR: 2.1) than their counterparts.**Conclusions**: The findings of the study highlight that FSW's food insufficiency is significantly associated with HIV risk behaviors and violence. This study underscores the need for community-led interventions focusing on food insufficiency and economic strengthening activities to reduce HIV vulnerability among FSWs. However, further evidence-based research and advocacies on food insufficiency is required to ensure that HIV prevention programs are appropriately addressed.

Keywords: food insufficiency, food insecurity, consistent condom use, violence, HIV risk, India

1. INTRODUCTION

Food insecurity as well as food insufficiency are now the known public policy concern for not only among food-poor countries, but also among food-rich countries. The estimates on global hunger indicate that about 795 million people are estimated to be chronically undernourished in 2012–14, and more than 90% of food-insecure individuals live in Asia (512 millions) and Africa (233 millions)[1]. Determinants of food insufficiency in the general population in both resource-rich and resource-poor countries include markers of low socioeconomic status (lower education, income, assets, and unemployment, age, larger household size, and number of children [2, 3, 4]. Women are invariably responsible for feeding household members, notably children and the infirm [5]. Lack of food can lead to risky coping strategies in the household, which may increase economic vulnerability or exposure to HIV (particularly among women), including the redirection of wage labor or the exchange of sex for money or food [6, 7, 8, 9, 10]. Due to food insufficiency, women may become involved in sex work or intergenerational relationships to gain access to money or food-related resources, where they lose the ability to negotiate safe sex practices [7, 11]. A study among South African women described that transactional sex was more likely among those who reported hunger than their counterparts [12]. Similar findings were reported in Nigeria, where 35% of female sex workers (FSWs) said that poverty and lack of means to obtain food caused them to join the sex trade, and to engage in unprotected sex with clients to earn quick money [13]. A population-based survey in Swaziland and Botswana found that women reporting food insufficiency in the past year had 80% increased odds of selling sex for money or resources, 70% increased odds of engaging in unprotected sex and reporting lack of sexual control, and 50% increased odds of intergenerational sex [8].

Food insufficiency and HIV are entangled in a vicious cycle that intensifies the vulnerability to and worsens the severity of, each condition [14]. Worldwide studies in various regions among FSWs have shown that food insufficiency is associated with inconsistent condom use [8, 15], sexual exchange [8], multiple sexual partnerships [16, 17, 18], a lack of control in sexual relationships [8], sexual relations with older or gang-affiliated partners [18]. Due to frequent engagement in risky sex, FSWs have a global HIV prevalence of 12%, which is 13.5 times higher than in the general population [19]. Further, evidence-based research studies across the globe highlighted that food insufficiency is also associated with sexual violence [20], symptoms consistent with sexually transmitted infections (STIs)[15, 21] and substance use before sex [18]. In San Francisco, food insufficiency was longitudinally associated with unprotected sexual activity and having multiple sexual partners among 154 homeless persons living with HIV [16]. For researchers, programmers and policymakers interested in food insufficiency, understanding the food insufficiency and risky sexual behavior and violence will be crucial for guiding policies for integrating nutrition support, and HIV and AIDS programming in ensuring that such programs target the priorities and needs of this vulnerable population. Although studies on debt, violence and risky sexual behavior has been conducted in India [22, 23, 24], studies exploring food insufficiency of FSWs and its relationship with HIV risk vulnerabilities and violence are scarce in India, despite having potential policy implications, and needs immediate attention. This study attempts to fill in this gap by understanding the food insufficiency and coping mechanism among FSWs, and assessing its association with HIV risk behaviors and violence in India.

2. MATERIALS AND METHODS

2.1. Study Settings and Design

We used data from the Avahan-III baseline evaluation survey - 2015 for this study. This is a cross-sectional survey conducted among FSWs during August to November 2015 in four high HIV prevalence states of India, including Andhra Pradesh/Telangana, Tamil Nadu, Karnataka and Maharashtra. The main focus of Avahan-III is to reduce the vulnerabilities (including HIV risk) among FSWs and men who have sex with men (MSM) by improving the access to financial security, social protection services, and to make the community-based organizations (COs) strong and sustainable. The baseline survey was designed to measure different vulnerabilities and capture the key behavioral indicators (e.g. HIV risk behaviors, social protection, financial security, violence, institutional development etc.).To sustain the impact of HIV prevention efforts in four states in India, Avahan-III program was initiated. Bill and Melinda Gates Foundation (BMGF) is partnering with Swasti and its group organizations from Catalyst Group (Catalyst Management Services and Vrutti) to implement the Avahan-III program. In this regard till the baseline survey time, a total of 87 COs were engaged in Avahan-III program; 75 COs are working towards FSWs population and 12 COs with MSM population.

2.2. Sampling and Sample Size

In Avahan-III baseline survey – 2015, sample size and power considerations were constructed based on our primary outcomes of interest: savings through formal sources, consistent condom use, and proportion experienced any violence. The sample size calculation assumed a 2-sided chi-square test with continuity correction, and a significance level of 0.05. We estimated the intra-class correlation of 0.15, and a non-response rate of 33% (based on the previous surveys). With this we calculated a sample size of 10 COs per state (to present state-level estimates), and minimum 3 outreach worker (ORW) areas per CO, and minimum 30 individual interviews per ORW area. With the assumption of 3 ORW areas within each CO, we estimated the sample size of 900 per state. However the technical committee anticipated that the power for the longitudinal analysis will be higher (as the baseline survey will be followed by mid-line and end -line survey), we inflated the sample size up to 10% and, we estimated the sample size of approximately 1000 FSWs per state. This translates to Pan-Avahan level sample size of 4000 individuals, recruited from 115

ORW areas within 39COs.The sampling frame was prepared based on a comprehensive list of FSWs who were administered with Membership Engagement Communication Tool (MECT) by implementing organization by 31st July 2015 in each CO. A three-stage cluster random sampling method was used to select respondents within a state. In the first stage, 10 COs were randomly selected within each state. In the second stage, three ORW areas (clusters) were randomly selected from each selected CO. In the third stage, the required numbers of FSWs were selected randomly from each selected ORW area (cluster). All clusters were selected under the COs where the numbers of clusters were below three and the size of individual sample is proportionately distributed. In Tamil Nadu state, all nine COs were selected as the total number of COs were under ten. A total of 4098 FSWs were interviewed across 39 COs from four states.

2.3. Methods of Data Collection

All interviews were conducted by trained female investigators with verbal and written skills in the local language of each state. The survey instrument (structured questionnaire for FSWs) was developed in English and translated into local languages. The questionnaire was pre-tested in communities similar to the survey sites, prior to the main survey. All the interviews were held in a private location specifically hired for the survey, or in a location convenient to the study participants. Field staff checked the data immediately after the interviews to ensure accuracy and completeness of the filled-in questionnaires. A user-written computer program in CSPro (version 5.0) was used for double data entry by trained data entry officers.

2.4. Ethics Statement

The overall study design, questionnaires and consent processes were reviewed and approved by the institutional review board for human research of population council in the USA and Sahara, centre for residential care and rehabilitation IRB/ethics board in India. Verbal consent was obtained from all respondents prior to participation in the interview, and steps were taken to ensure confidentiality. For ethical reasons, among the FSWs population, individuals aged 18 years or above were part of the sampling frame and among them, the information on selected participants was collected accordingly. No names and information were recorded on the questionnaires. Participants were not provided any compensation for their time in the study, but were referred to local CO project sites run by the implementing agency for more information and services. All the respondents were given contact details of the lead researchers at the Population Council to communicate their concerns on research, injuries and to get more information on the study. They were also provided the contact numbers of members of the accountability and transparency sub-committee for SWASTI (implementing agency) governing board to know their rights for being a participant in the research.

2.5. Measures

The measures and socio-demographic variables used in this study were selected as per the objectives of the paper, availability of variables in the data set and the review of literature. The socio-demographic variables considered in the analysis were age (<=30 years, > 30 years); marital status (never married, currently married, and others (widowed/divorced/separated/deserted)); education (illiterate, literate); place of solicitation for sex work (home, brothel/lodge/hotel, public places/street/highways, others), living status (living with family members/husband, living alone and living with others) and livelihood status (sex work only, other work with sex work); coping mechanism for food insufficiency (entertained more clients, defaulted on loans, borrowed money from informal sources, resorted to sex without using condoms, sold assets and others); consistent condom use with occasional clients (no, yes); consistent condom use with regular clients (no, yes); consistent condom use with non-regular partners (no, yes); consistent condom use with regular partners (no, yes); experienced STI symptoms in past six months (no, yes) and experienced any violence (physical and/or sexual) in past six months (no, yes) were also assessed. More details on the definitions of measures are given in the footnote of Table 3.

2.5.1. Food Insufficiency

Operational definitions of food insecurity vary between international organizations [25, 26, 27]. One of the most comprehensive definitions describes food in security as "the limited or uncertain availability of nutritionally adequate, safe foods or the inability to acquire personally acceptable foods in socially acceptable ways"[25]. Implicit in this general definition is the notion that a food-insecure individual may have one or several of the following characteristics: 1) insufficient quantity of food; 2) limited diversity of food groups; 3) poor safety of food; 4) feelings of hunger or anxiety regarding access to food; and 5) procurement of food in socially unacceptable manners, including begging, relying on charity, scrounging, stealing, exchanging sex for food, and other illicit activities [28]. The United States Department of Agriculture (USDA) defines food insufficiency as a state in which "consistent access to adequate food is limited by a lack of money and other resources at times during the year"[29]. Based on the USDA concept, in this study, food insufficiency status constitutes the dependent variable and was measured using the following two questions: In this survey, FSWs were asked two questions: First, in the past 6 months, did you or any of your household members ever eat less than the requirement because there wasn't enough money to buy food? Second, in the past 6 months, were you or any of your household members ever felt hungry, but didn't eat because you couldn't afford enough food? The answers were recorded in one of the following two categories, 0: no; 1: yes. Based on the above two questions, the composite index for food insufficiency was calculated (1= food insufficient) and (0= no).

2.6. Data Analysis

Descriptive statistics (i.e., means, standard deviations, and proportions) and bivariate analyses were used to describe the strength and association of socio-demographic characteristics, HIV risk behaviors, STI symptoms, violence, and food insufficiency among FSWs. The respective p-values for the bivariate analysis were calculated through chi-square test. Adjusted odds ratios (AOR) and their 95% confidence intervals (CI) were estimated through multivariate logistic regression, adjusting for socio-demographic characteristics, to assess the relationships of the degree of food insufficiency and with the potential HIV risk behavior variables. All analyses were conducted using STATA software (version 11.2).

3. RESULTS

More than three-fifths of FSWs included in the study were greater than 30 years of age (67%) and three-fifths were currently married (62%), literate (58%) and living with family members/husband (60%) (Table 2). A little less than one–fifth of FSWs (17%) reported experiencing food insufficiency in the past 6 months (Table 1). Among FSWs who reported facing food insufficiency, more than three-fifths were greater than 30 years of age (72%), currently married (63%), depends on other works with sex work for livelihood (65%), and living with family members/husband (62%); more than one-third of FSWs who reported experiencing food insufficiency were belonged to home based solicitation (33%) followed by rented room/massage parlour/others (30%), public place/street/highways (24%) and public place/street/highways (14%) solicitation respectively (Table 2). Among FSWs who reported facing food insufficiency, nearly half were illiterate and more than one-third were widowed/divorced/deserted/separated. Among FSWs who reported experiencing food insufficiency, more than half of the FSWs (53%) had two and more numbers of dependent children. More than 35% of FSWs had entertained more clients to cope with the situation of food insufficiency in past 6 months followed by defaulted on loans (24%), borrowed money from informal sources (20%), others (11%) and resorted to had sex without using condoms (7%) (Figure1).

Table 1. Food insufficiency status as reported by female sex workers in four survey states, India, 2015

Indicators	Percentage	N
In the past 6 months, did you or any of your household members ever eat less than the requirement because there wasn't enough money to buy food?		
No	85.4	3501
Yes	14.6	597
In the past 6 months, were you or any of your household members ever felt hungry, but didn't eat because you couldn't afford enough food?		
No	85.7	3511
Yes	14.3	587
Food insufficiency (Composite index)		
No	83.4	3420
Yes	16.6	678
Total	**100.0**	**4098**

Note: household member includes FSW herself, children and any adult member of the family; food insufficiency is a composite index.

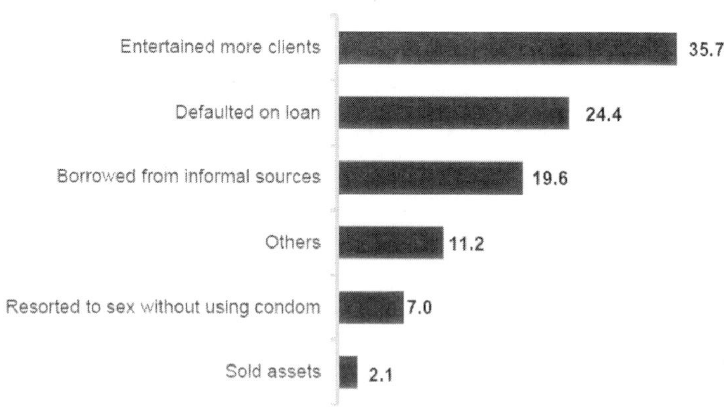

Figure 1. Coping mechanism for food insufficiency as reported by FSWs in past six months in four survey states, India, 2015

Table 2. Socio-demographic characteristics of FSWs who reported food insufficiency in four survey states, India, 2015

		Food insufficiency status		
Socio-demographic characteristics	**% (n) or Mean (SD)**	**No**	**Yes**	**p-value**
Age (Mean, SD)	34.4 (6.6)			
Age				0.000
<=30 years	33.5 (1374)	34.7 (1187)	27.6 (187)	
>30 years	66.5 (2724)	65.3 (2233)	72.4 (491)	
Education				0.013
Illiterate	42.5 (1740)	41.6 (1423)	46.8 (317)	
Literate	57.5 (2358)	58.4 (1997)	53.2 (361)	
Marital status				0.000
Currently married	62.1 (2545)	62.0 (2121)	62.5 (424)	
Never married	7.7 (314)	8.7 (298)	2.4 (16)	
Others[*]	30.2 (1239)	29.3 (1001)	35.1 (238)	
Typology (Place of solicitation)				0.000
Home-based	25.1 (1030)	23.7 (810)	32.5 (220)	
Brothel/lodge/hotel-based	29.9 (1227)	33.0 (1130)	14.3 (97)	
Public places/street/highways	21.6 (887)	21.3 (728)	23.5 (159)	
Others[¥]	23.3 (954)	22.0 (752)	29.8 (202)	
Living status				0.000
Living with family members/husband	59.9 (2453)	59.5 (2036)	61.5 (417)	
Living alone	21.8 (895)	21.2 (724)	25.2 (171)	
Living with others[$$]	18.3 (750)	19.3 (660)	13.3 (90)	
Livelihood status				0.000
Sex work only	47.8 (1959)	50.4 (1723)	34.8 (236)	
Other work with sex work	52.2 (2139)	49.6 (1697)	65.2 (442)	
Dependent children				0.000
No children	28.3 (1161)	29. 6 (1012)	22.0 (149)	
One	27.8 (1141)	28.3 (970)	25.2 (171)	
Two	33.6 (1377)	32.4 (1107)	39.8 (270)	
Three and above	10.2 (419)	9.7 (331)	13.0 (88)	
Total	**100.0 (4098)**	**100.0 (3420)**	**100.0 (678)**	

Note: p-values were calculated through chi-square test. [*]includes divorced/separated/deserted; [¥]includes rented room/massage parlour/others; [$$]includes living with madam/sex workers/partner.

The AORs in multivariate logistic regression models were adjusted for age, education, marital status, place of sex work solicitation, living arrangements and livelihood status (Table 3). Results show that the likelihood of consistent condom use with non-regular (67% vs. 77%; AOR: 0.6; 95% CI: 0.4-0.9) and regular partner (22% vs. 51%; AOR: 0.3; 95% CI: 0.2-0.4) were significantly lower among FSWs who reported food insufficiency than among those who did not. The likelihood of consistent condom use with occasional (AOR: 0.5; 95% CI: 0.4-0.7) and regular clients (AOR: 0.8; 95% CI: 0.6-0.9) was significantly lower among FSWs who experienced food insufficiency compared to those who did not. FSWs who reported food insufficiency were also significantly more likely to report any STI symptoms (28% vs. 13%; AOR: 2.7) and any violence (16% vs. 9%; AOR: 2.1) than their counterparts.

Table 3. Association between food insufficiency and HIV risk behaviors among FSWs in four survey states, India, 2015

		Food insufficiency	
HIV risk behaviors	**N = 4098**	**No**	**Yes**
Consistent condom use with occasional clients	% (n)	94.8 (2973)	89.8 (566)
	AOR (95% CI)	Reference	0.5 (0.4-0.7)**
Consistent condom use with regular clients	% (n)	91.3 (2949)	88.2 (563)
	AOR (95% CI)	Reference	0.8 (0.6-0.9)**
Consistent condom use with non-regular partner	% (n)	76.6 (1023)	66.9 (95)
	AOR (95% CI)	Reference	0.3 (0.2-0.4)***
Consistent condom use with regular partner	% (n)	50.9 (1249)	22.1 (103)
	AOR (95% CI)	Reference	0.6 (0.4-0.9)***
Experienced STI symptoms in past 6 months	% (n)	12.5 (427)	27.6 (187)
	AOR (95% CI)	Reference	2.7 (2.2-3.3)***
Experienced any violence in past 6 months	% (n)	8.8 (300)	15.5 (105)
	AOR (95% CI)	Reference	2.0 (1.6-2.6)***

Note: CI: Confidence Intervals; AOR: Adjusted Odds Ratios; *** and ** indicate values are significant at 1% and 5% level of significance respectively. AORs were adjusted for age, education, marital status, living arrangements, livelihood status and typology and dependent children. Consistent condom use refers to use of condom every time by the partners/clients while having sexual intercourse with the FSWs; Occasional clients refer to who pay every time but FSWs do not know them at all and remember their faces anyway; Regular clients refer to who pay every time they have sex with FSWs and FSWs know them well or recognize them as they visit them repeatedly; Non-regular partner refer to outside marital union or cohabiting; Regular partner refer to the main male sexual partner (either husband, boyfriend or live- in partner); STI symptoms refer to having symptoms of either of genital sore/ulcer, or yellowish/greenish discharge from vagina with or without foul smell, or lower abdominal pain when not suffering from diarrhea/ dysentary or combination of these symptoms; Any violence refer to either physical violence (hurt, hit, slapped, pushed, kicked, punched, choked, or burnt..etc) or sexual violence (forced to have sex by anyone when you didn't want to) or both.

4. DISCUSSION

The study findings indicate that nearly one-fifth of FSWs reported experiencing food insufficiency in their household in the past six months. The findings of the study show that FSWs' food insufficiency is significantly associated with experience of any violence and consistent condom use with different clients and partners. The food insufficiency is highly prevalent among FSWs who are more than 30 years of age, illiterate, currently married, divorced/deserted/separated, depends on other works with sex work for a livelihood, living with family members/husband, and among FSWs either belonged to the home based solicitation or public places/street based solicitation or rented room/massage parlour/others based solicitation. Our study findings extend previous findings by Oyefere (2007), who found that low socioeconomic status and food insufficiency played a strong role in influencing women to become sex workers, and sex workers described food insufficiency as a primary motivation for both joining and remaining in the trade [13]. In-depth analysis of the study adds further that FSWs with two or more children had 70% higher chances of reporting food insufficiency than others.

To overcome the situation of food insufficiency among the household of the FSWs, the study findings describe that more than one-third of FSWs had entertained more clients to cope with the situation of food insufficiency, while more than one-fifth have either defaulted on loans or borrowed money from informal sources, and a significant percentage had sex with clients without using condoms. The findings of the study show that FSWs who report of facing food insufficiency is significantly less likely to use condom consistently during the sexual act with regular and non-regular clients. Findings from the in-depth analysis also suggest that the average number of occasional clients per week is 4.1 (SD=5.7) among FSWs who reported food insufficiency compared to those who did not (3.1 (SD=3.4)), whereas the average number of regular clients per week is 3.4 (SD=4.6) among FSWs who reported food insufficiency compared to those who did not (3.1 (SD=3.3)). Previous studies also validate our findings in explaining that food insufficiency has significantly influenced the decision to use condoms among FSWs [13, 30]. Several previous studies have also shown strong associations of food insufficiency of women with HIV risk behaviors (inconsistent condom use, increase clients, unprotected sex, intergenerational sex, forced sex, and sex exchange) in sub-Saharan Africa [7, 12,30]. This study also shows that FSWs who faced food insufficiency are also more likely to report any STI symptoms. Previous studies have also described how food insufficiency contributes to STI and HIV acquisition risk in resource-poor settings among FSWs [15, 31, 32]. To the existing literature, our study further adds that FSWs who face food insufficiency are also defaulting on loans or borrowing money from informal sources, which is exacerbating their socioeconomic and mental conditions to even worst.

The study also shows that FSWs who faced food insufficiency were more likely to report violence than their counterparts. This finding is consistent with previous research in explaining that food insufficiency as a critical variable influencing women's risk of violence [33]. It is well known that the social and economic marginalization of FSWs' constrain their ability to engage in HIV risk reduction behaviors and also increase the risk of facing any violence as well [7, 33]. Further, these findings are well supported by an African study that FSWs who had experienced violence (particularly sexual violence) are lacking control over their sexual decision making [34, 35] and are more likely to engage in unprotected sex, to exchange sex for money or resources, to have multiple partners, and to be at HIV risk [36, 37, 38].

Findings from the study about food insufficiency and HIV risk add to the expanding research in India and elsewhere in emphasizing the importance of food insufficiency as a variable of central importance in HIV prevention activities. This study further highlights a strong need for programs to address food insufficiency, poverty, and income strengthening and employment in particular. Possible program focus should be in the long term, efforts at the national level to improve women's social, legal, and economic standing – including improved access to education, financial security, social protection schemes and employment – are needed to broaden women's economic options and to reduce the vulnerability of FSWs. In the shorter term, economic interventions such as microfinance and micro-enterprise projects can create an additional income source for FSWs and provide a buffer against financial crises and food insufficiency [39, 40].

In India, a micro-enterprise program was found to reduce HIV risk behaviors and provide a feasible and acceptable source of secondary income in a cohort of FSWs [41]. Some other best examples in India are the Sonangachi project in Kolkata, and the Pragati intervention in Bangalore, where community-led interventions not only helped in change community perceptions of HIV/AIDS and sex work, and reduce stigma, culminating in a political-legal change that helped FSWs organize and claim their rights, but also instrumental in economic strengthening of FSWs to reduce their vulnerability. Other examples from the southern states of India show that the HIV prevention programs have emphasized community mobilization for the economic strengthening of sex workers [24, 42] to reduce vulnerability among sex workers, including food insufficiency. Similar interventions, microfinance program and other social safety program in Cambodia, Kenya and sub-Saharan African countries have also shown a positive impact in reducing poverty and HIV risk behaviors among key populations, and improved their household food sufficiency, and ability to access health care services[43, 44, 45]. These types of interventions would likely to be more successful if considering the concept of "transformatory" interventions, where goals are more inclusive and set by beneficiaries as active agents, rather than "instrumental", where goals are set outside [39]. It can be underlined that mobilizing key populations were the first step towards generating change in the community, and economic strengthening activities (e.g. microfinance and vocational training) followed, based on the response from the community [24, 46, 47, 48].

5. LIMITATIONS

Although the study findings offer important insights on the relationship between food insufficiency, violence and HIV risk among FSWs in India, they must be interpreted in light of certain study limitations. The food insufficiency, violence and HIV risk indicators are based on self-reports which are susceptible to social desirability and recall biases. The analyses are cross-sectional and causality cannot be assumed as in the case of prospective research studies. The study findings cannot be generalized to the whole FSWs community as the study was conducted among selected FSWs, still can be generalized for FSWs belonged to the similar type of settings. Furthermore, food insufficiency is only one component of the broader concept of food insecurity, which also includes insufficient quality and diversity of foods, poor safety of food, feelings of deprivation or restricted choice about the amount and types of food available, and inability to procure food in a socially acceptable manner[27, 28]. More detailed studies among FSWs using more extensive and sensitive food security scales validated in the Indian context with attention to possible regional and cultural differences will be necessary for furthering the policies and programs.

6. CONCLUSION

In conclusion, the study findings offer important insights into the vulnerability of FSWs in terms of food insufficiency, violence and HIV risk, which require immediate program attention. This study recommends that protecting and promoting access to food should be an instant step taken forward by the government may sustain the food security and decrease the vulnerability to HIV among FSWs. Therefore, targeted food assistance and support for FSWs' subsistence farming and other means of food production should also be considered as strategies to reduce vulnerability among FSWs in India. Steps should also be taken for reducing the burden of upstream risk factors include a national recession, high unemployment, global climate change, and other factors beyond the control of individual sex workers. At the end, the study suggests for strengthening community-led interventions focusing on economic strengthening activities (e.g. microfinance, vocational training and access to financial services) and other social safety programs for addressing the food security as a path to a sustainable reduction of HIV risk. More importantly, HIV prevention programs and policies need to acknowledge that food insecurity is an important structural issue that needs to be addressed through integrated program approach and community mobilization interventions. More in-depth research is required to investigate the causal mechanisms of effective economic strengthening interventions, including their effect on poverty and food insecurity reductions, which have implications for ending the spread of HIV in India and elsewhere.

Conflict of Interest and Financial Disclosure Statements

None declared.

ACKNOWLEDGEMENTS

This paper was written as part of Avahan-III evaluation grant of the Bill & Melinda Gates Foundation through Avahan, its India AIDS Initiative. The views expressed herein are those of the authors and do not necessarily reflect the official policy or position of the Bill & Melinda Gates Foundation and Avahan. The funders had no role in study design, data collection and analysis, decision to publish, or preparation of the manuscript. We are grateful to other colleagues of Population Council for providing the necessary inputs for writing this paper.

AUTHOR CONTRIBUTIONS

Conceived and designed: SKP.

Performed the experiments: SKP, MB and RA.

Analyzed the data: SKP.

Contributed reagents/materials/analysis tools: SKP, MB and RA.

Wrote the paper: SKP, MB and RA.

REFERENCES

1. FAO, IFAD and WFP. The state of food insecurity in the World 2015. Meeting the 2015 international hunger targets: taking stock of uneven progress. Rome, FAO. 2015.

2. Laraia B, Siega-Riz A, Gunderson C, Dole N. Psychosocial factors and socioeconomic indicators are associated with household food insecurity among pregnant women. Journal of Nutrition 2006; 136(1):177-182.

3. Foley W, Ward P, Carter P, Coveney J, Tsourtos G, Taylor A. An ecological analysis of factors associated with food insecurity in South Australia, 2002-7. Public Health Nutrition 2010; 13(2): 215-221.

4. Mohammadzadeh A, Dorosty A, Eshraghian M. Household food security status and associate factors among high-school students in Esfahan, Iran. Public Health Nutrition 2010; 13(10):1609-1613.

5. Kadiyala S, Gillespie S. Rethinking food aid to fight AIDS. Washington, DC: International Food Policy Research Institute; 2003.

6. Fenton L. Preventing HIV/AIDS through poverty reduction: the only sustainable solution. Lancet 2005; 364(9440):1186-1187.

7. Gillespie, S., Kadiyala, S. HIV/AIDS and food and nutrition security: from evidence to action. Washington, DC: International Food Policy Research Institute; 2005.

8. Weiser S, Leiter K, Bangsberg D, Butler L, Pery-de Korte F, Phaladze N, Heisler M. Food insufficiency is associated with high-risk sexual behavior among women in Botswana and Swaziland. PLoS Medicine 2007; 4:1589-1597.

9. Ngo AD, McCurdy SA, Ross MW, Markham C, Ratliff EA, Pham HT. The lives of female sex workers in Vietnam: Findings from a qualitative study. Culture Health and Sexuality 2007; 9(6): 555-570.

10. Fitzgerald-Husek A, Martiniuk AL, Hinchcliff R, Aochamus CE, Lee RB. I do what I have to do to survive: an investigation into the perceptions, experiences and economic considerations of women engaged in sex work in Northern Namibia. BMC Womens Health 2011; 11: 35.

11. Gillespie S, Kadiyala S, Greener R. Is poverty or wealth driving HIV transmission? AIDS 2007; 21(Suppl 7):S5-S16.

12. Dunkle KL, Jewkes RK, Brown HC, et al. Transactional sex among women in Soweto, South Africa: prevalence, risk factors and association with HIV infection. Social Science and Medicine 2004; 59:1581-1592.

13. Oyefara JL. Food insecurity, HIV/AIDS pandemic and sexual behaviour of female commercial sex workers in Lagos metropolis, Nigeria. Journal of Social Aspects of HIV/AIDS 2007; 4(2): 626-635.

14. WHO. Nutrient requirements for people living with HIV/AIDS: Report of a technical consultation. Geneva: World Health Organization; 2003.

15. Tsai AC, Weiser SD. Population-based study of food insecurity and HIV transmission risk behaviors and symptoms of sexually transmitted infections among linked couples in Nepal. AIDS and Behavior 2014; 18 (11):2187-97.

16. Vogenthaler NS, Kushel MB, Hadley C, Frongillo EA, Jr., Riley ED, Bangsberg DR, et al. Food insecurity and risky sexual behaviors among homeless and marginally housed HIV-infected individuals in San Francisco. AIDS and Behavior 2013; 17 (5):1688-93.

17. Eaton LA, Cain DN, Pitpitan EV, Carey KB, Carey MP, Mehlomakulu V, et al. Exploring the relationships among food insecurity, alcohol use, and sexual risk taking among men and women living in South African townships. The Journal of Primary Prevention 2014; 35 (4):255-65.

18. Raiford JL, Herbst JH, Carry M, Browne FA, Doherty I, Wechsberg WM. Low prospects and high risk: structural determinants of health associated with sexual risk among young African American women residing in resource-poor communities in the south. American Journal of Community Psychology 2014; 54(3-4):243-50.

19. Kerrigan DL, Fonner VA, Stromdahl S, Kennedy CE. Community empowerment among female sex workers is an effective HIV prevention intervention: A systematic review of the peer-reviewed evidence from low- and middle-income countries. AIDS and Behavior 2013; 17(6): 1926-1940.

20. Tsai AC, Leiter K, Heisler M, Iacopino V, Wolfe W, Shannon K, et al. Prevalence and correlates of forced sex perpetration and victimization in Botswana and Swaziland. American Journal of Public Health 2011; 101 (6):1068-74.

21. Tsai AC, Hung KJ, Weiser SD. Is food insecurity associated with HIV risk? Cross-sectional evidence from sexually active women in Brazil. PLoS Medicine 2012; 9 (4):e1001203.

22. Reed E, Gupta J, Biradavolu M, Devireddy V, Blankenship KM. The context of economic insecurity and its relation to violence

and risk factors for HIV among female sex workers in Andhra Pradesh, India. Public Health Reports 2010; 125 Suppl. 4: 81-89.

23. Saggurti N, Jain AK, Sebastian MP, Singh R, Modugu HR, Halli SS, Verma RK. Indicators of mobility, socio-economic vulnerabilities and HIV risk behaviours among mobile female sex workers in India. AIDS and Behavior 2012; 16:952-959.

24. Patel SK, Prabhakar P, Jain AK, Saggurti N, Adhikary R. Relationship between community collectivization and financial vulnerability of female sex workers in southern India. PLoS ONE 2016; 11(5): e0156060.

25. UNSN. Nutrition and HIV/AIDS. Statement by the Administrative Committee on Coordination, Sub-committee on Nutrition at its 28thsession. United Nations Sub-committee on Nutrition: Nairobi, Kenya; 2001.

26. Save the Children. Food security, livelihoods and HIV/AIDS: A Guide to the linkages, measurement and programming implications. Westport, CT: Save the Children; 2004.

27. UNFAO. The state of food insecurity in the World: high prices and food security--threats and opportunities. United Nations Food and Agriculture Organization; 2008.

28. Keenan DP, Olson C, Hersey JC, et al. Measures of food insecurity/security. Journal of Nutrition Education 2001; 33:S49-S58.

29. [29] Bickel G,Nord M,Price C, Hamilton W, Cook J. Guide to measuring household food security (PDF). USDA Food and Nutrition Service. Retrieved 23 April 2016; 2000.

30. In article PubMed

31. Hargreaves JR, Morison LA, Chege J, Rutenburg N, Kahindo M, et al. Socioeconomic status and risk of HIV infection in an urban population in Kenya. Tropical Medicine and International Health 2002; 7: 793-802.

32. Miller CL, Bangsberg DR, Tuller DM, Senkungu J, Kawuma A, Frongillo EA, et al. Food insecurity and sexual risk in an HIV endemic community in Uganda. AIDS and Behavior 2011; 15(7):1512-9.

33. Fielding-Miller R, Mnisi Z, Adams D, Baral S, Kennedy C. There is hunger in my community: a qualitative study of food security as a cyclical force in sex work in Swaziland. BMC Public Health 2014; 14:79.

34. de Waal A, Whiteside A. New variant famine: AIDS and food crisis in southern Africa. Lancet 2003; 362: 1234-1237.

35. Stillwaggon E. HIV transmission in Latin America: Comparison with Africa and policy implications. South African Journal of Economics 2000; 68: 985-1011.

36. Ambrus JL Sr., Ambrus JL Jr. Nutrition and infectious diseases in developing countries and problems of acquired immunodeficiency syndrome. Experimental Biology and Medicine 2004; 229: 464-472.

37. Kalichman SC, Simbayi LC. Sexual assault history and risks for sexually transmitted infections among women in an African township in Cape Town, South Africa. AIDS Care 2004; 16: 681-689.

38. Koenig MA, Zablotska I, Lutalo T, Nalugoda F, Wagman J, et al. Coerced first intercourse and reproductive health among adolescent women in Rakai, Uganda. International Family Planning Perspectives 2004; 30: 156-163.

39. Weiser SD, Leiter K, Heisler M, McFarland W, Percy-de Korte F, et al. A population-based study on alcohol and high-risk sexual behaviors in Botswana. PLoS Medicine 2006; 3: e392.

40. UNAIDS, UNAIDS guidance note on HIV and sex work. Geneva, Switzerland: UNAIDS, 2012.

41. Kennedy CE, Fonner VA, O'Reilly KR, Sweat MD. A systematic review of income generation interventions, including microfinance and vocational skills training, for HIV prevention. AIDS Care 2014; 26 (6):659-73.

42. Sherman SG, Srikrishnan AK, Rivett KA, Liu SH, Solomon S, Celentano DD. Acceptability of a microenterprise intervention among female sex workers in Chennai, India. AIDS and Behavior 2010; 14(3):649-657.

43. Pillai P, Bhattacharjee P, Ramesh BM, Isac S. Impact of two vulnerability reduction strategies - collectivisation and participation in savings activities - on HIV risk reduction among

female sex workers: Karnataka Health Promotion Trust, Bengaluru, Karnataka, India; 2012.

44. Lee H, Pollock G, Lubek I, Niemi S, O'Brien K, Green M, Bashir S, Braun E, Kros S, Huot V, et al. Creating new career pathways to reduce poverty, illiteracy and health risks, while transforming and empowering Cambodian women's lives. Journal of Health Psychology 2010; 15(7):982-992.

45. Odek WO, Busza J, Morris CN, Cleland J, Ngugi EN, Ferguson AG. Effects of micro-enterprise services on HIV risk behaviour among female sex workers in Kenya's urban slums. AIDS and Behavior 2009; 13(3):449-461.

46. Baird SJ, Garfein RS, McIntosh CT, Oezler B. Effect of a cash transfer programme for schooling on prevalence of HIV and herpes simplex type 2 in Malawi: a cluster randomised trial. Lancet 2012; 379(9823):1320-1329.

47. Basu I, Jana S, Rotheram-Borus MJ, Swendeman D, Lee SJ, Newman P, Weiss R. HIV prevention among sex workers in India. Journal of Acquired Immune Deficiency Syndromes 2004; 36(3): 845-852.

48. Souverein D, Euser SM, Ramaiah R, Ram P, Gowda N, Gowda CS, et al. Reduction in STIs in an empowerment intervention programme for female sex workers in Bangalore, India: the Pragatiprogramme. Global Health Action 2013; 6: 22943.

49. Vejella S, Patel SK, Saggurti N, Prabhakar P. Community collectivization and consistent condom use among female sex workers in southern India: evidence from two rounds of behavioral tracking surveys. AIDS and Behavior 2016; 20(4): 776-87.

11

ECONOMETRIC ANALYSIS OF RURAL HOUSEHOLDS' RESILIENCE TO FOOD INSECURITY IN WEST SHOA, ETHIOPIA

Temesgen Kebede[1,], Jema Haji[1], Belaineh Legesse[1], Girma Mammo[2]

[1]School of Agricultural Economics, Haramaya University, Dire Dawa, Ethiopia

[2]Ethiopian Institutes of Agricultural Research, Melkassa, Ethiopia

ABSTRACT

The major objective of this study is to analyze rural households' capability to absorb the negative consequences of unexpected shocks using seven resilience blocs based on the framework of resilience analysis. Resilience index was defined as a function of agricultural inputs and technology, social safety nets, access to public services, access to food and income, access to assets, stability and adaptive capacity. The estimation of each bloc was made separately using different multivariate techniques, where the result becomes covariates in the measurement of resilience index. The estimation of resilience index was done using factor analysis and three factors were retained. Under the first factor, all blocs, except access to public services, are positively correlated with resilience. The negative correlation between access to public services and resilience is because observed variables like health services and education qualities decreases as households become poorer. In terms of importance to rural household's resilience index, the result indicates that asset ownership play significant role followed by access to food and income, as well as social safety nets. These resilience blocs show the likelihood of recovering from any form of climatic shocks that a household experiences. In the second factor, access to public services becomes positive, which shows that it is a positive characteristic of resilience. Adaptive capacity is positive in the first factor and negative in the second factor. The third factor triggers hidden information of the resilience bloc as stability and adaptive capacity are positive, which likely tells common story in terms of food security situations. In conclusion, poor households have limited or no access to physical and financial assets, little education, and often suffer from human illness and livestock diseases/death. Poor households lack access to sufficient, high-quality land and other natural resources or to remunerative resources of income and agricultural production boosting activities. Therefore, it is recommended that households should have supplements with preconditions and options available to them in terms of capabilities and activities such as agricultural production boosting and income-generating activities, access to assets, improving the quality of public services, social safety nets and adaptive capacity.

Keywords: resilience, food insecurity, smallholders, West Shoa, Ethiopia

1. INTRODUCTION

Climate is a key natural resource for sustenance of life. The change in climate is a complex biophysical process and difficult concept. It is slippery to empirically demonstrate the climatic events that are attributable outside the ideal world of computer models [1]. In fact, there is a scientific understanding that has been established on the significant rising of greenhouse gases (GHG) arising mainly from anthropogenic activities [2] results in the atmosphere and oceans to warmer, glaciers to melt, sea levels to increase and the climate continue to change [3].

The climate is continually changing regardless of human intervention for at least the next decades and beyond [4]. Consequently, there are observable global and regional temperature change; as well as hydrological cycle getting disrupted; including the change in the atmospheric water vapor, precipitation, stream flows; cryosphere changes, and changes in ocean properties. The effects of the change with the implication for nature and human lives have been observed scientifically [5]. This negative impact of climate change becomes a serious concern in particular in developing countries' agricultural production and the food systems [6, 7].

Climate related shocks are the major causes of persistent hunger, frequent famine, [8] and widespread undernourishment and stifled rural households' food security in developing countries. The global unfavorable climate variability show the most recent trend in food security challenges. For Ethiopia, there exists strong correlation between the overall gross domestic product (GDP), agriculture contribution to GDP and the rainfall pattern, showing how plentiful rain events associated with bountiful agricultural production and food security, while a "poor" or limited rains in amount, distribution and duration means a poor harvest for most [9, 10]. The amount of rainfall below the long run average by 10% in Ethiopia, for instance, leads to a 4.4% reduction in the food production [11].

Rainfall distribution and pattern is correlated to agricultural production which remains crucial challenge [12] even after twenty five years of von Braun conclusion. The perdition of failed rainfall accompanied with ever exploding population growth, declining of soil fertility and rising erosion mainly arising from tilling of the steep slopes causes great damages to the life and livelihoods of rural smallholder farmers. The stride for livelihood from charcoal marketing and expanding farm land, and over-grazing has led to deforestation. These cumulative effects contribute negatively to agricultural production, which led to subsistence harvest.

Poor agricultural harvest due to drought induced calamites primarily owed to successive failed rains left a significant number of people in Ethiopia to emergency food handout. Owing to the continued ocean warming effect of El *Nino,* Ethiopia is facing one of the worst crises. From June 2015 onwards; the effect left an estimated 10.2 million people to emergency food aid [13] and hence, rural households are dipping into food insecurity.

These demands for the shift in attention from the crises management, shift in mental model construct of the society itself and identifying the key actors for building households resilience to such deep rooted chronic food insecurity. Some pioneer scholars [12, 13] and international organization [16]have tried to examine household level food security issues through short term and long term strategic combinations from resilience perspective. Resilience is a broad concept of measurement of systems' ability to withstand unpredictable shocks. In this regard, the government needs to have moral and political responsibilities to establish communities that withstand the challenge before it happens or quickly recover from the shocks or exploit benefit from crisis.

The government of Ethiopia has quite progressive programs that enable rural households to withstand climate related shocks like the productive safety net program (PSNP), household asset building (HAB) and other policy oriented programs. The major aim of these programs is to lever households from food insecurity and even leading to economic and decent life. Conversely, as in [17] document reports that the support for livelihoods due to crises affected rural households has been insufficient. This reveals albeit endeavor for making rural households to lead a decent life, looking for sustainable solutions through resilience building remains crucial.

The notion of resilience is a complex process more often than not requiring people to adapt completely new orientation of life and to transform existing social and institutional structures. In such cases, those well established and institutionalized patterns of social agency will have to be discarded and new organizational settings beyond the framework of familiar strategies will have to be developed and put in practice. Two basic facts as in [15] can be coined. The first is related to the fact that resilience has multidimensional nature and the second fact is associated with the unpredictable nature of shocks to households to which they are exposed.

This empirical household level study on resilience to food insecurity was conducted in five woredas of West Shoa zone of Ethiopia. In this study, resilience was defined as the current states of affairs and its ability to withstand shocks. Accordingly, five resilience blocs with two additional capability dimensions were used. These resilience blocs are access to agricultural input and technology, social safety nets, access to public services, access to food and income, access to asset, stability and adaptive capacity.

2. RESEARCH METHODOLOGY

2.1. Description of the Study Area

This study was carried out in West Shoa zone, one of the 18 zones located at the center of Oromia National Regional States. Its capital is Ambo and has 528 rural and 43 urban kebeles. As in [18]population and housing survey projection, it has a population of 2,500,482. The zone has 18 districts and among these, four districts are located in highland agro ecology, eight districts are located in mid altitude and six of them are located in lowland.

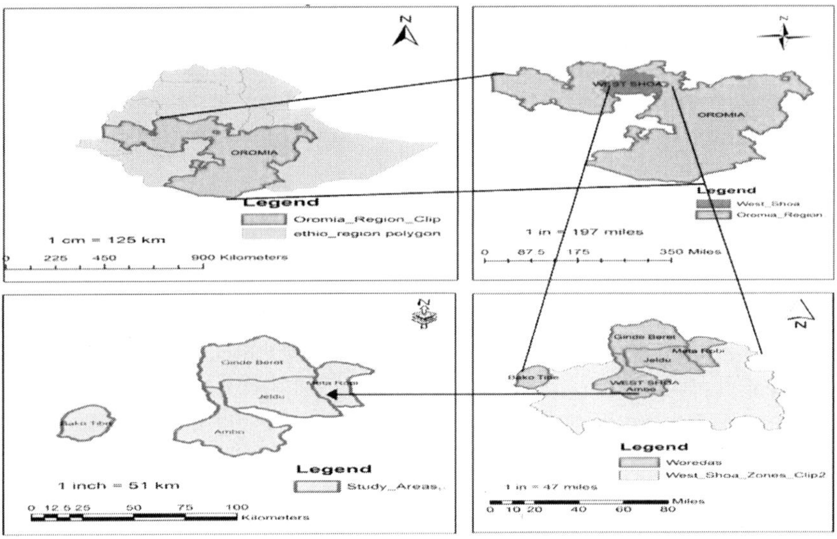

Figure 1. Map of the study area

The zone has area of 14,349.29 square kilometers. The zone consists of 47.7% of the total area as leveled field which is an ideal place for agriculture. Gorges (4.6%), mountainous area (16.8%) and other (30.9%) take the topography share of the zone. Agriculture is the major means of the livelihood. Around 70% of income of the rural households is generated from crop production, and about 20% from livestock rearing. The major crops produced are wheat, *teff*, barley, maize, sorghum, bean, pea, *noug* and sesame. In addition, there are a large number of livestock (1.86 million cattle), small ruminants (1.55 million goats and sheep), donkey, mule and horses (more than 300,000 equines); poultry, bee colonies: - traditional, transitive and modern beehive.

The altitude of West Shoa zone ranges from 1000 to 3288 meters above sea level, where the largest area lies above 2000 meters above sea level. The zone experiences maximum temperature ranging from 18°C to 30°C with minimum temperature ranging from 7°C to 22°C. Rainfall distribution also varies from minimum of 250 mm to a maximum of 2610 mm. Almost half of the soil type of the zone is red,

29% of the soil is grey, 27% of the soil type is categorized under red brown and the remaining 6% constitutes other soil types.

2.2. Sampling and Data Description

In this study, both primary and secondary data were collected. Primary data collection was mainly based on a survey, which was formulated at household level and conducted face to face to obtain firsthand information.

To administer the survey, multistage sampling techniques was used. First, districts in the zone were clustered based on agro-ecology into three as highland, mid-altitude and lowland. Again, each district was classified into two based on relief recipient and non relief recipient districts. Accordingly, from the four districts located in the highland agro ecology, two of them are more frequent relief receivers (in thirteen years juncture, the districts receive relief more than 7 times) and the remaining two districts are less frequent relief receivers (received relief less than 3 times) for the time period ranging from 2003 to 2015. Similarly, among the eight districts which are located in the mid-altitude, three of them are more frequent relief receivers and the remaining five districts are less relief receiver districts. Likewise, out of the six districts located in lowland agro-ecology, one district is a more frequent relief receiver and the remaining five districts are less relief receivers.

Therefore, there are six clusters of more relief and less relief receiver districts. Two round of non-repetitive selection procedure were taken from each cluster to give second chance of selecting every district. In each cluster, a value of one and zero was assigned, with the name of the district having a value of 1 to be included and otherwise to be rejected. Then, using lottery method, picking up one at a time from each cluster was made. Accordingly, from the cluster of relief receiver highland agro-ecology districts, Jaldu district was selected randomly. From mid-altitude agro-ecology, Gindeberet and Meta Robi districts were more frequent relief receivers and Ambo from less frequent relief receiver clusters were selected. The three districts, Meta Robi, Gindeberet, and Jaldu make around 60% the total number of beneficiaries. From less relief receiver lowland agro-ecology districts, Bako Tibe was also included randomly. The total districts sum up to five, one district from highland agro-ecology, three districts from midlands and one district from low land agro-ecology.

Kebeles in each randomly selected district was again clustered based on agro-ecologies. Then, one representative kebele from each agro-ecology in the district was selected using simple random sampling technique. Kebeles in Gindeberet are either lowland or midland while other districts have three agro-ecologies. Therefore, the total kebeles selected sum up to fourteen.

There are 330,772 rural households in the zone. From the total kebeles in the zone, each year 50% of them are experiencing shocks associated with rainfall variability. Finally, the sample size is determined following [19] formula as:

$$n = \frac{Z^2 pqN}{e^2 (N-1) + Z^2 pq} \tag{1}$$

Where n is the required sample size, Z is the inverse of the standard cumulative distribution that correspond to the level of confidence, e is the desired level of precision, p is the estimated proportion of kebeles exposed to rainfall variability. N is the total number of rural households inhabiting in the zone.

$$= \left[\frac{(1.96^2)(0.5)(0.5)(330{,}772)}{(0.05^2)(330{,}771) + (1.96)^2 (0.5)(0.5)} \right]$$

$$= \frac{317673.4288}{827.8879}$$

$$= 383.72 \approx 384. \tag{2}$$

Therefore, the total sample size is determined to be 384 rural households. Finally, sample respondents were selected from each kebele randomly based on probability proportion to size.

Secondary data were also collected from zonal office of agriculture, zonal risk prevention and preparedness office, and each respective district office of agriculture. Data on climatic variables were collected from National Meteorological Agency Stations at different locations.

3. MODELING RESILIENCE TO FOOD INSECURITY

Resilience of rural households depends on options available to them to lead a decent life [15]. Those options are preconditions for the households' response mechanisms to the negative effects of unforeseen climate related shocks [20]. For instance, agricultural inputs and technology constitutes of the provisions of agricultural service packages, agricultural input supplies and scientific knowledge. These aggregate forms of agricultural inputs and technology play significant role in increasing agricultural production henceforth enhance their resilience to food insecurity. Social safety nets as social protections component has also been an essential mechanism that enables households' recovering capability and increase household's resilience to food insecurity.

Resilience is a latent variable defined indirectly, using seven resilience blocs. To measure household resilience, two options are available: measure all dimensions simultaneously through structural equation modeling (SEM) or measure each bloc separately using different multivariate techniques[15].

The SEM is an extension of general linear modeling procedure like analysis of variance (ANOVA) and multiple regression analysis [15, 20]. The model measures all the components simultaneously and assumes that residuals are distributed normally. Hence, it is limited to the normally distributed observed variables in continuous form [21]. However, data collected at household level is either ordinal or categorical, which inhibit the use of SEM to measure resilience. Measurement of latent variable with the help of multivariate techniques is advantageous [15].

Multivariate statistical techniques to generate these latent variables depend on the scale of observed variables where, household level survey data are qualitative in nature, non-continuous type variables. Hence, a separate multivariate technique is relevant to employ for the analysis like factorial analysis, and principal component analysis. This is because, it is related to the assumptions that variables may not be normally distributed and measuring different component separately enables the model to be more flexible [15, 20]. In this paper both principal component analysis and factor analyses were used to estimate unobserved variables of the resilience bloc [20].

To estimate resilience, two stages were followed. In the first stage each resilience bloc was estimated separately. Nonetheless, each bloc is latent variable, not observed directly, in a given survey but possible to estimate them through multivariate techniques [20, 22]. In the second stage, resilience index was computed from the result of the first stage. The blocs that enable to estimate resilience are agricultural input access and technology, social safety nets, access to public services, access to food and income, access to assets, stability and adaptive capacity.

3.1. Access to Agricultural Inputs and Technology (AIT)

This resilience bloc is directly related to the household's degree of production capacity. Observable variables that are expected to define access to agricultural inputs and technology include fertilizer, herbicide and extension contacts. Farmers that are using fertilizer as one form of agricultural input enable them to improve their farm productivity through increasing crop per unit area, which would improve total production per household and more food to be available for the household, and hence enhance their resilience.

Herbicide use has likely control plant diseases and hence increase household level of food production thereby enhances resilience to food insecurity. Extension contacts are the average number of contacts that the household head received during the last 12 months. Access to agricultural inputs and technology is a critical resilience bloc for the success of resilience to climate variability. Factor analysis was run using principal factor method.

3.2. Social Safety Net (SSN)

Social safety nets are crucial aspect for the poor to make life simple and lessen the impact of climate related shocks to them. In West Shoa zone, social safety nets as social protection, in the form of relief that consists of grain, oil and pulses, assistances in cash and in kind was given to households affected with climate related shocks. Households that receive assistance were asked about the quality of assistance, job assistance, frequency of assistance and overall attitude on targeting assistance to the needy. The observed variables to generate the unobserved (latent) variables were diverse indicators ranging from discrete values (like job assistance) to categorical (assistance targeted to the needy; including some not needy; and targeted without distinction) to continuous (cash assistance). In order to estimate social safety nets latent variable principal component analysis was used.

3.3. Access to Public Services (APS)

Access to public services encompasses key responses provided by the public that is expected to enhance household's resilience. The provisions of public services are exogenous to households, but it remains fundamental to manage risk and respond accordingly and enhancing household's resilience.

Observed variables to estimate the latent variable (in this case access to public services) included are access to information (dummy variable: 1 if the household head access to information through television, radio or any other means of accessing information), access to credit (dummy variable: 1 if the household head has borrowed credit over the last 12 months period), access to irrigation, infrastructure like roads, hospitals and schools. Access to drinking water, electricity and telecommunications networks and mobility and transport constraints (ordinal scale from 1 (less constraints) to 3 (more constraints) were also included in estimation of this latent variable.

3.4. Access to Food and Income (AFI)

Income and food access are directly related to households capacity to absorb shocks. Food access is the economic capacity of a household to afford food, which requires a household to have income for food consumption expenditure; therefore, we have calculated it as the per capita income of the household computed from total household's income to the family size. Average dietary energy consumption is included to take caloric adequacy at household level, which is calculated from average kilo calorie intake per AE per day. To account for perception of food access, household heads were asked nine generic questions of the Household Food Insecurity Access Scale (HFIAS) developed by Food and Nutrition Technical Assistance (FANTA) [23]. Household dietary diversity score (HDDS) was also included as an indicator of the household's nutritional proxies applied to the two weeks consumption of different food items. The consumption of 12 food groups for dietary diversity score, which can also be used as a proxy indicator for food access [24, 25, 26]. To estimate income and food access latent variable, factor analysis was used.

3.5. Access to Assets (A)

Smallholder farmers possess agricultural assets like land, livestock and non agricultural assets like estimated amount of nonfarm income earned in *Birr,* house structure and number of rooms. Land holding and livestock ownership are veritable assets that improve quality of life by supporting and enabling to generate diversified sources of income, encourage productions of both crop and livestock, improves mechanism to access nutritious food, and enhances resilience of smallholder farmers.

3.6. Stability (S)

Stability refers to household's options and capacity to withstand as a whole to external shocks and stressors during shock prevalence time. It is one bloc of resilience responds to perturbation, confront climate related shocks and recovering quickly. Household's survival depends on the interaction components that enable them to react to such external stimuli and continue their life and livelihoods operations indifferently. Stability is an important dimension of household's resilience.

The bedeviled nature of notoriously unpredictable climate variability causes instability. It progressively worsens resilience of smallholder farmers' and severely hamstrung their life and livelihoods. Even smaller external event can bring nefarious outcome like catastrophe destruction. Households with high stability have likely illustrates high resilience to food insecurity, while those showing low stability will have low resilience.

Socio-economic and ecological variables were captured to estimate this latent variable like perceptions to drought over the last two to three decades, the rainfall variability that elapsed similar period of time, livestock diseases and crop failure due to climate variability causes, output price volatility, water shortages. Moreover, human related disturbances like chronic illness, violence, death were also taken into account.

To estimate stability, observed variables are, indeed, an indicator of instability. Thus, we multiplied each of the observed variables by negative 1 in order to make them consistent with the meaning of the latent variable S.

3.7. Adaptive Capacity (AC)

Adaptive capacity refers to the level of access to and exploits benefit therein from resources in order to deal with shocks [27]. Adaptive capacity is the ability to react to shocks, which ranges from institutional framework that enables to learn, generate experience and store knowledge to create power structure to solve *ex ante* and *ex post* problems through learning processes. One basic mechanism to create knowledge and power structure is the existence of institutional framework like being a member of idir or equib by increasing households' trust among themselves. Education average was also used in the estimation of adaptive capacity, which is the average of years of education completed by household members, is sources for accumulating knowledge. Stock of knowledge made through average education of years completed by household members increase adaptive capacity of that particular household.

The other variable included to estimate this latent variable is diversified sources of income. It was based on the premises that a diversified sources of income leads to a greater adaptive capacity. Engagement in economic activities also enhances household's adaptive capacity, which was taken into account using the ratio of the number of households aged 15 to 60 to the total family size.

Health matters for adaptive capacity, which was captured as it is a dummy variable taking value equal to one if member of the households are healthy, otherwise zero.

3.8. Assessment Procedure of Resilience to Food Insecurity

In the second stage, resilience index is estimated from resilience blocs anticipated in the previous sub-sections. In mathematical notation, resilience index is represented as a function of the blocs as:

$$Ri = f(AIT, SSN, APS, AFI, A, S, AC) \quad (2)$$

Where Ri – Resilience index, AIT – Agricultural Inputs and Technology, SSN – Social Safety Nets, APS – Access to Public Services, AFI – Access to Food and Income, A – Assets, S – Stability, AC – Adaptive capacity. Hence, resilience index is the weighted sum of the factors generated and specified as:

$$R_i = \sum_{i=1} W_j F_j \quad (3)$$

Where W_j is the weight of variable j and F_j is the factor under consideration of the variable j. The weights are the proportions of variance explained by each factor.

4. RESULTS AND DISCUSSION

In this section, we present summary of the results of the observed variables contribute to assessing the value of the latent variables representing the resilience blocs under the first stage. Under the second stage resilience index estimation result is made from the resilience blocs.

4.1. Access to Agricultural Inputs and Technology (AIT)

Table 1 presents eigen values for each factor and Table 2 shows the factor loadings for the original variables. The three variables play important role in estimation of access to agricultural inputs and technology (AIT). Table 1 depicts factor analysis using principal component factors and Kaiser Criterion suggests to retain Factor1 with eigenvalues higher than 1. Here, one factor is retained and it explains more than 42% of the variation.

Table 1. Eigen values for each factor

Factor	Eigenvalue	Difference	Proportion	Cumulative
Factor1	1.2646	0.32725	0.4215	0.4215
Factor2	0.93736	0.13932	0.3125	0.734
Factor3	0.79804	.	0.266	1

LR test: independant vs. saturated: chi2(3) =21.22 Prob>chi2=0.0001

Access to fertilizer and the number of extension services play significant role in estimation of AIT. The correlations between each variable and AIT is higher whereas herbicide is less important. These variables are the most import inputs boosting agricultural production where food access, one dimension of food security, depends on production. The more the agriculture performs well the greater is the households have the options and the capability to escape from food insecurity. Therefore, we can conclude that fertilizer use, herbicide use and extension contacts enhances agricultural production, ensure food security and thereby households become more resilient to food insecurity.

Table 2. Factor loadings (pattern matrix) and unique variances

Variable	Factor1	Uniqueness	AIT
Fertilizer use	0.7353	0.4593	0.58144
Herbicide use	0.5279	0.7213	0.41743
Extension frequency	0.6673	0.5547	0.52768

4.2. Social Safety Nets (SSN)

The first component obtained explains 91% of the variation and it is acceptable for estimating the latent variable SSN.

Table 3. Eigen value for SSN

Component	Eigenvalue	Difference	Proportion
Comp1	4.524	4.318	0.905
Comp2	0.206	0.046	0.041
Comp3	0.160	0.086	0.032
Comp4	0.074	0.037	0.015
Comp5	0.037	.	0.007

Table 4 below illuminates the correlation between observed variables and the latent variable (SSN). In the first component, all the observed variables are positively correlated with SSN and play important role in the estimation.

Table 4. Principal components (eigenvectors) for SSN

Variable	Comp1	Unexplained	SSN
Job assistance	0.463	0.032	0.984
Frequency of assisted	0.451	0.079	0.960
Cash and in kind assistance	0.445	0.105	0.946
Quality of assistance	0.434	0.150	0.922
Assistance target the needy	0.443	0.111	0.943

Each indicator of SSN has similar importance in the estimation. SSN as the social protection scheme constitutes job assistance and its frequency, amount in cash and in-kind and the quality associated with service as well as assistance targeting the needy are important variables. Job assistance is the major among the generated variables to estimate SSN.

4.3. Access to Public Services (APS)

The following table (Table 5) shows the eigen values for running principal component analysis. Four components are retained. The four components explain 58.6% of the variation.

Table 5. Eigen value for APS

Component	Eigenvalue	Difference	Proportion
Comp1	2.711	1.261	0.246
Comp2	1.450	0.285	0.132
Comp3	1.165	0.046	0.106
Comp4	1.118	0.119	0.102
Comp5	0.999	0.126	0.091
Comp6	0.873	0.058	0.079
Comp7	0.815	0.052	0.074
Comp8	0.763	0.061	0.069
Comp9	0.703	0.422	0.064
Comp10	0.281	0.159	0.026
Comp11	0.122	.	0.011

Access to phone networks, access to drinking water and access to electricity are correlated with component one. Access to education is correlated negatively with component two. Physical access to human health, physical access to livestock health, sanitation facilities, quality of education and access to education are correlated with the third component. Physical access to livestock health, perception to security and mobility and transport constraints variables are correlated with the fourth component (Table 6).

Table 6. Eigen vector for access to public services

Variable	Comp1	Comp2	Comp3	Comp4	Unexplained	APS
Physical access to human health	0.040	-0.030	0.626	0.191	0.497	0.067
Physical access to livestock health	0.080	-0.205	0.327	0.336	0.671	0.132
Quality of human health services	-0.047	0.550	0.274	-0.034	0.468	-0.078
Access to education	0.150	-0.442	0.321	-0.146	0.512	0.247
Quality of education	-0.056	0.557	0.307	-0.108	0.420	-0.093
Perception to security	-0.038	0.225	0.068	0.515	0.621	-0.063
Mobility and transport constraints	-0.057	-0.073	-0.198	0.730	0.342	-0.094
Access to drinking water	0.571	0.096	-0.114	0.035	0.086	0.941
Access to electricity	0.535	0.135	-0.070	0.112	0.177	0.882
Access to phone networks	0.546	0.126	-0.115	-0.047	0.152	0.898
Sanitation facilities	0.220	-0.225	0.393	-0.061	0.612	0.362

Access to phone network by household head or any members in the household enable them to obtain updated information on local and regional climate statistics, on agricultural input prices such as price of fertilizer, insecticides and pesticides. This helps farmers to make precautious and alert them to bounce back from potential future shocks.

The table above (Table 6) shows that the original variables like access to drinking water, electricity and phone networks are, as expected, positively correlated with the estimated APS. Weak correlation of the observed variables like physical access to health service to both human and livestock, and perceptions to security, mobility and transport with the first component are observed. This can be explained by the fact that physical access to health services and the quality therein are characterized by few numbers of well educated physicians, and physical equipments in the process of health service provisions to both human and livestock.

Under the second component in the estimation of APS, access to education is negatively correlated. This is because the school location is far consuming their time and efforts. Conversely, the quality of education is positively correlated APS. The more the school is equipped with professionals the more the quality is increasing.

4.4. Access to Food and Income (AFI)

Table 7 below shows the eigen-values for each factor and the subsequent table (Table 8) show the factor loading for the original variables. Factor one is retained which explains 49% of the variations. The factor produced is quite meaningful and it is possible to consider it the underlying latent variable for food and income access.

Table 7. Eigen value of food and income

Factor	Eigenvalue	Difference	Proportion
Factor1	1.96072	1.09563	0.4902
Factor2	0.86509	0.12919	0.2163
Factor3	0.7359	0.2976	0.184
Factor4	0.4383	.	0.1096

The factor loadings presented for the original variables that consists of HFIAS, kilo calorie available per day per adult equivalent, HDDS and per capita income per day. All these variables aim to measure food access. HFIAS has a negative correlation with AFI because it increases as food security decreases. HDDS and per capita income of the household remains less important than HFIAS and kilo calorie intake per AE per day. This involves that the high correlation of HFIAS and Kcal per day per AE with the IFA blocs, but even the HDDS, and per capita income have a meaningful correlation.

Table 8. Factor loadings (pattern matrix) and unique variances

Variable	Factor1	Uniqueness	AFI
HDDS	0.6212	0.6141	0.546
Per capita income	0.5815	0.6619	0.512
HFIAS	-0.7459	0.4436	-0.757
Kcal day AE	0.8248	0.3197	0.892

4.5. Access to Asset (A)

Table 9 shows the eigen values of the assets and two components are retained in the estimation of this latent variable. The retained components explain 62% of the variation.

Table 9. Eigen value for assets

Component	Eigenvalue	Difference	Proportion
Comp1	1.642	0.204	0.328
Comp2	1.438	0.536	0.288
Comp3	0.902	0.272	0.180
Comp4	0.630	0.242	0.126
Comp5	0.388	.	0.078

Table 10 below shows the eigen vector for estimation of the latent variable, which is access to assets. Landholding and livestock ownership measured in terms of TLU play significant role and their signs are positive as expected. Land holding and livestock ownership measured in TLU are strongly related to the first component of assets of smallholder farmers. Number of rooms is negatively related to the second component whereas house structure related positively to access to assets.

Table 10. Eigen vector for assets

Variable	Comp1	Comp2	Comp3	Comp4
landholding	0.652	0.275	0.021	-0.012
TLU	0.662	0.227	0.127	0.014
Nonfarm income	-0.242	0.389	0.833	-0.307
House structure	-0.230	0.624	-0.084	0.742
Number of rooms	0.159	-0.577	0.532	0.595

Under the component two, nonfarm income and house structure contribute in the estimation of resilience and the sign is positive as expected but the sign of the number of rooms turned negative. This is due to the fact that smallholder farmers do not tell the exact number of rooms they have in their compound.

4.6. Stability (S)

Table 11 shows the eigen values and the subsequent table (Table 12) depicts the coefficient loadings. To estimate the value of these latent variables, the loss due to shocks like livestock loss due to theft or dead, crop loss due to drought, water shortages, and outbreak of diseases and fall in price in the market, other shocks like member of household death, illness, and losses of job. It is the capacity as a whole to external shocks and stressors, where the household's survival depends on the interaction components that enable them to react to such external stimuli.

Table 11. Eigenvalue of stability

Factor	Eigenvalue	Difference	Proportion
Factor1	1.956	0.200	0.196
Factor2	1.756	0.166	0.176
Factor3	1.590	0.575	0.159
Factor4	1.016	0.115	0.102
Factor5	0.900	0.057	0.090
Factor6	0.844	0.174	0.084
Factor7	0.670	0.128	0.067
Factor8	0.542	0.127	0.054
Factor9	0.415	0.105	0.042
Factor10	0.310	.	0.031

Table 12 shows that the most variables like drought, rainfall and livestock disease are more common and stable. On the other hand, illness and water availability is instable. The table (Table 12) shows that the most variables like drought, rainfall and livestock disease are more common and stable. On the other hand, illness and water availability is instable.

Table 12. Rotated factor loadings (pattern matrix) and unique variances

Variable	Factor1	Factor2	Factor3	Factor4	Uniqueness
Drought	0.802	-0.130	-0.044	-0.229	0.286
Rainfall variability	0.247	0.324	-0.096	0.476	0.599
Snow	0.023	0.616	0.350	0.085	0.491
Livestock diseases	0.620	0.356	0.004	-0.116	0.475
Crop failure	-0.134	-0.112	0.856	-0.053	0.234
Output price volatility	0.235	0.259	0.759	-0.156	0.277
Water short	-0.371	0.727	-0.032	-0.110	0.321
Illness	-0.741	0.216	-0.091	-0.209	0.352
Crime	0.144	0.416	-0.142	0.611	0.414
Death	-0.187	-0.183	-0.098	0.829	0.234

4.7. Adaptive capacity (AC)

Table 13. Eigenvalue for adaptive capacity

Component	Eigenvalue	Difference	Proportion	Cumulative
Comp1	1.244	0.155	0.249	0.249
Comp2	1.090	0.166	0.218	0.467
Comp3	0.923	0.045	0.185	0.652
Comp4	0.878	0.013	0.176	0.827
Comp5	0.865	.	0.173	1

Two components are retained. The first two components explain 47% of the variation.

Table 14. Eigen vector of adaptive capacity

Variable	Factor1	Factor2	Factor3
Diversified income sources	-0.2728	0.6495	0.4498
Household education average	0.5721	0.1311	-0.0112
Employment ratio	-0.2088	0.667	-0.5544
Health situations	-0.5423	-0.1643	0.4667
Institutions participations	0.5105	0.2985	0.5219

The table above shows the correlation of the estimated AC with transformed variables. Labor force participation is the most important variable followed by diversified income sources and average education of members in the household.

4.8. Estimation Result of Resilience

Under the section above emphasis was given to estimate each resilience bloc separately using different multivariate techniques mainly principal component and factor analyses. Now, it is necessary to pool each bloc to estimate resilience of smallholder farmers. The resilience blocs estimated above become covariates in the estimation of resilience index. Assuming all the blocs are normally distributed with mean zero and variance one, it is possible to run factor analysis using principal component factor method.

The following table summarizes results obtained after factor analysis is run using principal component factor method. The table shows that factor 1 explains 25% of the variations. Factor 2 and factor 3 explains 18% and 14%, respectively.

Table 15. Eigenvalues and variance explained

Factor	Eigenvalue	Difference	Proportion
Factor1	1.768	0.483	0.253
Factor2	1.286	0.256	0.184
Factor3	1.030	0.076	0.147
Factor4	0.954	0.097	0.136
Factor5	0.857	0.263	0.122
Factor6	0.594	0.083	0.085
Factor7	0.511	.	0.073

The first factor represents resilience bloc except access to public services (APS), which is negatively correlated with other variables. This can be imagined given that weak APS increases when households becomes poorer. In the second factor, APS becomes positive, which shows that it is a positive characteristic of resilience. Adaptive capacity (AC) is positive in the first factor and negative in the second factor. AC shows the likely that when a household becomes poor, put the poor in difficulty to acquire resources that they did not have before. The third factor triggers hidden information of the resilience bloc s. From all the building bloc s under the third factor, stability (S) and adaptive capacity (AC) are positive. This is likely tells common story in terms of food security and vulnerability situations.

Resilience estimation cannot be a one dimension and Table 16 below shows the factor loadings taking into consideration three factors. Asset holding is the most important component in resilience of smallholder farmers, which represent household's level of wellbeing. Among the blocs of resilience, APS is negatively related to the first factor. This is evident that poor accesses to public services increases household's vulnerability to shocks and exacerbate their food insecurity situations.

Table 16. Factor loadings (pattern matrix) and unique variances

Variable	Factor1	Factor2	Factor3	Uniqueness
AIT	0.467	0.703	-0.030	0.287
SSN	0.470	-0.558	-0.044	0.466
APS	-0.378	0.319	-0.089	0.748
AFI	0.652	0.504	-0.171	0.292
A	0.740	-0.298	-0.210	0.319
S	0.107	0.116	0.894	0.175
AC	0.450	-0.146	0.382	0.630

Table 17. Means and standard deviations for resilience and its components in different agro ecology

Variable	Lowlands		Midlands		Highlands		Total	
	Mean	Std. Dev.	Mean	Std. Dev.	Mean	Std. Dev.	Mean	Std. Dev.
AIT	-0.079	0.993	0.114	0.997	-0.041	1.007	0.000	1
SSN	0.041	0.536	-0.028	0.730	-0.004	0.825	0.002	0.709
APS	-0.044	0.355	0.018	0.337	0.024	0.349	0.000	0.347
AFI	-0.013	0.790	0.086	0.838	-0.075	0.700	0.000	0.779
A	0.021	0.826	0.012	0.777	0.010	0.634	0.014	0.747
S	0.019	0.816	-0.030	0.903	0.013	0.872	0.000	0.863
AC	0.051	0.698	-0.040	0.535	-0.010	0.860	-0.001	0.708
R	0.033	1.303	-0.035	1.333	0.005	1.205	0.000	1.278

Among the three agro ecology classification, Components of resilience is presented as shown in the figure above, where midland agro ecology is better resilient, which depends on access to inputs and technology and, income and food. Adaptive capacity and social safety nets seem to be weak in midland unlike lowlands agro ecology.

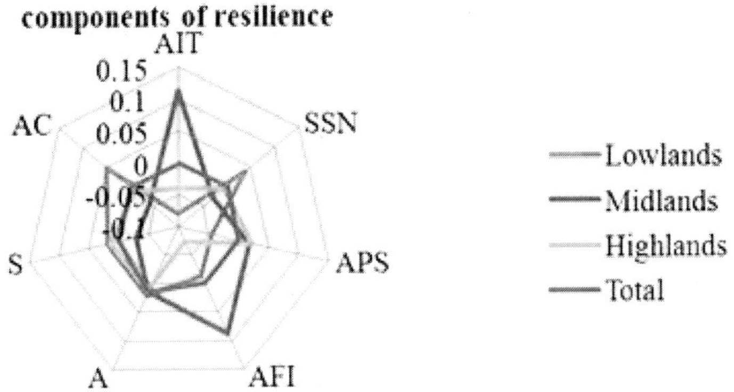

Figure 2. Radar graph for resilience components

5. CONCLUSIONS

Food insecurity in Ethiopia, like most developing countries, is a dominant problem. Climate related shocks are the major causes and stifled rural households' food security. The way a household withstands climate related shocks depends on the preconditions and options available to them in terms of capabilities and activities. The best option to withstand the effects of climate related shocks is through resilience.

Using resilience analysis framework, resilience index was defined as a function of agricultural inputs and technology, social safety nets, access to public services, access to food and income, access to assets, stability and adaptive capacity. Each bloc was a latent variable; unobserved per se. Therefore the estimation was made separately using different multivariate techniques. The result of the estimation of each bloc becomes covariates in the measurement of resilience index. In the estimation of resilience each resilience bloc was pooled based on the fact that all the blocs were normally distributed.

Hence, factor analysis was run using principal component factor method and three factors were retained. Under the first factor, all blocs, except access to public services, are positively correlated with resilience. The negative correlation between access to public services and resilience is because access to public services like health services and education qualities decreases as households becomes poorer. In terms of importance to rural household's resilience index, the result indicates that asset ownership play significant role followed by access to food and income, as well as social safety nets. These resilience blocs show the likelihood of recovering from any form of climatic shocks that a household experiences. In the second factor, access to public services becomes positive, which shows that it is a positive characteristic of resilience. Adaptive capacity is positive in the first factor and negative in the second factor. The third factor triggers hidden information of the resilience bloc as stability and adaptive capacity are positive, which likely tells common story in terms of food security situations.

Asset holding is the most important component in resilience of smallholder farmers, which represent household's level of wellbeing. Among the building blocs of resilience, APS is negatively related to the first factor. This is evident that poor accesses to public services increases household's vulnerability to shocks and exacerbate their food insecurity situations. This means, in the specific case of smallholders found in lowlands agro ecology of the West Shoa zone need to be made, such as livestock related initiatives and water-related interventions.

ACKNOWLEDGMENTS

This publication was made possible by financial support provided in part by the Swedish International Development Cooperation Agency (SIDA) and Ethiopian Ministry of Education. All views, interpretations, recommendations, and conclusions expressed in this paper are those of the authors and not necessarily those of the supporting or collaborating institutions.

REFERENCES

1. M. Pelling, Adaptation to climate change: from resilience to transformation, 1st ed. London: Routledge, 2011.

2. R. Hasan and U. Habiba, "Anthropogenic Causes: Population Pressure, Demographic Changes, Urbanization and Its Implication on Food Security," in Food Security and Risk Reduction in Bangladesh: Methods, Approaches and Practices, U. Habiba, A. Abedin, A. W. R. Hassan, and R. Shaw, Eds. Kyoto University , Japan: Springer Japa, 2015.

3. IPCC, Climate Change 2014 Impacts, Adaptation , and Vulnerability Part A: Global and Sectoral Aspects Working

Group II Contribution to the Fifth Assessment Report of the Intergovernmental Panel on Climate Change. 2014.

4. IPCC, "Climate Change 2014 Synthesis Report Summary Chapter for Policymakers," Ipcc, p. 31, 2014.

5. IPCC, "Climate Change 2013 The Physical Science Basis Working Group I Contribution to the Fifth Assessment Report of the Intergovernmental Panel on Climate Change Summary for Policymakers," p. 33, 2013.

6. C. Arndt, W. Farmer, K. Strzepek, and J. Thurlow, "Climate Change, Agriculture and Food Security in Tanzania," The World Bank Development Research Group Agriculture and Rural Development Team, WPS6188, 2012.

7. M. E. Brown, Food Security, Food Prices and Climate Variability. London and New York: Routledge, 2014.

8. W. N. Adger, "Approches to Vulernability to Climate Change," CSERGE Working Paper GEC 96-05, 1996.

9. W. Bank, "Economics of Adaptation to Climate Change: Synthesis Report," 2010.

10. Nahu-Senaye, "Weather Insurance for Farmers: Experience from Ethiopia," in New Direction for Smallholder Agriculture, 2011.

11. J. von Braun, "A policy Agenda for Famine Prevention in Africa," 1991.

12. T. Asaminew and K. Diriba, "Recent Changes in Rainfall , Temperature and Number of Rainy Days over Northern Oromia Zone , Ethiopia," vol. 3, no. 6, pp. 62-70, 2015.

13. USAID, "Ethiopia – Complex Emergency Fact Sheet #2, December 18, 2015, USAID Ethiopia." 2015.

14. C. Folke, S. Carpenter, T. Elmqvist, L. Gunderson, C. S. Holling, and B. Walker, "Resilience and sustainable development: building adaptive capacity in a world of transformations," Ambio, vol. 31, no. 5, pp. 437-440, 2002.

15. L. Alinovi, E. Mane, and D. Romano, "Measuring Household Resilience to Food Insecurity: Application to Palestinian Households," 2009.

16. WFP, "Resilience Measurement Principles: Towards an agenda for Measurement Design," 2014.

17. (Federal Democratic Republic of Ethiopia) FDRE, "NATIONAL POLICY AND STRATEGY ON DISASTER RISK MANAGEMENT," 2009.

18. (Central Statistical Agency) CSA, "Population Projection of Ethiopia for All Regions At Woreda Level from 2014 - 2017," Addis Ababa, 2013.

19. C. R. Kothari, Research Methodology: Methods and Techniques. 2004.

20. L. Alinovi, E. Mane, and D. Romano, "Towards the measurement of household resilience to food insecurity: applying a model to Palestinian household data," 2008.

21. P. Lei and Q. Wu, "Introduction to structural equation modeling: Issues and practical considerations," Educational Measurement: issues and practice, vol. 26, no. 3, pp. 33-43, 2007.

22. L. Alinovi, M. D'Errico, E. Mane, and D. Romano, "LiveLihoods strategies and househoLd resiLience to Food insecurity: an empiricaL anaLysis to Kenya," in Promoting Resilience through Social Protection in Sub-Saharan Africa, 2010.

23. J. Coates, A. Swindale, and P. Bilinsky, "Household Food Insecurity Access Scale (HFIAS) for Measurement of Food Access: Indicator Guide, Version 3," Food and Nutrition Technical Assistance Project, no. August, 2007.

24. Swindale and P. Bilinsky, "Household Dietary Diversity Score (HDDS) for Measurement of Household Food Access: Indicator Guide," no. March, 2005.

25. P. Bilinsky and A. Swindale, "Household Dietary Diversity Score (HDDS) for Measurement of Household Food Access: Indicator Guide VERSION 2 Anne Swindale Household Dietary Diversity Score (HDDS) for Measurement of Household Food Access: Indicator Guide VERSION 2," 2006.

26. J. Hoddinott and Y. Yohannes, "Dietary Diversity as a Household Food Security Indicator," Food and Nutrition Technical Assistance Project, Academy for Educational Development, vol. 53, no. May, p. 160, 2002.

27. T. Frankenberger, T. Spangler, S. Nelson, and Mark Langworthy, "Enhancing Resilience to Food Security Shocks in Africa," no. November, 2012.

13

FOOD PURCHASING BEHAVIORS AND FOOD INSECURITY AMONG COLLEGE STUDENTS AT THE UNIVERSITY OF TEXAS AT SAN ANTONIO

Lesli Biediger-Friedman[1], Bonnie Sanchez[2], Meizi He[2], Jianmin Guan[2], Zenong Yin[2]

[1]School of Family and Consumer Sciences, Texas State University, 601 University Dr., San Marcos, TX 78666, USA

[2]Department of Health and Kinesiology, University of Texas at San Antonio, San Antonio, TX, USA

ABSTRACT

A decline in diet quality observed in college students can be attributed to consuming less than the recommended amounts of primary food groups (dairy, fruit, vegetables, and grains) and higher intakes of sweetened beverages. The investigation of food purchasing behaviors may help explain the potential influences, like food security and access to healthy food that may be causing the shift in dietary patterns. This study used receipt analysis and assessed food security in a cross-sectional sample of 258 undergraduate and graduate students. Food security questionnaires and seven-day food and beverage receipt logs were analyzed. Over half of the sampled population were between 21-25 years of age, of which a majority were undergraduates and lived off campus. Results showed that almost a third of the students were classified as having either very low (11.6%) or low (19.4%) food security. The largest amount of money was spent on grocery store purchases. The highest frequency of purchases occurred at fast-food venues and included a sugar-sweetened beverage and fried food. Gender differences were found in fast-food purchases, with males spending an average of $19.27 and females spending an average of $18.29 per week. However, no significant gender differences in the frequency of purchases made at grocery stores, convenience stores, fast-food restaurants, sit-down restaurants or campus dining venues. Moreover, students living in off-campus apartments purchased significantly more fruits and vegetables than students living with parents. The study findings indicate that purchasing patterns persist across levels of food security and for all levels are compounded by less than optimal purchasing of fruit and vegetables.

Keywords: food security, college student health, food purchasing

1. INTRODUCTION

Food purchasing behavior influences and may provide insight into dietary intake of a selected population. Food purchasing behavior among undergraduate and graduate-level college students is intriguing as changes to dietary patterns often result in a decrease in overall diet quality [1]. Dietary pattern changes that occur during the transition into young adulthood often result in a decrease in overall diet quality. Numerous studies have identified the trends of limited fruit and vegetable consumption and high fatty food consumption by college students [2, 3, 4]. In fact, college students often report consuming less than the recommended amounts of primary food groups, including grains, fruits, vegetables, dairy and meat(s) [2, 5, 6]. The 2010 National College Health Assessment found that only 6% of college students consumed the recommended daily serving of fruits and vegetables [2]. Furthermore, previous research has indicated caloric imbalance and high intake of sweetened beverages is common among college students [7, 8] and has been associated with weight gain [9]. Overall, serious health issues may arise with limited fruit and vegetable intake and high intake of sugar-sweetened beverages. This shift in dietary patterns away from nutrient dense foods may stem from a variety of factors that influence food purchasing behavior, including food security, access to healthy food and low income level. In 2012, 41% of US 18 to 24 year olds attended a two or four year degree-granting institution with many depending on financial aid [10].

The 2014 Hunger in America report stated that out of 33.7 million of their clients receiving food assistance 2.1 million of them were full time college students [11]. By examining the food purchasing behaviors of college students, appropriate environmental, educational, and dietary intervention methods can be developed[12]. Food insecurity is common among college students and indicates inadequate access to food, as related to income, location, or food cost [13, 14].

In 2013, 14.3% of US households and 18.0% of Texas households were reported as food insecure, with household income at or below the poverty line as a primary risk factor [13, 15]. In contrast, almost a third (31%) of the participants in this study were classified as having very low or low food security. Research suggests that food insecurity, including college student food insecurity, is associated with causal factors such as low income, poor financial management and poor time management, and results in a variety of health and academic issues [16]. Food insecurity is also associated with overeating and obesity [16]. Understanding the degree of food insecurity among college students, and its association with food purchasing, supports effective intervention planning for this population.

Purchasing behavior can be defined through trends and patterns, which are determined by evaluating food and beverage purchases [17]. These patterns can be observed through various methods, including 24-hour recalls, food frequency questionnaires and receipt analysis, which evaluates type, expense, and location of food purchases. Most research on health among college students focuses on assessing dietary patterns through self-report. Research that assesses actual food purchases does not also assess related factors like food security [3, 5, 18, 19].

Documenting food purchasing behaviors such as where and what type of food is purchased, and how much money is spent per food outlet, can enhance the understanding of college students' dietary habits [20]. This study (1) used receipt analysis to determine food purchasing behavior among college students attending the University of Texas at San Antonio, (2) explored food security levels among the study population, and (3) determined if food purchasing behavior is associated with food security levels among the study population.

2. METHODS

This cross-sectional study included undergraduate and graduate students from a large university (30,258 students) in the south central region of the US. Emails were sent to 15 instructors of undergraduate and graduate courses from a variety of study areas to recruit classes. Eight classes total participated in this convenience sample of the target population. Recruitment emails with study instructions and informed consent language were sent to all students in the selected classes. Students were asked to complete an online questionnaire and a receipt log. Participation was incentivized through the offer of extra credit; students were also provided an alternative extra credit opportunity. Students were given a two-week period of time to complete the study documents and each participant was identified by a randomly assigned code upon submission of study materials. Data were excluded if online questionnaire and receipt log were incomplete, or the personal identification codes did not match. The study was approved by the Institutional Review Board of the University of Texas at San Antonio.

2.1. Measurement

Participants completed an online questionnaire with questions about demographic variables, purchasing patterns, sources of income and methods of payment for purchases. Participants also completed the US Adult Food Security Survey Module (AFSSM), which was validated in 2006 by Gulliford, Nunes and Rocke [21]. The AFSSM was modified by the National Center for Health Statistics (NCHS) into a 6-question assessment. The survey classified participants into three groups based on food security score: 0-1 (very low food security), 2-4 (low food security), and 5-6 (high or marginal food security).

A receipt log was used to collect all food and beverage purchasing data for a 7-day period of time. The receipt analysis methodology was selected and adapted based on previous research assessing food purchasing behaviors. [17, 22, 23] Study participants attached receipts from food purchases to the pages of a logbook that posed three questions concerning each purchase: 1) what was purchased? 2) for whom was the purchase made? and 3) how was the food purchased? The cost per week of food and beverage purchases was calculated by totaling the amount spent per receipt throughout the 7-day period of time. Additionally, all purchases made at each of the seven following locations were summed: grocery store, fast-food restaurant, sit-down restaurant, on-campus food outlet, convenience store, vending machine, and bar. To categorize purchases, a coding structure of themes and subthemes was developed based on a food index adapted by the research team [17]. Two coders were given background information on the study, a list of the potential index categories and a rating sheet. The rating sheet was used to assess the feasibility of coding food items for this study. After food and beverage items from submitted receipts were coded, the principle investigator and lead coder met and reconciled differences.

Statistical analyses were conducted using SPSS version 20 [24]. Descriptive statistics were utilized to assess demographic characteristics of the sample. Independent t-tests and one-way analysis of variance were used to examine the differences and associations between food purchasing behaviors and food security levels.

2.2. Strength and Limitations

This study has a variety of strengths. This study incorporated two methods to evaluate purchasing behavior: (1) online questionnaire and (2) receipt analysis, and the latter incorporated all possible food outlets. Only one known study has included such a breadth of food outlets in receipt analysis[17]. Additionally, the present study assessed level of food security and included an analysis of weekly spending patterns to capture typical food purchasing behavior. The only other known assessment of food security on a college campus collected general monthly spending patterns [25]. Finally, evaluating food and beverage purchasing behavior provides an objective measure of dietary patterns [17].

Limitations of this study include the collection of cross-sectional survey data, the use of a convenience purposeful sampling technique, small sample size, short duration, and unknown reliability of receipt collection. Additionally, while the week-long duration of receipt analysis provides specific information about purchasing behavior, the data collected might be impacted by the timing of the participant's income cycle, financial aid distribution, current job status, inconsistent shopping patterns, and monthly schedule. Finally, the index categories were based on the categories identified in the literature and populated by emergent data, however, the index is not able to pick up on all food categories.

3. RESULTS

3.1. Participants

A total of 258 college students (155 female/103 male) completed both the questionnaire and receipt log. The sample was majority Hispanic 129 (50%), which is reflective of the south Texas region. Participants represented a wide age range, with over half of the sampled population between 21-25 years of age. Additionally, both undergraduate 215 (83%) and graduate 39 (15%) students were included in the study.

Results from the online questionnaire indicated that the majority of the students lived in an off-campus apartment or house, with about a quarter living with a parent or relative. Study participants reported a variety of income sources, with many indicating multiple sources of income. Almost a third of the participants were classified as having either very low (29 or 12%) or low (49 or 19%) food security; however, only nine participants (4%) reported receiving aid from government assistance programs. In total, 178 (69%) participants were classified as high or marginal food security.

Table 1. Study population and food security levels

Food Security Classifications	Study populationn (%)	Texas %	United States %
Very low/low food security	80 (31)	17.4	14.7
High/marginal food security	178 (69)		
Total	258 (100)		
Age	n		%
18-20	37		14.3
21-25	159		61.6
26-55	49		24
Gender	n		%
Male	103		39.9
Female	155		60.1
Marital Status	n		%
Single	230		89.2
Married	28		10.9
Student Classification	n		%
Graduate	39		15.1
Freshman	2		0.8
Sophomore	26		10.1
Junior	89		34.5
Senior	98		38
Special student	4		1.6
Ethnicity	Study population (%)	University population (%)	US College student population (%)
Asian	9 (3.5)	5	6
African American	32 (12.4)	8.1	14
White	76 (29.5)	33.1	61
Hispanic	129 (50)	44.1	13
Other	12 (4.7)	9.5	6

3.2. Receipt Log Analysis

Analysis of receipt log data revealed weekly patterns in location, category and frequency of food and beverage purchases. Of the 258 study participants, 209 (81%) submitted at least one receipt for fast-food venues, 216 (83.7%) purchased at least one sugar-sweetened beverage, and 184 (71.3%) purchased at least one fried item (Table 2). Fruit and vegetable purchases were made by 143 (55.4%) of participants. On average, $18.68 (SD = $20.39) was spent at fast-food venues per week, $43.98 (SD = $54.70) at grocery stores and $15.97 (SD = $26.15) at restaurants (Table 2). Overall, the receipt logs identified no significant differences between the total amount spent on fast food, restaurant, and grocery purchases. Minimal differences were found based on gender for fast-food purchases, with males spending an average of $19.27 and females spending an average of $18.29 per week.

3.3. Food Purchasing Questionnaire

Participants reported monthly spending patterns for grocery and fast-food purchases using the online questionnaire. As reported on the questionnaire, most (81%) participants reported visiting fast-food restaurants 1-2 times per week, 37.6% of participants reported purchasing meals on campus 1-2 times per week, and 78.7% reported shopping at a full grocery store 1-2 times per week. Participants reported that they most typically purchased food from fast-food venues (81%), grocery stores (71.7%) and restaurants (48.8%), but some also purchased food from on-campus fast-food venues (33.3%), on-campus dining venues (29.1%) and convenience stores (22.5%).

3.4. Food Purchasing Behaviors

Each category of food and beverage purchasing behavior was compared with student characteristics to assess differences. No significant differences were found between the frequency of purchases made at grocery stores, convenience stores, fast-food restaurants, sit-down restaurants or campus dining venues based on gender, living arrangement, student classification or level of food security. In contrast, significant differences were found among the frequency of restaurant purchases based on student classification, with graduate students purchasing from restaurants significantly more than undergraduate students (Table 3, $t = 2.80$, $p < 0.01$) and undergraduate students purchasing from on-campus dining significantly more than graduate students (Table 3, follow-up Tukey test, $t = 3.04$, $p < 0.01$). Significant differences were also found based on living arrangement, with students living in off-campus apartments purchasing on-campus dining significantly more than students living with parents (Table 4, post-hoc Tukey test, $F [2,255] = 4.08$ $p<0.05$, $\eta = 0.018$).

Table 2. Frequencies of Food Purchasing Behavior as Per Receipt Analysis

Receipts by Venue (number of participants that submitted at least one receipt per venue)		
Food Venue Type	N	%
Fast-Food Venues	209	81.0
Grocery Stores	185	71.7
Restaurants	126	48.8
On-campus Fast-Food	86	33.3
On campus Dining	75	29.1
Convenience Stores	58	22.5
Food index categories		
Entrees	Side items	Combo meals
Value/dollar menu items	Fried items	Tex/Mex items
Water/no calorie beverage	Alcohol	Caffeinated beverages
Sweetened beverages	Grocery items	Vegetables/fruit
Grocery entrée/mixed dish	Discretionary salty/sweet	Meat/poultry/legumes
Dairy	Grains	Eggs
Significant findings from food index categories		
	N	%
Fruits/Vegetables	143	55.4
Caffeinated Beverages	74	28.7
Sweetened Beverages	216	83.7
Fried items	184	71.3
Fast-food Value/Dollar menu items	37	14.3

Money Spent per Venue by Receipts					
Venue	Minimum	Maximum	Mean	Median	Std. Deviation
Grocery	$.00	$300.63	$43.98	$23.88	$54.70
Fast-Food	$.00	$152.90	$18.68	$12.76	$20.39
Restaurant	$.00	$150.31	$15.97	$.00	$26.15
Campus Dining	$.00	$36.69	$4.78	$.00	$7.42
Vending Machine	$.00	$1.50	$.01	$.00	$0.13
Convenience Store	$.00	$77.84	$1.85	$.00	$6.29
Bar	$.00	$37.50	$.92	$.00	$4.92

Table 3. Food Purchasing Behaviors by Student Classification (n=258)

Food purchasing behaviors	Mean per week (SD)			*F*	*P* < .05
	On-campus	Off-campus	Off-campus with Parents		
Campus dining frequency	1.50 (1.73)	1.48 (1.80)	.90 (1.33)	4.08	0.018
Fruit/vegetable purchases	4.17 (6.60)	3.91(4.85)	2.05 (3.59)	3.88	0.022
Money spent on campus dining	$7.62 ($9.77)	$6.61 ($9.43)	$3.96 ($6.27)	4.01	0.019

Table 4. Food Purchasing Behaviors by Students' Living Arrangement (n=258)

Food purchasing behaviors	Mean per week (SD)		t	p
	Undergraduate	Graduate		
Restaurant frequency	.72 (1.01)	1.28 (1.78)	2.80	< .01
Campus dining frequency	1.19 (.97)	.41 (1.54)	3.04	< .01
Money spent on restaurants	$14.33 ($23.66)	$25.17 ($36.19)	2.41	< .05
Money spent on campus dining	$5.31 ($7.76)	$1.76 ($3.96)	2.79	< .01

No significant differences were found between purchases of foods in the index categories (fruits and vegetables, sugar-sweetened beverages, fried items, caffeinated beverages and value/dollar menu items) based on gender, student classification or level of food security. In contrast, significant differences were found based on living arrangement, (Table 4, post-hoc Tukey test, $F[2,255] = 3.88$, $p < 0.05$, $\eta = .022$), with students living in off-campus apartments purchasing significantly more fruits and vegetables than students living with parents.

No significant differences were found between the amount of money spent at grocery stores, fast-food restaurants, sit-down restaurants and campus dining venues based on gender, living arrangement, student classification, or level of food security. Significant differences were found between the amount of money spent on food and beverage purchases based on living arrangement, with graduate students spending more at restaurants than undergraduates (Table 3, $t = 2.41$, $p < .05$), students residing in off-campus apartments spending more at campus dining venues than students living with parents (Table 4, follow up Tukey test, $F[2,255] = 4.01$, $p < 0.05$, $\eta = .019$) and undergraduate students spending more at campus dining venues than graduate students (Table 3, $t = 2.79$, $p < .01$).

4. DISCUSSION

The present study revealed several key findings. The students surveyed most frequently purchased food and beverages from fast-food venues, although they spent more money at grocery stores. During the week in which they logged receipts, most of the students purchased at least one sugar-sweetened beverage and one fried item, and almost half did not purchase any fruits or vegetables. Significant differences were found for food purchasing behaviors based on living arrangement and student classification, which suggests food availability differences among these groups. Student both living on-campus and off-campus spent more money of fruits and vegetables than did students living off-campus with parents. In contrast, no significant differences were found for food purchasing behaviors based on gender or level of food security.

In the present study, a majority of the students purchased food from fast food restaurants at least once a week. Previous studies have demonstrated that college students purchase fast-food approximately 1-3 times per week, but purchase frequency can be as high as 6-8 times per week [26,27]. Suggested reasons for the high frequency include convenience [28], time constraints, inclination to eat with others and the belief that fast-food is inexpensive [26]. Moreover, if fast-food is a major part of the college student lifestyle, nutrition education programs should focus on informing students about the nutritional content of fast-food menu items in order to help them make healthier choices when purchasing at these venues. Eating patterns are commonly maintained from college throughout adulthood [6].

The variation in food purchasing behaviors found based on living arrangement could be attributed to the difference in primary shopper of the household. The small difference between grocery and non-grocery (on average $1.77) suggests that college students contribute a comparable amount of money to both.

Food security was a concern within the group of students surveyed. This finding is consistent with other studies that have demonstrated almost a quarter of college students in the US to be food insecure [25]. Rarely is food purchasing behavior evaluated based on level of food security; therefore, little is known about the relationship between these two variables. In a study using concept mapping to determine the influence of food security on food purchases, Walker and Kawachi demonstrated similarities in purchasing patterns between food secure and insecure populations [29]. Most interestingly, the present study revealed no significant differences between food purchasing behavior based on level of food security, indicating that both food secure and insecure individuals have similar purchasing patterns. One possible explanation for this similarity is the influence of environmental factors on food purchasing behavior. Environmental factors such as food availability, marketing, convenience, and social pressure may lead college students to purchase similar types of foods regardless of financial status [30].

Significant differences were found in food purchasing behavior based on living arrangement and student classification. Graduate students purchased more often from and spent more money at restaurants compared to undergraduate students. This could be explained by potentially higher income among graduate students. Undergraduate students purchased more often from and spent more money at on-campus dining venues compared to graduate students. This could be explained by class schedules that offer undergraduate classes during the day, multiple times per week, placing undergraduate students on campus more often during daytime hours. Furthermore, graduate students living on their own could struggle with the skills needed for meal preparation [31]. This study did not find significant differences in food purchasing behavior based on gender or other demographic characteristics, and this could be due to the similarity of food environments experienced by students across these groups.

Receipt analysis is a promising method for assessing food purchasing behaviors, and provides an alternative to methods that rely on self-reporting of data. Although the collection and analysis of receipts is labor intensive, it is less time consuming than food diaries. Technological improvements like smartphone applications and scanning of receipts could make the process more efficient. Additionally, previous research indicates that even with limited reminders from researchers and minimal incentives, participants complete receipt collection [23].

5. CONCLUSION

Based on results from receipt analysis, this study demonstrates that college students typically spend similar amounts of money on grocery and non-grocery foods, while visiting fast-food restaurants more frequently than other venues. Analysis of purchases by food index category indicates that college students are commonly purchasing at least one sugar-sweetened beverage and one fried item per week, yet only a little over half of the students purchase fruits and vegetables. In addition, a high incidence of food insecurity exists within this population.

Documenting college student food purchasing behaviors may assist nutrition professionals in targeting educational efforts to improve food and beverage choices and food budget management. Due to the high amount of money spent by college students on grocery purchases, educational programs should address the types of foods and beverages purchased from grocery stores, emphasizing a cost-effective shopping strategy that increases fruit and vegetable purchases and decreases sugar-sweetened beverage purchases. By developing strategies to decrease fast-food consumption and increase fruit and vegetable intake, college students may learn to sustain positive behaviors throughout their life.

It is important to understand that there is a large interaction between individuals, their living situation, and their food environments. The influences of environmental factors (e.g. food costs, food policy and food culture) are interrelated and always changing, which may impact individual food purchasing behavior. In the present study, only the individual and community level factors (location of purchases, amount of money spent and specific items purchased) were examined. Research employing a social-ecological approach is needed to examine the influence of upper-level environmental factors on food purchasing behaviors among college students. Such an approach would yield insight about all levels of the university food environment.

ACKNOWLEDGEMENT

The authors acknowledge the students and faculty who volunteered to assist with data collection on this project.

STATEMENT OF COMPETING INTERESTS

The authors have no competing interests.

REFERENCES

1. Racette, S.B., Deusinger, S.S., Strube, M.J., Highstein, G.R., and Deusinger, R.H., "Weight changes, exercise, and dietary patterns during freshman and sophomore years of college," Journal of American College Health, 53(6), 245-251, May - June 2005.

2. American College Health Association, "American College Health Association-National College Health Assessment II: Reference Group Executive Summary Spring 2010," Linthicum, MD: American College Health Association. [Online] Available: http://www.acha-ncha.org/docs/ACHA-NCHA-II_ReferenceGroup_ExecutiveSummary_Spring2010.pdf. [Accessed April 27, 2016].

3. Townsend, M..S., Peerson, J., Love, B., Achterberg, C., and Murphy, S.P., "Food insecurity is positively related to

overweight in women," Journal of Nutrition, 131(6), 1738-1745, June 2001.

4. Wiley, D. and James, G., "Assessing the health behaviors of Texas college students," Journal of American College Health, 44(4), 167-71, January 1996.

5. Demory-Luce, D., Morales, M., Nicklas, T., Baranowski, T., Zakeri, I., and Berenson, G., "Changes in food group consumption patterns from childhood to young adulthood: the Bogalusa Heart Study," Journal of American Dietetic Association, 104(11), 1684-91, November 2004.

6. Haberman, S. and Luffey, D., "Weighing in college students' diet and exercise behaviors," Journal of American College Health, 46(4), 189-91, January 1998.

7. West, D.S., Bursac, Z., Quimby, D., Prewitt, T. E., Spatz, T., Nash, C., Mays, G. and Eddings, K., "Self-reported sugar-sweetened beverage intake among college students," Obesity, 14, 1825-1831, October 2006.

8. Huffman, L. and West, D.S., "Readiness to change sugar sweetened beverage intake among college students," Eating Behavior, 8, 10-14, January 2007.

9. Ludwig, D., Peterson, K., and Gortmaker, S., "Relation between consumption of sugar-sweetened drinks and childhood obesity: a prospective, observational analysis," Lancet, 357, 505-508, February 2001.

10. U.S. Department of Commerce, Census Bureau, Current Population Survey (CPS), October, 1967 through 2012. Available: http://nces.ed.gov/programs/digest/d13/tables/dt13_302.60.asp. [Accessed May 19, 2016].

11. Weinfield, N., Mills, G, Borger, C., Gearing, M., Macaluso, T., Montaquila, J., Zedlewski, S., "Hunger in America 2014 National Report," Feeding America. 2014. Available: http://help.feedingamerica.org/HungerInAmerica/hunger-in-america-2014-full-report.pdf. [Accessed May 19, 2016].

12. Lowry, R., Galuska, D.A., Fulton, J.E., Wechsler. H., Kann, L., and Collins, J.L., "Physical activity, food choice, and weight management goals and practices among U.S. college students,"

American Journal of Preventive Medicine, 18(1), 18-27, January 2000.

13. Nord, M. and Hopwood, H., U.S. Dept. of Agriculture, Economic Research Service. "A comparison of household food security in Canada and the United States ERR-67. 2008," Available: http://www.ers.usda.gov/publications/err-economic-research-report/err67.aspx#.UkXGiqyWbAo. [Accessed May 2, 2016].

14. United States Census Bureau. Statistical Abstract of the United States: 2012, 2011. United States Census Bureau. [Online]. Available: http://www.census.gov/compendia/statab/2012edition.html. [Accessed May 1, 2016].

15. Coleman-Jensen, A., Nord, M., and Singh, A., "USDA Household Food Security in the United States in 2012," Available: http://www.ers.usda.gov/publications/err-economic-research-report/err155.aspx#.UsnAZRbvzRO. [Accessed July 22, 2014].

16. Olson, C.M. and Holben, D.H., "Position of The American Dietetic Association: Domestic food and nutrition security," Journal of American Diet Association, 102, 1840-1847, December 2002.

17. Cullen, K., Baranowski, T., Watson, K., Nicklas, T., Fisher, J., O'Donnell, S., Baranowski, J., Islam, N. and Missaghian, M., "Food category purchases vary by household education and race/ethnicity: Results from grocery receipts," Journal American Dietetic Association, 107(10), 1747-1752, October 2007.

18. Brevard, P.B. and Ricketts, C.D., "Residence of college students affects dietary intake, physical activity, and serum lipid levels," Journal American Dietetic Association, 96(1), 35-38, January 1996.

19. Brunt, A.R. and Rhee, Y.S., "Obesity and lifestyle in US college students related to living arrangements," Appetite, 51, 615-621, May 2008.

20. Driskell, J., Meckna ,B., and Scales, N., "Differences exist in the eating habits of university men and women at fast-food restaurants," Nutrition Research, 26(10), 524-530, October 2006.

21. Gulliford, M., Nunes, C., and Rocke, B., "The 18 Household Food Security Survey items provide valid food security classifications for adults and children in the Caribbean," BMC Public Health, 6, 26-33, February 2006.

22. DeWalt, K., D'Angelo, S., McFadden, M., Danner, F., Noland, M., and Kotchen, J., "The use of itemized register tapes for analysis of household food acquisition patterns prompted by children," J Am Diet Assoc, 90, 559-562, April 1990.

23. French, S., Shimotsu ,S., Wall, M., and Gerlach, A., "Capturing the spectrum of household food and beverage purchasing behavior: A review," Journal American Dietetic Association, 108, 2051-2058, December 2008.

24. IBM Corp. Released 2011. IBM SPSS Statistics for Windows, Version 20.0. Armonk, NY: IBM Corp.

25. Chaparro, M., Zaghloul, S., Holck, P., and Dobbs, J., "Food insecurity prevalence among college students at the University of Hawaii at Manoa," Public Health Nutrition, 12(11), 2097-2103, August 2009.

26. Morse, K. and Driskell, J., "Observed sex differences in fast-food consumption and nutrition self-assessments and beliefs of college students," Nutrition Research, 9, 173–179, March 2009.

27. Larson, N.I., Neumark-Sztainer, D., Laska, N.M., and Story, M., "Young adults and eating away from home: Associations with dietary intake patterns and weight status differ by choice of restaurant," Journal American Dietetic Association, 111(11), 1696-1703, November 2011.

28. Driskell, J.A., Kim, Y.N., and Goebel, K.J., "Few differences found in the typical eating and physical activity habits of lower-level and upper-level university students," Journal American Dietetic Association, 105(5), 798-801, May 2005.

29. Walker, R.E., and Kawachi, I., "Use of concept mapping to explore the influence of food security on food buying practices," Journal of the Academy of Nutrition and Dietetics, 112(5), 711-717, April 2012.

30. Nestle, M. Food Politics: How the food industry influences nutrition and health. University of California Press, Berkeley, CA, 2002.

31. Larson, N.I., Story, M., Eisenberg, M.E., and Neumark-Sztainer, D., "Food preparation and purchasing roles among adolescents: Associations with sociodemographic characteristics and diet quality," Journal American Dietetic Association, 106, 211-218, February 2006.

14

BELLAGIO REPORT ON HEALTHY AGRICULTURE, HEALTHY NUTRITION, HEALTHY PEOPLE

Artemis P. Simopoulos [1,*], Peter G. Bourne [2] and Ole Faergeman[3]

[1]The Center for Genetics, Nutrition and Health, Washington, DC 20009, USA

[2]Green Templeton College, University of Oxford, Oxford OX2 6HG, UK

[3]Department of Internal Medicine and Cardiology, Aarhus Sygehus University Hospital Tage Hansens Gade 2, 8000 Aarhus C, Denmark

ABSTRACT

The Bellagio Report on Healthy Agriculture, Healthy Nutrition, Healthy People is the result of the meeting held at the Rockefeller Foundation Bellagio Center in Lake Como, Italy, 29 October–2 November 2012. The meeting was science-based but policy-oriented. The role and amount of healthy and unhealthy fats, with attention to the relative content of omega-3 and omega-6 fatty acids, sugar, and particularly fructose in foods that may underlie the epidemics of non-communicable diseases (NCD's) worldwide were extensively discussed. The report concludes that sugar consumption, especially in the form of high energy fructose in soft drinks, poses a major and insidious health threat, especially in children, and most diets, although with regional differences, are deficient in omega-3 fatty acids and too high in omega-6 fatty acids. Gene-nutrient interactions in growth and development and in disease prevention are fundamental to health, therefore regional Centers on Genetics, Nutrition and Fitness for Health should be established worldwide. Heads of state and government must elevate, as a matter of urgency, Nutrition as a national priority, that access to a healthy diet should be considered a human right and that the lead responsibility for Nutrition should be placed in Ministries of Health rather than agriculture so that the health requirements drive agricultural priorities, not *vice versa*. Nutritional security should be given the same priority as food security.

Keywords: omega-3 and omega-6 fatty acids; fructose; non-communicable diseases; nutrition security; nutrition policy; gene-nutrient interactions

1. INTRODUCTION

The meeting on *Healthy Agriculture, Healthy Nutrition, Healthy People* took place at the Rockefeller Foundation Bellagio Center in Italy, 30 October–1 November 2012. The meeting was sponsored by The Center for Genetics Nutrition and Health, The Rockefeller Foundation, Green Templeton College of the University of Oxford, W.K. Kellogg Foundation, Nutrilite Health Institute, Health Studies Collegium, Hellenic American University, and Hellenic American Union. The focus of the meeting was the Implementation of the Action Plan on Healthy Agriculture, Healthy Nutrition, Healthy People, which had been developed at the meeting on Healthy Agriculture, Healthy Nutrition, Healthy People, held at Ancient Olympia, Greece, 5–8 October 2010 [1,2].

The meeting in Bellagio was science-based but policy-oriented. There were 19 participants from 9 countries, including distinguished physicians, nutritionists, agriculturists, economists, policy experts, lawyers, representatives of industry and representatives from United States Agency for International Development (USAID), Pan American Health Organization (PAHO), and the W.K. Kellogg Foundation. This international constellation of expertise provided a superb opportunity for in depth discussions of the most current scientific evidence on sustainable agriculture and nutrition security for health.

The group's broad, overall concerns were with human health, particularly child health, with societal economics, and with planetary ecosystems. Our lifestyles—including where we live, our activity levels, economic well-being and exposure to stress—all affect human health. We are also embedded in larger systems of agriculture, food cultures and food supply chains that can increase as well as decrease our chances of becoming and remaining healthy. At the same time that some children starve, others (sometimes in the same societies) are prone to obesity and other chronic diseases that stem from poor nutritional content of foods.

While many substances in the diet may affect health, the meeting focused primarily on those elements where the scientific evidence shows the link to be strongest and where the impact on the epidemic of non-communicable diseases (NCDs) worldwide is greatest.

2. GOALS

1. To develop strategies that would translate the current state of scientific knowledge on nutrition into specific interventions that will result in people eating healthier diets.

2. Agronomic, nutritional and medical sciences should not be subservient to business interests.

3. THE MEETING FOCUSED ON THE FOLLOWING ISSUES

1. Health-oriented agriculture is needed to tailor the food chain to eradicate critical deficiencies and imbalances (e.g., change animal feeds to balance the omega-6/omega-3 fatty acid ratio, decrease the excessive production of high fructose corn syrup (HFCS) [3,4,5,6].

2. Agronomic, nutritional and medical sciences should be independent of business interests.

3. Need for new forms of agriculture such as agroecology and urban agriculture.

4. Future dietary guidelines to be based on ecological (including climatological) as well as nutritional science.

5. Nutrition research should be the basis of food sciences research and not the reverse as it is now.

4. NOVEL ASPECTS OF THE MEETING

Over the past 10 years there have been many reports on diet and chronic diseases, obesity, global health, and non-communicable diseases (NCD's) issued by WHO-FAO, national governments, scientific institutions, medical associations and foundations. However, the novelty of this meeting was the emphasis on:

1. The vital role of political leadership in translating the current well-documented level of scientific knowledge into national and international policies that will change the composition of the food people consume.

2. The importance of specific nutrients such as the balance of omega-6 and omega-3 fatty acids in the diet and the excessive production and consumption of fructose and its detrimental effects on growth and development of children and the development of chronic diseases [7].

3. The importance of developing national food composition tables. To date, only a few countries have these data, and as a result FAO and WHO depend on data per capita consumption of major food groups for policy making [8].

4. The differences and similarities between more affluent countries and developing countries, and what needs to be done going forward that is practical, feasible, and sustainable.

5. The economic and political contexts in which meaningful actions affecting population nutrition must occur.

6. The role of genetics. Gene expression patterns and their frequencies differ geographically between populations and within populations, but the effect of genetic variants on disease is modified by environmental factors including diet. For example, the dietary intake of vegetable oils high in omega-6 fatty acids increases the risk for cardiovascular disease as a function of genetic variation in European populations and perhaps even more so in populations of African ancestry with genetic variants affecting rates of metabolism of omega-6 fatty acids due to their higher frequency [9,10]. Gene/diet interactions should be considered in all studies relating diet to health and diseases such as diabetes, obesity, cardiovascular disease and African sleeping sickness. Recently the NIH and Wellcome Trust have joined

forces to fund large-scale population studies by African researchers on African populations.

5. MEETING CONTENT

One of the important issues included in all the presentations, given over three days, was the obstacles governments face in implementing policies that would lead to optimal scientifically based diets for their populations. The sources of opposition to those policies were also discussed. Participants were asked to consider the complexities for government adoption of policy, including regional considerations, leadership issues (academic institutions, medical school education, industry, including agribusiness); management; economic issues (which was discussed in detail by Dr. Ole Faergeman of Denmark); and nutritional determinants of health. Specific attention was also given to commercial considerations with attention to developing policies without unnecessary negative impact on the food industry. However, it was agreed government must not be influenced by industry to pursue policies contrary to the health and nutrition needs of its people.

6. LOCAL INITIATIVES TO ENLIGHTEN INDUSTRY

Two countries have initiated nutritional programs with demonstrable benefit on the nutrition and health of their peoples. In both instances a pre-condition for success was a high level of political commitment to assuring a strong food supply with optimal nutritional content. Dr. Dan L. Waitzberg (Brazil) gave a presentation of how Brazilian government policy, under presidential direction, has resulted in the "right to nutrition and food" for all of its citizens, and how this new policy has had an impact on the health of the Brazilian people [11]. Similarly, Dr. Kraisid Tontisirin (Thailand) provided an exciting presentation on how the nutrition, agriculture and health departments of the Thai government have worked together to develop nutritional policies based on consideration of all three disciplines [12].

7. ROLE OF SPECIFIC FOOD GROUPS

One of the more hotly discussed topics was on the role of the nutritional content of foods. This included a discussion of the role of healthy and unhealthy fats, with attention to the relative content of omega-3 and omega-6 fatty acids in food by Dr. Artemis P. Simopoulos (USA) [13,14,15,16,17]. In addition, Dr. Richard J. Johnson (USA) reviewed the evidence that the worldwide increase in added sugars containing fructose may underlie the epidemics of obesity and diabetes [7,18,19,20].

8. CONCLUSIONS

8.1. General Conclusions

1. Good health requires food of good quality. Access to optimal nutrition and health are fundamental human rights. They apply to us all, rich and poor, young and old.

2. Malnutrition remains common. One in seven humans is malnourished because of poverty. The poor live in poor countries, but they also live in rich countries with major inequalities in wealth. The poor have little choice about what is available for them to eat. In contrast, the affluent suffer from overnutrition having a wide selection of foods with both poor and good nutritional content, but inadequate knowledge or government guidance to avoid a diet that impacts adversely on their health.

3. Malnutrition is a societal issue, and it is a gigantic one. The last 30 years have seen a dramatic growth of economic and geopolitical powerof emerging markets—Brazil, China, India, Indonesia, Mexico, Russia, South Africa—and the magnitude of the nutrition and health issues facing those countries will soon exceedthat in wealthycountries. The issues include simultaneously both the continuously growing chronic non-communicable diseases of the affluent, and the infectious diseases of the poor. The dietary choices made by the affluent in these countries will have a steadily increasing negative impact on the health of their populations. There is an opportunity to prevent this.

4. Malnutrition is also a function of what food we choose to produce, how we produce it, and whether and how we make it available to us all. Farmers, industrial agriculture and food processing and distribution profoundly affect ecosystems and climate, moreover, and they are major actors in our economic

and financial systems. These players also directly determine the quality of the dietary options available.

5. Good nutrition and malnutrition are understood by scientists, and they should have a key role in the adoption of good nutrition, ecology and agronomy policies by governments.

6. Governments are influenced to varying degrees by corporate interests. The task of government leaders is to work out policies for food and nutrition with appropriate respect to culture and agricultural tradition as well as the food industry.

7. Adding to the difficulties of formulating policy, the ivory tower of unadulterated university research no longer exists. The food industry including agriculture also performs research, it contributes to and influences research performed in universities, and it understandably exploits the results of research in choosing what to produce and bring to market. All of these various complexities continue to affect if not determine debates about nutrition and human health.

8. Chronic non-communicable diseases such as atherosclerosis, type 2 diabetes, obesity, respiratory diseases, and certain cancers are common in rich countries and on the increase in countries on the way to affluence. All of these conditions are more or less determined by what we eat, and the debates about what to eat to avoid disease are almost countless. Some of them are nevertheless scientifically well informed by studies at many different levels of nutrition understanding.

9. Well performed epidemiological studies have documented effects of micronutrients on health. Vitamin D is an example. Still other studies have been performed on the level of the three major sources of food energy: *carbohydrates, fats and proteins*. The following discussion is an attempt to exemplify aspects of this particular branch of nutrition research that are relevant for policy.

10. Advancing science has provided convincing evidence that providing food solely based on calorie content is not enough to provide good health and nutrition. Rather, the choice of carbohydrates, fats, and proteins affect risk of disease. Even obesity is not a simple function of caloric intake. Increasing evidence, for example, suggests that large amounts of a sugar such as fructose in processed foods and beverages may increase the risk for developing diabetes and liver disease.

The adverse effects of excessive sugar consumption had been known for more than fifty years but we have failed to intervene appropriately.

8.2. Specific Conclusions

8.2.1. Fructose from Added Sugars

1. Fructose is a monosaccharide found in honey, ripened fruits and vegetables. Table sugar is sucrose, a disaccharide composed of fructose chemically coupled to glucose, another monosaccharide. Sources of fructose are sugar cane, sugar beets and corn. It is an effective and low-cost sweetener, and it is therefore extensively used in food and beverages (high-fructose corn syrup, HFCS). It does have a dependence producing effect making it hard for people to reduce or eliminate it from their diet [21,22,23].

2. Intake of sugar and sweeteners containing fructose has increased markedly in many countries throughout the world. The U.S. National Health and Nutrition Examination Survey (NHANES), for example, reported that about 15% of Americans consume greater than 25% of their energy from added sugars. Annual intake of added sugars in the United States is approximately 35 kg/capita or about one sixth of food energy.

3. There is increasing evidence from experimental and clinical studies that intake of added sugars not only increases the well-known risk of caries, but also risk of cardiovascular disease, non-alcoholic fatty liver disease, obesity, diabetes, and possibly even cancer. While some authorities, primarily those funded by the food industry, have argued that the high amounts of added sugars in food and beverages may contribute to health risks solely as a consequence of their caloric content, there is also mounting evidence that fructose may have a specific ability to cause fatty liver (which can progress to cirrhosis of the liver), high triglycerides in blood (which can contribute to cardiovascular disease), insulin resistance (leading to type 2 diabetes) and increased appetite (which obviously can lead to obesity) [5,6]. Obesity itself promotes cardiovascular disease, type 2 diabetes and certain cancers, moreover. Immoderate intake of added sugars,

fructose in particular, may therefore increase health risks with important public health implications.

8.2.2. Fatty Acids

1. Studies performed since the middle of the 20th century indicated that saturated fat increased, and polyunsaturated fat lowered, the risk of disease, cardiovascular disease in particular. That understanding encouraged farmers and the food industry to increase production of vegetable oils rich in polyunsaturated fats from soy, sunflower and, particularly in the United States, corn (maize).

2. Fat in food is mainly fatty acids chemically coupled to glycerol. Fatty acids can be saturated with hydrogen. If not, they are more or less unsaturated. The polyunsaturated fatty acids contribute importantly to average diets, but the balance of two kinds of polyunsaturated fatty acids in modern diets is quite different from that in diets during human evolution [3,16]. Whereas the latter contained about one omega-3 fatty acid for every four omega-6 fatty acids, modern diets can contain as much as fifty to a hundred times more omega-6 than omega-3 polyunsaturated fatty acids. The evidence that this imbalance contributes to disease is now convincing, and governments should formulate policies for agriculture and food to affect costs and availability of various fatty acids to the general public so that the ratio of omega-6 to omega-3 fatty acids can once again approach that to which we are genetically adapted, *i.e.* four to one [4,24]. High omega-6/omega-3 ratios typify Western diets and, increasingly, diets throughout the world, and they are associated with increased risk for cardiovascular disease, obesity, type 2 diabetes and cancer of the breast and prostate, particularly in individuals who are genetically predisposed. Of concern, animal experiments indicate that low intakes of docosahexanoic acid, an omega-3 fatty acid, in combination with a high intake of fructose, leads to metabolic syndrome in the brain [25].

8.2.3. All Calories Are Not the Same

1. We use the apparent self-contradiction, "a calorie is not a calorie", to emphasize that different nutrients with the same amount of food energy (calories) can differ in their effects on body weight. Fructose, for example, increases appetite more effectively than glucose [6,26]. One calorie of fructose is

therefore more obesogenic than one calorie of glucose. Similarly, omega-6 fatty acids may be more obesogenic than omega-3 fatty acids. Weight loss regimens must therefore take nutritional as well as overall caloric concerns into account [27,28].

2. The metabolic effects of whole food calories also differ from those of processed and restructured foods [29].

8.2.4. Nutrition Is Part of a Larger Picture

1. We acknowledge the monetary importance of agriculture and food production, but we also acknowledge the importance of agriculture for societal fabric and the impact of agriculture on the ecosystems on which we depend. World-wide increased agricultural production is ascribed to the further industrialization of agriculture since the mid 20th century ("Green Revolution"), but industrial agriculture is also an important reason that mankind has now passed several planetary boundaries for sustainability.

2. They include disruption of the nitrogen cycle, loss of biodiversity, and global warming. Demand for chemical fertilizers is also rapidly depleting known deposits of phosphorus, and profligate use of phosphorus, nitrogen and pesticides is an important cause of destruction of ecosystems including those in soil. Others compromising soil health are erosion by wind and water, compaction by heavy machinery, and pollution by effluents from intensive production of livestock.

3. The allocation of farm land to raising biofuels and feed for animals rather than food for humans increases demand for and transnational purchases of farm land in poor countries by rich countries. Such allocation also increases the price of food. Food prices have fluctuated, moreover, because of the speculation in agricultural commodities made possible by deregulation of financial markets. Most of these complexities affect nutrition detrimentally, and they all make life more difficult and precarious for the poor.

8.2.5. The Brazilian Model

1. Brazil is a good example of how presidential leadership can mobilize all aspects of government, national agriculture and public health to achieve better health through dramatically

improved nutrition. President Luiz Ignacio Lula da Silva publicly announced the very high priority he attached to ending hunger and reducing poverty in the country. This set in motion changes throughout the society that enhanced the availability and nutritional quality of food. The government provided leadership in supporting local food production. Legislation required that 30% of meals served at schools must come from local markets, thus supporting local farmers and providing fresh and nutritious foods consistent with the culture of the various local communities.

2. Brazil has sought original ways to eliminate hunger and poverty, obliging the state to implement public policies that guarantee fundamental human rights to minimum income, food, health, education and work.

3. Some of the key lessons learned include: (i) the importance of participatory pacts related to concepts and principles; (ii) the appropriateness of the choice of a systemic and intersectoral approach; (iii) the relevant role of civil society ensured through formal spaces of social dialogue (CONSEAs); (iv) the importance of the state in the protection of human rights above market interests; (v) the necessary practice of intersectoral coordination in the design and management of public policies on food and nutrition security; (vi) the strategic role of women in the struggle to guarantee food sovereignty as well as the conservation and sustainable management of natural resources; and (vii) the respect for and guarantee of ethno-development principles in the design and implementation of public policies for indigenous peoples, blacks, traditional peoples and communities.

4. The continuity of the main public policies that have contributed to this progress and the convergence of political and social forces are indispensable conditions to overcoming the challenges that still hinder the elimination of all forms of social inequality and violation of rights.

5. Brazil provides a model that other countries can emulate.

8.2.6. The Thai Model

1. Thailand, an emerging economy with a distinctive heritage of a unique cultural cuisine, is today one of the leaders in the progressive management of food production, marketing, nutrition and human health. Under the nation's *Strategic*

Framework for Food Management, nutrition policy is formulated in a way that goes well beyond the office of any one department or ministry of government. As in Brazil Thailand has shown high level government commitment to food and nutrition policy. Ministers and secretaries of health, food, agriculture, urban and rural planning, commerce, foreign aid, and finance all have responsibilities and rights to guide policy agendas with implications for food. Food policy has therefore been elevated to the highest levels, and the head of government serves as chairperson of the strategic planning group. Perhaps even more progressive is the assumption that the highest levels of government are there to support self-directed community-based leaders in fulfilling locally defined objectives for food production, health promotion and environmental stewardship.

9. RECOMMENDATIONS

1. Heads of state and government must elevate, as a matter of urgency, nutrition as a national priority (e.g., Brazil and Thailand).

2. Good nutrition is a human right, but it is impossible to achieve for whole populations without good policies for food, health, nutrition, agriculture, ecology, economy and commerce. It is therefore the responsibility of heads of state and government to provide the leadership that will lead to an "all society" approach for good nutrition.

3. Advance public understanding of the following key aspects of nutrition:

(1) With the increasing decline in infectious diseases most experts believe that poor nutrition is now the single most important obstacle to better health worldwide.

(2) Under-nutrition and malnutrition primarily affect the developing world where people with no choice have inadequate intake of calories and micronutrients. It differs from the problem in industrialized nations where many people knowingly and unknowingly choose a diet with a composition that leads to serious chronic disease and premature death.

(3) Emerging market countries such as Brazil, China, India and Russia simultaneously face the nutritional problems of both developed and developing countries.

(4) Sugar consumption, especially in the form of high energy fructose in soft drinks, poses a major and insidious health threat, especially to children. The health threat is comparable to that from cigarette smoking.

(a) Most diets, although with regional differences, are deficient in omega-3 fatty acids and too high in omega-6 fatty acids.

(b) Access to a healthy diet should be considered a human right.

1. Place the lead responsibility for nutrition in ministries of health rather than agriculture so that the health requirements drive agricultural priorities not vice versa. Nutritional security should be given the same priority as food security.

2. The American Heart Association warnings on the "overconsumption" of added sugar should be strongly promoted (no more than 6 teaspoons for an adult woman and 9 teaspoons for adult men daily) [30]. As an example, this would limit the average woman to one 8-oz sugar-sweetened beverage per day or its equivalent. Health warnings on all sugar-sweetened beverages should be considered.

3. A concerted effort is needed to decrease the ratio of omega-6 to omega-3 fatty acids in the diet. Education and if necessary government intervention should be used to get populations to switch from oils high in omega-6 such as corn, safflower, and sunflower oils, to those high in omega-3 such as rapeseed, flax seed and oils high in monounsaturated fatty acids such as olive oil, hazelnut oil in combination with rapeseed oil. Increased fish consumption should be stressed. Scientists should collaborate with the fishing industry to achieve this end. A ratio of 4:1 of omega-6 to omega-3 in the diet should be the goal.

4. Governments through their agricultural policies, taxation, subsidies, pricing and controls at the point of distribution should support the availability of foods rich in healthful components. They should also strongly consider penalizing those who put on the market products that are harmful to health. In so doing governments should place a higher emphasis on the health of the population over market

interests. They should also foster and support cultivation at the local level including urban agriculture. The production of vegetables and fruits high in anti-oxidants should be stressed.

5. In view of the limited knowledge most physicians and other health providers have concerning nutrition, a major initiative should be launched to incorporate nutrition into curricula stressing its crucial role in the epidemic of non-communicable diseases. A similar initiative should be launched with those already practicing.

6. Food consumption patterns vary around the globe as a result of food availability, cultural determinants, and economic circumstances. A series of Research Centers on Genetics, Nutrition and Fitness for Health should be established in different regions, along with educational components for professionals and the public. They would collect and analyze food consumption data focusing particularly on the chemical content of the food consumed in their regions.

7. The Center for Genetics Nutrition and Health representing the Bellagio group will work to implement the conclusions reached at the meeting of 29 October–2 November 2012. This will include:

(1) Distributing copies of the Bellagio Report to a wide diversity of academic and non-academic outlets.

(2) Consulting and collaborating with other groups concerned with mal-nutrition and under-nutrition, food security, access to a nutritionally adequate diet for the economically deprived, and particularly the health and nutrition of children.

(3) Working with leaders of national governments, both executive and legislative, and international organizations such as FAO, WHO and its regional organizations, especially PAHO, the World Bank and other agencies of the UN to achieve the incorporation of the recommendations above into their policies and programs.

(4) Establishing a coalition with the WHO Commissions on Non-Communicable Disease and the Social Determinants of Health to insure that the essentiality of nutrition for normal growth and development and in combating chronic non-communicable diseases is always considered in their deliberations.

ACKNOWLEDGMENTS

The Bellagio Report was approved by the Participants of the Bellagio Meeting on "Healthy Agriculture, Healthy Nutrition, Healthy People": Conference Chairs: Artemis P. Simopoulos, Peter G. Bourne, Ole Faergeman; Honorary Co-Chairs: Dan Glickman, Philip R. Lee; Participants: Jon Andrus, Gail C. Christopher, Sarath Gopalan, Russell Jaffe, Richard J. Johnson, Leonidas Koskos, Philippe Legrand, Duo Li, Ascensión Marcos, Anne M. Peniston, Sam Rehnborg, Laura A. Schmidt, Ian Scott, Kraisid Tontisirin, Dan L. Waitzberg.

REFERENCES

1. Simopoulos, A.P. Healthy Agriculture, Healthy Nutrition, Healthy People; World Review of Nutrition and Dietetics Volume 102; Karger: Basel, Switzerland, 2011.

2. Simopoulos, A.P.; Faergeman, O.; Bourne, P.G. Action Plan for a Healthy Agriculture, Healthy Nutrition, Healthy People. J. Nutrigenet. Nutrigenomics 2011, 4, 65–82.

3. Simopoulos, A.P. The importance of the omega-6/omega-3 Fatty Acid ratio in cardiovascular disease and other chronic diseases. Exp. Biol. Med. (Maywood) 2008, 233, 674–688.

4. Simopoulos, A.P. Omega-6/Omega-3 Essential Fatty Acids: Biological Effects. In Omega-3 Fatty Acids, the Brain and Retina; World Review of Nutrition and Dietetics Volume 99; Simopoulos, A.P., Bazan, N.G., Eds.; Karger: Basel, Switzerland, 2009; pp. 1–16.

5. Stanhope, K.L.; Schwarz, J.M.; Keim, N.L.; Griffen, S.C.; Bremer, A.A.; Graham, J.L.; Hatcher, B.; Cox, C.L.; Dyachenko, A.; Zhang, W.; et al. Consuming fructose-sweetened, not glucose-sweetened, beverages increases visceral adiposity and lipids and decreases insulin sensitivity in overweight/obese humans. J. Clin. Invest. 2009, 119, 1322–1334.

6. Stanhope, K.L.; Bremer, A.A.; Medici, V.; Nakajima, K.; Ito, Y.; Nakano, T.; Chen, G.; Fong, T.H.; Lee, V.; Menorca, R.I.; Keim, N.L.; Havel, P.J. Consumption of fructose and high fructose corn syrup increase postprandial triglycerides, LDL-cholesterol, and apolipoprotein-B in young men and women.J. Clin. Endocrinol. Metab. 2011, 96, E1596–E1605.

7. Te Morenga, L.; Mallard, S.; Mann, J. Dietary sugars and body weight: Systematic review and meta-analyses of randomised controlled trials and cohort studies. BMJ 2012, 346, e7492.

8. Simopoulos, A.P.; Butrum, R.R. International Food Data Bases and Information Exchange: Concepts, Principles and Designs; World Review of Nutrition and Dietetics Volume 68; Karger: Basel, Switzerland, 1992.

9. Sergeant, S.; Hugenschmidt, C.E.; Rudock, M.E.; Ziegler, J.T.; Ivester, P.; Ainsworth, H.C.; Vaidya, D.; Case, L.D.; Langefeld, C.D.; Freedman, B.I.; Bowden, D.W.; Mathias, R.A.; Chilton, F.H. Differences in arachidonic acid levels and fatty acid desaturase (FADS) gene variants in African Americans and European Americans with diabetes or the metabolic syndrome. Br. J. Nutr. 2012, 107, 547–555.

10. Mathias, R.A.; Sergeant, S.; Ruczinski, I.; Torgerson, D.G.; Hugenschmidt, C.E.; Kubala, M.; Vaidya, D.; Suktitipat, B.; Ziegler, J.T.; Ivester, P.; et al. The impact of FADS genetic variants on ω6 polyunsaturated fatty acid metabolism in African Americans. BMC Genet. 2011, 12, 50.

11. Leao, M.; Maluf, R.S. Effective Public Policies and Active Citizenship: Brazil's Experience of Building a Food and Nutrition Security System; Ação Brasileira pela Nutrição e Direitos Humanos (ABRANDH): Brasília, Brazil, 2012; p. 73.

12. The Thailand Food Committee. Strategic Framework for Food Management in Thailand. Available online: http://www.tnfc.in.th (accessed on 12 August 2012).

13. Daak, A.A.; Ghebremeskel, K.; Hassan, Z.; Attallah, B.; Azan, H.H.; Elbashir, M.I.; Crawford, M. Effect of omega-3 (n-3) fatty acid supplementation in patients with sickle cell anemia: Randomized, double-blind, placebo-controlled trial. Am. J. Clin. Nutr. 2013, 97, 37–44.

14. Skilton, M.R.; Mikkilä, V.; Würtz, P.; Ala-Korpela, M.; Sim, K.A.; Soininen, P.; Kangas, A.J.; Viikari, J.S.; Juonala, M.; Laitinen, T.; Lehtimäki, T.; Taittonen, L.; Kähönen, M.; Celermajer, D.S.; Raitakari, O.T. Fetal growth, omega-3 (n-3) fatty acids, and progression of subclinical atherosclerosis: preventing fetal origins of disease? The Cardiovascular Risk in Young Finns Study. Am. J. Clin Nutr. 2013, 97, 58–65.

15. Li, J.; Xun, P.; Zamora, D.; Sood, A.; Liu, K.; Daviglus, M.; Iribarren, C.; Jacobs, D., Jr.; Shikany, J.M.; He, K. Intakes of long-chain omega-3 (n-3) PUFAs and fish in relation to incidence of asthma among American young adults: the CARDIA study. Am. J. Clin. Nutr. 2013, 97, 173–178.

16. Gibson, R.A.; Neumann, M.A.; Lien, E.L.; Boyd, K.A.; Tu, W.C. Docosahexaenoic acid synthesis from alpha-linolenic acid is inhibited by diets high in polyunsaturated fatty acids. Prostaglandins Leukot. Essent. Fatty Acids. 2013, 88, 139–146.

17. Ramsden, C.E.; Hibbeln, J.R.; Majchrzak, S.F.; Davis, J.M. n-6 fatty acid-specific and mixed polyunsaturate dietary interventions have different effects on CHD risk: a meta-analysis of randomised controlled trials. Br. J. Nutr. 2010, 104, 1586–1600.

18. Johnson, R.J.; Segal, M.S.; Sautin, Y.; Nakagawa, T.; Feig, D.I.; Kang, D.H.; Gersch, M.S.; Benner, S.; Sánchez-Lozada, L.G. Potential role of sugar (fructose) in the epidemic of hypertension, obesity and the metabolic syndrome, diabetes, kidney disease, and cardiovascular disease. Am. J. Clin. Nutr. 2007,86, 899–906.

19. Page, K.A.; Chan, O.; Arora, J.; Belfort-Deaguiar, R.; Dzuira, J.; Roehmholdt, B.; Cline, G.W.; Naik, S.; Sinha, R.; Constable, R.T.; Sherwin, R.S. Effects of fructose vs. glucose on regional cerebral blood flow in brain regions involved with appetite and reward pathways. JAMA 2013, 309, 63–70.

20. Purnell, J.Q.; Fair, D.A. Fructose ingestion and cerebral, metabolic, and satiety responses. JAMA 2013,309, 85–86.

21. Handbook of Food and Addiction; Brownell, K., Gold, M., Eds.; Oxford University Press: New York, NY, USA, 2012.

22. Green, S.M.; Blundell, J.E. Effect of fat- and sucrose-containing foods on the size of eating episodes and energy intake in lean dietary restrained and unrestrained females: potential for causing overconsumption. Eur. J. Clin. Nutr. 1996, 50, 625–635.

23. Green, S.M.; Burley, V.J.; Blundell, J.E. Effect of fat- and sucrose-containing foods on the size of eating episodes and energy intake in lean males: potential for causing overconsumption. Eur. J. Clin. Nutr.1994, 48, 547–555.

24. Simopoulos, A.P.; Cleland, L.G. Omega-6/Omega-3 Essential Fatty Acid Ratio: The Scientific Evidence; World Review of Nutrition and Dietetics Volume 92; Karger: Basel, Switzerland, 2003.

25. Agrawal, R.; Gomez-Pinilla, F. "Metabolic syndrome" in the brain: deficiency in omega-3 fatty acid exacerbates dysfunctions in insulin receptor signalling and cognition. J. Physiol. 2012, 590, 2485–2499.

26. Ishimoto, T.; Lanaspa, M.A.; Le, M.T.; Garcia, G.E.; Diggle, C.P.; Maclean, P.S.; Jackman, M.R.; Asipu, A.; Roncal-Jimenez, C.A.; Kosugi, T.; et al. Opposing effects of fructokinase C and A isoforms on fructose-induced metabolic syndrome in mice. Proc. Natl. Acad. Sci. USA 2012, 109, 4320–4325.

27. Moon, R.J.; Harvey, N.C.; Robinson, S.M.; Ntani, G.; Davies, J.H.; Inskip, H.M.; Godfrey, K.M.; Dennison, E.M.; Calder, P.C.; Cooper, C. The SWS Study Group. Maternal Plasma Polyunsaturated Fatty Acid Status in Late Pregnancy Is Associated with Offspring Body Composition in Childhood. J. Clin. Endocrinol. Metab. 2013, 98, 299–307.

28. Massiera, F.; Saint-Marc, P.; Seydoux, J.; Murata, T.; Kobayashi, T.; Narumiya, S.; Guesnet, P.; Amri, E.Z.; Negrel, R.; Ailhaud, G. Arachidonic acid and prostacyclin signaling promote adipose tissue development: a human health concern? J. Lipid Res. 2003, 44, 271–279.

29. Ludwig, D.S. The glycemic index: physiological mechanisms relating to obesity, diabetes, and cardiovascular disease. JAMA 2002, 287, 2414–2423.

30. Johnson, R.K.; Appel, L.J.; Brands, M.; Howard, B.V.; Lefevre, M.; Lustig, R.H.; Sacks, F.; Steffen, L.M.; Wylie-Rosett, J. American Heart Association Nutrition Committee of the Council on Nutrition, Physical Activity, and Metabolism and the Council on Epidemiology and Prevention. Dietary sugars intake and cardiovascular health: a scientific statement from the American Heart Association.Circulation 2009, 120, 1011–1020.

15

HIV/AIDS, UNDERNUTRITION, AND FOOD INSECURITY

Louise C. Ivers,[1,2,3] Kimberly A. Cullen,[2] Kenneth A. Freedberg,[3,4] Steven Block,[5,6] Jennifer Coates,[5] and Patrick Webb[5]

[1]Partners In Health, Boston, Massachusetts

[2]Brigham and Women's Hospital, Boston, Massachusetts

[3]Center for AIDS Research, Harvard Medical School, Boston, Massachusetts

[4]Massachusetts General Hospital, Boston, Massachusetts

[5]Friedman School of Nutrition Science and Policy, Boston, Massachusetts

[6]Fletcher School of Law and Diplomacy, Tufts University, Boston, Massachusetts

ABSTRACT

Despite tremendous advances in care for human immunodeficiency virus (HIV) infection and increased funding for treatment, morbidity and mortality due to HIV/AIDS in developing countries remains unacceptably high. A major contributing factor is that >800 million people remain chronically undernourished globally, and the HIV epidemic largely overlaps with populations already experiencing low diet quality and quantity. Here, we present an updated review of the relationship between HIV infection, nutritional deficiencies, and food insecurity and consider efforts to interrupt this cycle at a programmatic level. As HIV infection progresses, it causes a catabolic state and increased susceptibility to other infections, which are compounded by a lack of caloric and other nutrient intake, leading to progressive worsening of malnutrition. Despite calls from national and international organizations to integrate HIV and nutritional programs, data are lacking on how such programs can be effectively implemented in resource-poor settings, on the optimum content and duration of nutritional support, and on ideal target recipients.

Morbidity and mortality related to human immunodeficiency virus (HIV) infection in the developing world remain unacceptably high, despite major advances in HIV therapy and increased international funding for care [1,2]. People living with HIV infection (themselves or among family members) face not just sickness but also impaired productivity, declining income, and increasingly difficult choices among essential but competing expenses, such as food versus health care or schooling versus rent [3]. The physiological complications of progression of HIV infection are compounded by the problems associated with poverty, because it translates into insufficient consumption of a diet of adequate quality and quantity to bolster immune function and support medical therapy. Recently, several international agencies emphasized that targeted nutritional interventions should be systematically linked to antiretroviral interventions [4-11]. The World Bank has called for a scaling up of action on nutrition and AIDS through "action research" and "learning by doing" [10, p 12]. A recent review of approaches to nutrition in HIV programs in Africa concluded that current HIV/AIDS policies "have tended toward highly medicalized approaches" and called for "a comprehensive approach to link health strategies with community-oriented food-based strategies" [12, p 2–3]. Despite this, few data exist to help guide the development of effective programs that integrate HIV care and nutrition.

Food insecurity (defined as a persistent lack of access to adequate food in needed quantity and quality), undernutrition (including deficiencies in micronutrients as well as macronutrients), and HIV/AIDS overlap and have additive effects [4]. More than 800 million people worldwide are chronically undernourished, and >33 million are living with HIV infection [1, 2, 13]. Combating undernutrition and HIV/AIDS are 2 of the 8 United Nations Millennium Development Goals to be achieved by 2015—international targets that form a blueprint for galvanizing priorities for the world's poor. The complex interaction between HIV infection and nutrition seriously threatens the achievement of these goals.

HIV Care in Developing Countries

Advances in the treatment of HIV infection during the last 20 years have resulted in antiretroviral therapy (ART) combinations that can result in reduced HIV RNA level and improved immunologic function, leading to dramatic improvements in health, reductions in morbidity, and prolonged life [14-17]. Increased funding has become available for HIV treatment in the developing world, and the vast majority of such programs have demonstrated excellent clinical outcomes [18, 19]. Despite this, optimism is tempered by the fact that HIV infection remains a major cause of morbidity and mortality [20] when at the same time malnutrition remains the main cause of child mortality across the developing world [12]. The largest burden of HIV disease still exists in low- and middle-income countries, where >2 million deaths due to AIDS occurred in 2007 alone and just 31% of patients requiring ART have access to treatment [1]. Early mortality while receiving ART is a common feature in many programs, with individuals presenting for care with very advanced disease and multiple comorbid conditions [18, 21]. Comorbidities such as tuberculosis, undernutrition, diarrheal disease, and malaria are highly prevalent in these areas, and all have a negative interaction with HIV infection [22, 23].

Barriers to effective HIV care in the developing world are many, including a lack of trained health care professionals, a lack of infrastructure, and a lack of resources devoted to health [24]. The financial cost of care to individuals also has an important effect on HIV care in resource-constrained environments—paying for care has been associated with both worse outcomes and worse adherence to therapy [25-28]. Both households and governments face competing choices for their expenditures: food (often accounting for as much as 75% of total household spending), health care, and education are frequent competitors [3]. In this context, the complex interaction between HIV infection, undernutrition, and food insecurity can be a critical barrier to effective HIV care, and the development of evidence-based programmatic solutions to these issues becomes essential.

Undernutrition and HIV feedback

Undernutrition and HIV status have negative feedback loops, resulting in severe effects on the resilience of individuals, households, and communities. Such interactions manifest at both the level of the HIV-infected individual and the level of the affected household in terms of clinical, nutritional, quality-of-life, and economic outcomes.

At the individual level, a lack of access to appropriate food and the direct effect that HIV has on impaired metabolic functions in absorption, storage, and utilization of nutrients can translate into compromised immunity, nutrient deficiencies, and increased vulnerability to infectious diseases [29, 30]. Lack of sufficient food intake and/or malabsorption leads to weight loss, which further exacerbates the catabolic nature of HIV infection [31, 32]. Weight loss is itself a significant, independent risk factor for AIDS-related mortality, and HIV-associated wasting often persists even with use of ART [33, 34].

HIV infection reduces the efficiency of nutrient absorption and utilization partly because of frequent diarrhea due to compromised immunity [35-37]. Malabsorption of fats and carbohydrates is common, with the former adversely affecting the absorption and utilization of fat-soluble vitamins, compromising immunity and worsening nutrient deficiencies [38]. Infections and nutritional deficiencies cause an increase in levels of prooxidants that results in oxidative stress, which may indirectly accelerate HIV replication [38]. Metabolic changes, including changes in insulin and glucagon levels, result from both reduced food intake and the immune response to infection and may lead to muscle wasting [37]. Because HIV infection increases resting energy expenditure as a function of HIV load, people living with HIV infection have higher protein requirements than do their noninfected counterparts [35, 37-40], and HIV-infected children experiencing weight loss have energy requirements 50%-100% above normal [40]. ART itself increases resting energy expenditure independently of viral load, further contributing to HIV-associated weight loss [33, 39]. As HIV infection progresses, it can cause a catabolic state that is compounded by a lack of caloric intake, increasing the severity of preexisting undernutrition [30, 32, 41]. In children, advanced HIV infection often presents with clinical features that are indistinguishable from severe undernutrition [42]. These facts further highlight the particular need to ensure adequate caloric and multivitamin intake in adults and children living with HIV infection.

Of critical importance is the growing recognition that individuals receiving ART face serious adverse effects, resulting in lack of adherence when faced with a lack of food in the household [43-45]. Undernutrition increases the probability of developing hepatic toxicity to nevirapine [46]. Food facilitates the absorption and effectiveness of drugs, and increased appetite is an intended and desirable effect of drug therapy—one that is needed to reverse loss of body mass and to promote recuperation and enhanced immune function [47, 48].

At the household level, a lack of food can lead to the adoption of risky coping strategies, such as sale of assets, redirection of (wage) labor, or exchange of sex for money or food, all of which increase exposure to HIV and increase economic vulnerability [49-51]. Reduced food intake in the HIV-affected household can also result from loss of income and food-production capacity in the family due to labor loss, psychosocial factors, or adverse effects of medication (such as dizziness and nausea) [36, 37,52]. ART is difficult to take on an empty stomach, travel to a health facility may become impossible because of weakness and lethargy, time in the fields or at work cannot be spared for medical visits, and migration in search of work affects continuity of care [53, 54]. In other cases, assets are sold to pay for medical care or children are removed from school because of a lack of funds or the need for additional labor, leading families into worsening cycles of poverty [55, 56]. A lack of access to food drives families into social crisis, migration, and displacement, which subsequently puts them at increased risk of HIV infection and its consequences [53, 57]. Rural communities with a high prevalence of HIV infection may face aggregate reductions in the local food supply and increased labor costs [58]. The result of these interactions is a series of ripple effects extending far beyond the infected individual to the household and societal levels [59]. The overall loss of productivity contributes significantly to hunger and poverty for families and communities. The total economic loss from HIV/AIDS worldwide is estimated at US $25 billion per year and rising [60].

In other words, HIV/AIDS substantially complicates the already multidimensional problem of global undernutrition, and undernutrition in turn complicates the global fight against the HIV epidemic [36, 55].

Interventions to Interrupt the Cycle

Targeted food and nutritional assistance to individuals with HIV infection and their families has the potential to improve nutrition [10, 61] and may decrease susceptibility to HIV infection [36, 49, 61, 62]. Targeted food rations, for example, may allow infected individuals to improve adherence to therapy while preserving assets by not having to sell possessions to purchase food [61]. In the United States, nutritional interventions to prevent weight loss and wasting in HIV-infected patients have often focused on counseling and nutrient supplements rather than food rations to increase energy and protein intake [47, 63]. Many have been shown to be very successful [47, 64]. Interventions that seek to enhance the knowledge and behaviors of mothers with respect to nutrition have been recognized for decades as being valuable for child nutrition [65, 66]. Although techniques and message content vary widely across programs, communicating specific information on nutrition is consistently associated with a positive outcome [67]. Targeted food interventions may also enable increased labor supply and the productivity of that labor, the benefits of which might include increased home production of food and increased wage earning, both of which contribute to household food security. In other words, food and other nutritional assistance programs have the potential to improve the course of HIV disease in developing countries, where undernutrition and food insecurity are major coexisting factors.

Clinical and Nutritional Effects of Food Assistance in HIV Care

Despite the current understanding of the complex interaction between HIV infection, food intake, and low income, the quantitative clinical benefits of providing food assistance to individuals with HIV infection, the appropriate enrollment criteria for targeted food programs, the appropriate duration of food assistance, and the effects of such programs on household members remain largely undocumented [68-70]. A recent Cochrane systematic review reported that, on the basis of the current evidence, no conclusions could be drawn regarding the effect that macronutrient supplementation has on morbidity and mortality in people with HIV infection [71]. A pilot study of food ration supplementation in Zambia suggested that food assistance is associated with better adherence to ART; however, no significant effect was observed for weight gain or CD4 cell count. This may in part be attributable to a small sample size; the authors called for a large randomized study to demonstrate the clinical outcomes of food supplementation [72]. Prevention of any adverse effects of food assistance is also important. Although data on the incidence of refeeding syndrome among those with severe wasting due to HIV infection are lacking, these individuals may be at risk for potentially fatal shifts in fluid and electrolyte balance during rapid refeeding [73, 74]. In addition to the direct health benefits of food assistance for the individual, attention must also be paid to the effects that interventions have on households, such as labor productivity and broader measures of household welfare. Understanding these effects will be critical to the development of effective and sustainable food programs [75, 76].

A detailed discussion of interventions other than assistance in the form of food rations is beyond the scope of this review. However, the role played by such potentially complementary interventions as agricultural interventions, socioeconomic assistance, accompaniment, education, and training [59, 77-79] are of the utmost importance and need to receive critical consideration to improve the livelihoods of people living with HIV infection and food insecurity.

Ideal Beneficiaries of Food Assistance

Efficient targeting of food assistance is critical to the management of scarce resources, but few data exist to guide programs as to which individuals or households to target in locations where there is both high food insecurity and a high prevalence of HIV infection. Programs are often targeted to individuals receiving ART, but it is highly plausible that food assistance would benefit those not yet requiring ART, potentially preventing the progression of HIV disease and delaying the need for ART. It is not clear how food or other nutritional support (whether supplements or nutritional education) is shared *within* families. Households are not unitary decision-making bodies; food is shared and allocated differently within different types of households depending on demographic composition, who within the household is sick or has died, social standing, socioeconomic status, and other factors [80]. Understanding the differing bases for sharing food is critical to improving the targeting of therapeutic food versus food intended for general household consumption [81-83].

Optimal Components of Food Assistance

Although agreement is growing that nutritional support is beneficial, the optimal form of such support remains unknown and largely unstudied [75]. A recent training manual developed in Ethiopia asserts that food-based approaches to increasing vitamin and mineral intake and optimizing immune function are "the most preferred strategy" and that foods should include local vegetables and fortified staple products [81, 84]. However, there is no international consensus on a universal HIV food ration, making it difficult to determine programmatically what any food basket should contain [81, 85]. Furthermore, food rations require resources, but few data exist on the cost-effectiveness of nutritional interventions in the context of HIV care in developing countries [86-88]. This may differ substantially from that of more-general studies of the returns of nutritional interventions [47, 89]. It is increasingly argued that more attention is needed on the importance of complementary community outreach in tandem with food—that is, seeking to empower caregivers or individuals by imparting tailored knowledge about causes and solutions to these conditions.

Recently, the use of ready-to-use therapeutic foods (RUTFs) has received growing attention in food support, with a particular focus on spreads that are semisolid variants of F100 therapeutic milk (a milk formulation used for the treatment of severe childhood malnutrition). The most widely used spread is a mixture of milk powder, sugar, vegetable oil, peanuts, vitamins, and minerals—an energy-dense product that resists bacterial contamination and requires no cooking [90, 91]. Providing a RUTF to HIV-infected individuals in addition to food rations to affected family members appears to have the potential to affect nutritional gains across the household. The RUTF provides a nutrient-dense supplement that can be targeted to the HIV-infected individual, with other foods in the basket serving to protect other family members from consumption inadequacy. That fortified blended foods and RUTFs have significant effects on morbidity and nutritional outcomes has been shown among refugees in Algeria [92, 93], Nepal [94], Bangladesh [95], and Zambia [96]. In Angola, the prevalence of anemia among children decreased from 48% to 24% over a period of 12 months, and vitamin A deficiency among adolescents was reduced from 47% to 20% [97]. RUTFs are also increasingly being used in HIV programs [98, 99].

Quantity of calories is important, but so is quality in terms of the nutrient components and mixes within food baskets. There is growing scientific consensus that food sufficiency is a critical component of the treatment of both malnutrition and malnutrition-mediated disease outcomes and that sufficiency requires close attention to diet quality, not merely quantity or adequacy. By further linking the clinical and nutritional effects of food interventions to determinants of household welfare, one could extend our understanding of the benefits of both to HIV-infected individuals and their household members.

There is considerable debate and uncertainty over the nutritional and health effects of generic food rations, which are used for many programmatic purposes around the world. Their role in preventing starvation in emergencies and in buffering household-level consumption among the very poor is clearly important; however, not only do these uses have different objectives than those of food-assistance programs for chronic diseases such as HIV/AIDS, but the nutritional effect of the so-called standard rations has been questioned [100, 101]. For example, recent research in Haiti demonstrated that one of the common "nutritionally enhanced" components of World Food Programme rations—a micronutrient-fortified corn-soya-blend—had little or no effect on childhood anemia unless additionally fortified with a powdered micronutrient mix added to the food at the time of serving [102]. Thus, the World Food Programme and other food-assistance agencies have argued strongly for a need for more insight into appropriate food formulations and nutritional packages that may achieve measurable nutrition and health outcomes in the context of HIV programs [76, 103].

Economists have long proposed the possibility that, in addition to the direct health benefits for individuals and their households, increased caloric intake and improved nutritional status may lead to higher wages and labor productivity (ie, the "efficiency wage hypothesis") [104]. Strong empirical support for this hypothesis has been established in countries as diverse as Sierra Leone [105] and India [106]. As the labor force in countries with a high prevalence of HIV infection becomes depleted by disease—with potentially devastating economic consequences [107]—understanding and measuring the productivity cost of HIV infection and how food supplementation may affect it is also critical in the design of public health responses.

CONCLUSIONS

HIV infection constitutes a global public health emergency and is most prevalent in areas of the world where undernutrition is also a serious concern. The concept of enhancing access to food among undernourished people, regardless of HIV status, is long-standing; however, critical questions remain as to the most effective ways to incorporate nutritional interventions into HIV programs. The differentiation between food and nutrition must be emphasized, as must the concept that quantity of food is not synonymous with nutritional value. This has been less of a focus because of the urgency of the situation and the understandable reflex to get whatever food is available to those who are hungry during emergencies. The negative interactive effects of undernutrition, inadequate food consumption, and HIV infection demand special focused efforts to ensure that effective cross-sectorial solutions are devised and implemented.

ACKNOWLEDGMENTS

Financial support. National Institute of Allergy and Infectious Diseases (grant K23 AI063998 to L.C.I. and grant K24 AI062476 to K.A.F.) and the Harvard Center for AIDS Research (grant P30 AI060354-02S1).

REFERENCES

1. Joint United Nations Programme on HIV/AIDS (UNAIDS). Report on the global AIDS epidemic. Geneva: UNAIDS and the World Health Organization, 2008.

2. Joint United Nations Programme on HIV/AIDS (UNAIDS). AIDS epidemic update. Geneva: UNAIDS and the World Health Organization, 2007.

3. Oldewage-Theron W, Dicks E, Napier C. Poverty, household food insecurity and nutrition: coping strategies in an informal settlement in the Vaal Triangle, South Africa. Public Health 2006; 120:795–804.

4. World Health Organization (WHO). Nutrition and HIV/AIDS. Geneva: WHO, 2005.

5. United Nations Administrative Committee on Coordination/Subcommittee on Nutrition (ACC/SCN). Nutrition and HIV/AIDS. Geneva: ACC/SCN, 2001.

6. United Nations Administrative Committee on Coordination/Subcommittee on Nutrition. Fifth report on the world nutrition situation: nutrition for improved development outcomes. Geneva: United Nations System Standing Committee on Nutrition, 2004.

7. United States Agency for International Development (USAID). USAID programs: HIV/AIDS and nutrition. USAID Issue Briefs, 2003. Available at: http://www.usaid.gov/our_work /global_health/aids/ TechAreas/nutrition/nutrfactsheet.html. Accessed 27 March 2008.

8. World Food Programme, World Health Organization, UNAIDS. Policy brief: HIV, food security and nutrition. Geneva: United Nations, 2008.

9. United Nations Millennium Development Goals report. Geneva: United Nations, 2006.

10. World Bank. Repositioning nutrition as central to development: a strategy for large-scale action. Washington, DC: World Bank, 2006.

11. World Health Organization (WHO). WHO Nutrition: Nurturing Health. Regional consultation on nutrition and HIV/AIDS in

French speaking countries in Africa region: evidence, lessons and recommendations for action. Geneva: WHO, 2008.

12. Panagides D, Graciano R, Atekyereza P, Gerberg L, Chopra M. Discussion paper 48: a review of nutrition and food security approaches in HIV and AIDS programmes in eastern and southern Africa. Regional Network for Equity in Health in East and Southern Africa, 2007.

13. The state of food insecurity in the world: 2006. Rome: Food and Agriculture Organization of the United Nations, 2006.

14. Palella FJ Jr, Delaney KM, Moorman AC, et al. Declining morbidity and mortality among patients with advanced human immunodefi- ciency virus infection. HIV Outpatient Study Investigators. N Engl J Med 1998; 338:853–60.

15. Hammer S, Squires K, Hughes M, et al. A controlled trial of two nucleoside analogues plus indinavir in persons with human immunodeficiency virus infection and CD4 cell counts of 200 per cubic millimeter or less. AIDS Clinical Trials Group 320 Study Team. N Engl J Med 1997; 337:725–33.

16. Gulick R, Ribaudo H, Shikuma C, et al. Triple-nucleoside regimens versus efavirenz-containing regimens for the initial treatment of HIV- 1 infection. N Engl J Med 2004; 350:1850–61.

17. Moore R, Keruly J, Gebo K, Lucas G. An improvement in virologic response to highly active antiretroviral therapy in clinical practice from 1996 through 2002. J Acquir Immune Defic Syndr 2005; 39: 195–8.

18. Ivers LC, Kendrick D, Doucette K. Efficacy of antiretroviral therapy programs in resource-poor settings: a meta-analysis of the published literature. Clin Infect Dis 2005; 41:217–24.

19. Coetzee D, Hildebrand K, Boulle A, et al. Outcomes after two years of providing antiretroviral treatment in Khayelitsha, South Africa. AIDS 2004; 18:887–95.

20. Joint United Nations Programme on HIV/AIDS (UNAIDS). 2006 Report on the global AIDS epidemic. Geneva: UNAIDS, 2006.

21. Braitstein P, Brinkhof M, Dabis F, et al. Mortality of HIV-1-infected patients in the first year of antiretroviral therapy: comparison between low-income and high-income countries. Lancet 2006; 367:817–24.

22. Niyongabo T, Henzel D, Ndayishimyie JM, et al. Nutritional status of adult inpatients in Bujumbura, Burundi (impact of HIV infection). Eur J Clin Nutr 1999; 53:579–82.

23. van Lettow M, Fawzi W, Semba R. Triple trouble: the role of malnutrition in tuberculosis and human immunodeficiency virus coinfection. Nutr Rev 2003; 61:81–90.

24. Furber AS, Hodgson IJ, Desclaux A, Mukasa DS. Barriers to better care for people with AIDS in developing countries. BMJ 2004; 329: 1281–3.

25. van Oosterhout J, Bodasin N, Kumwenda J, et al. Evaluation of antiretroviral therapy results in a resource-poor setting in Blantyre, Malawi. Trop Med Int Health 2005; 10:464–70.

26. Byakika-Tusiime J, Oyugi JH, Tumwikirize WA, Katabira ET, Mugyenyi PN, Bangsberg DR. Adherence to HIV antiretroviral therapy in HIV+ Ugandan patients purchasing therapy. Int J STD AIDS 2005; 16:38–41.

27. Weiser S, Wolfe W, Bangsberg D, et al. Barriers to antiretroviral adherence for patients living with HIV infection and AIDS in Botswana. J Acquir Immune Defic Syndr 2003; 34:281–8.

28. Ilyasu Z, Kabir M, Abubakar IS, Babashani M, Zubair ZA. Compliance to antiretroviral therapy among AIDS patients in Aminu Kano Teaching Hospital, Kano, Nigeria. Niger J Med 2005; 14:290–4.

29. Katona P, Katona-Apte J. The interaction between nutrition and infection. Clin Infect Dis 2008; 46:1582–8.

30. Piwoz E. Nutrition and HIV/AIDS: evidence, gaps and priority actions. Washington, DC: Academy for Educational Development, 2004.

31. Gorbach S, Tamsin A, Roubenoff R. Interactions between nutrition and infection with human immunodeficiency virus. Nutr Rev 1993; 51:226–34.

32. Wheeler DA. Weight loss and disease progression in HIV infection. AIDS Read 1999; 9:347–53.

33. Mangili A, Murman DH, Zampini AM, Wanke CA. Nutrition and HIV infection: review of weight loss and wasting in the era of

highly active antiretroviral therapy from the Nutrition for Healthy Living cohort. Clin Infect Dis 2006; 42:836–42.

34. Tang AM, Forrester J, Spiegelman D, Knox TA, Tchetgen E, Gorbach SL. Weight loss and survival in HIV-positive patients in the era of highly active antiretroviral therapy. J Acquir Immune Defic Syndr 2002; 31:230–6.

35. de Waal A, Whiteside A. New variant famine: AIDS and food crisis in southern Africa. Lancet 2003; 362:1234–7.

36. Haddad L, Gillespie S. Effective food and nutrition policy responses to HIV/AIDS: what we know and what we need to know. J Int Dev 2001; 13:487–511.

37. Piwoz E, Preble E. HIV/AIDS and nutrition: a review of literature and recommendations for nutritional care and support in sub-Saharan Africa. Washington, DC: Academy for Educational Development, 2000.

38. Semba RD, Tang AM. Micronutrients and the pathogenesis of human immunodeficiency virus infection. Br J Nutr 1999; 81:181–9.

39. Shevitz AH, Knox TA, Spiegelman D, Roubenoff R, Gorbach SL, Skolnik PR. Elevated resting energy expenditure among HIV-sero- positive persons receiving highly active antiretroviral therapy. AIDS 1999; 13:1351–7.

40. World Health Organization (WHO). Nutrient requirements for people living with HIV/AIDS: report of a technical consultation. Geneva: WHO, 2003.

41. Wig N, Bhatt SP, Sakhuja A, Srivastava S, Agarwal S. Dietary adequacy in Asian Indians with HIV. AIDS Care 2008; 20:370–5.

42. Beisel W. Nutrition in pediatric HIV infection: setting the research agenda. Nutrition and immune function: overview. J Nutr 1996; 126: 2611S–5S.

43. Au J, Kayitenkore K, Shutes E, et al. Access to adequate nutrition is a major potential obstacle to antiretroviral adherence among HIVinfected individuals in Rwanda. AIDS 2006; 20:2116–8.

44. Castleman T, Seumo-Fosso E, Cogill B. Food and nutrition implications of antiretroviral therapy in resource limited settings. Report 7. Washington, DC: Food and Nutrition

Technical Assistance Project, Academy for Educational Development, 2004.

45. Unge C, Johansson A, Zachariah R, Some D, Van Engelgem I, Ekstrom AM. Reasons for unsatisfactory acceptance of antiretroviral treatment in the urban Kibera slum, Kenya. AIDS Care 2008; 20:146–9.

46. Sanne I, Mommeja-Marin H, Hinkle J, et al. Severe hepatotoxicity associated with nevirapine use in HIV-infected subjects. J Infect Dis 2005; 191:825–9.

47. McDermott AY, Shevitz A, Must A, Harris S, Roubenoff R, Gorbach S. Nutrition treatment for HIV wasting: a prescription for food as medicine. Nutr Clin Pract 2003; 18:86–94.

48. Raiten D, Grinspoon S, Arpadi S. Nutritional considerations in the use of ART in resource limited settings. Durban, South Africa: Department of Nutrition for Health and Development, World Health Organization, 2005.

49. Gillespie S, Kadiyala S. HIV/AIDS and food and nutrition security: from evidence to action. Washington, DC: International Food Policy Research Institute, 2005.

50. Fenton L. Preventing HIV/AIDS through poverty reduction: the only sustainable solution? Lancet 2004; 364:1186–7.

51. Weiser SD, Leiter K, Bangsberg DR, et al. Food insufficiency is associated with high-risk sexual behavior among women in Botswana and Swaziland. PLoS Med 2007; 4:1589–97.

52. Bukusuba J, Kikafunda JK, Whitehead RG. Food security status in households of people living with HIV/AIDS (PLWHA) in a Ugandan urban setting. Br J Nutr 2007; 98:211–7.

53. Loevinsohn M, Gillespie S. HIV/AIDS, food security and rural livelihoods: understanding and responding. Discussion paper. Washington, DC: International Food Policy Research Institute, 2003.

54. Mukherjee JS, Ivers LC, Leandre F, Farmer P, Behforouz H. Antiretroviral therapy in resource-poor settings: decreasing barriers to access and promoting adherence. J Acquir Immune Defic Syndr 2006; 43(Suppl 1):S123–6.

55. Stokes SC. Measuring impacts of HIV/AIDS on rural livelihoods and food security. Rome: Sustainable Development Department, Food and Agricultural Organization of the United Nations, 2003.

56. Piot P, Pinstrup-Andersen P, Gillespie S, Haddad L. AIDS and food security: essays. Washington, DC: International Food Policy Research Institute, 2002.

57. Rollins N. Food insecurity—a risk factor for HIV infection. PLoS Med 2007; 4:1576–7.

58. Jayne T, Villarreal M, Pingali P, Hemrich G. Interactions between the agricultural sector and the HIV/AIDS pandemic: implications for agricultural policy. East Lansing, MI: Department of Agricultural Economics, Michigan State University, 2004.

59. Gillespie S. AIDS, poverty, and hunger: challenges and responses. Washington, DC: International Food Policy Research Institute, 2006.

60. The state of food insecurity in the world: 2005. Rome: Food and Agriculture Organization of the United Nations, 2005.

61. Kadiyala S, Gillespie S. Rethinking food aid to fight AIDS. Food Nutr Bull 2004; 25:271–82.

62. Cohen D. Achieving food security in vulnerable populations. BMJ 2005; 331:775–7.

63. Stack JA, Bell SJ, Burke PA, Forse RA. High-energy, high-protein, oral, liquid, nutrition supplementation in patients with HIV infection: effect on weight status in relation to incidence of secondary infection. J Am Diet Assoc 1996; 96:337–41.

64. Association of Nutrition Services Agencies (ANSA). The power of nutrition. Washington, DC: ANSA, 2006.

65. Berg A. Malnutrition: what can be done? Washington, DC: World Bank, 1987.

66. Andersen JE. What should be next for nutrition education? J Nutr 1994; 124:S828–32.

67. Webb P, Block S. Nutrition information and formal schooling as inputs to child nutrition. Econ Dev Cult Change 2004; 52:801–20.

68. Vanable PA, Carey MP, Blair DC, Littlewood RA. Impact of HIVrelated stigma on health behaviors and psychological adjustment among HIV-positive men and women. AIDS Behav 2006; 10:473–82.

69. Marchione TJ. Interactions with the recipient community in targeted food and nutrition programs. J Nutr 2005; 135:886–9.

70. Agnarson AM, Ericson J, Ekstrom AM, Thorson A. Antiretroviral therapy: what about food? AIDS 2007; 21:1225–6.

71. Mahlungulu S, Grobler LA, Visser ME, Volmink J. Nutritional interventions for reducing morbidity and mortality in people with HIV. Cochrane Database Syst Rev 2007:CD004536.

72. Cantrell RA, Sinkala M, Megazinni K, et al. A pilot study of food supplementation to improve adherence to antiretroviral therapy among food-insecure adults in Lusaka, Zambia. J Acquir Immune Defic Syndr 2008; 49:190–5.

73. Mehanna HM, Moledina J, Travis J. Refeeding syndrome: what it is, and how to prevent and treat it. BMJ 2008; 336:1495–8.

74. Nyirenda C, Zulu I, Kabagambe EK, et al. Acute hypophosphataemia and hypokalaemia in a patient starting antiretroviral therapy in Zambia—a new context for refeeding syndrome? BMJ Case Reports 2009: bcr0720080469.

75. Arrehag L, de Waal A, Whiteside A. 'New variant famine' revisited: chronic vulnerability in rural Africa. Humanitarian Exchange 2006; 33:7–10.

76. Food and Nutrition Technical Assistance (FANTA) project and World Food Programme (WFP). Washington DC: FANTA project, Academy for Educational Development, 2007.

77. Behforouz H, Farmer P, Mukherjee J. From directly observed therapy to accompagnateurs: enhancing AIDS treatment outcomes in Haiti and Boston. Clin Infect Dis 2004; 38:S429–36.

78. Byron E, Gillespie S, Nangami M. Integrating nutrition security with treatment of people living with HIV: lessons being learned in Kenya. Washington, DC: International Food Policy Research Institute, 2006.

79. Egge K, Strasser S. Measuring the impact of targeted food assistance on HIV/AIDS-related beneficiary groups: monitoring

and evaluation indicators. In: Gillespie S, ed. AIDS, poverty, and hunger: challenges and responses. Washington, DC: International Food Policy Research Institute, 2006:305–24.

80. Haddad L, Pen˜a C, Nishida C, Quisumbing A, Slack A. Food security and nutrition implications of intrahousehold bias: a review of literature. Washington, DC: International Food Policy Research Institute, 1996.

81. Collins S, Sadler K, Dent N, et al. Key issues in the success of community-based management of severe malnutrition. Food Nutr Bull 2006; 27:S49–82.

82. Report on food and nutrition for people living with HIV/AIDS. Washington, DC: President's Emergency Plan for AIDS Relief, 2006.

83. Samuels F, Rutenberg N. HIV, food and drugs: livelihoods, nutrition and anti-retroviral therapy (ART) in Kenya and Zambia. London: Overseas Development Institute, 2008.

84. Ministry of Agriculture and Rural Development (MoARD), Government of Ethiopia, Food and Agriculture Organization of the United Nations (FAO). Nutritional care and support for people living with HIV/AIDS: a training course. Addis Ababa: MoARD/FAO, 2005.

85. Sanchez P, Palm C, Sachs J, et al. The African millennium villages. Proc Natl Acad Sci U S A 2007; 104:16775–80.

86. Blinkoff P, Bukanga E, Syamalevwe B, Hughes A. Under the mupundu tree: volunteers in home care for people with HIV/AIDS and TB in Zambia's copperbelt. Oxford: Strategies for Hope Trust, 2005.

87. Fakande I, Malomo O. Home care of AIDS patients from the medical and nursing viewpoint—a project in Ife-Ijesa zone, Osun State, Nigeria [abstract 42423]. In: Program and abstracts of the XII International AIDS Conference (Geneva). Geneva: International AIDS Society, 1998.

88. Mamlin J, Kimaiyo S, Lewis S, et al. Integrating nutrition support for food-insecure patients and their dependents into an HIV care and treatment program in western Kenya. Am J Public Health 2009; 99: 215–21.

89. Caldwell R, Huddle J, Luma J. Food aid and chronic illness: insights from the community and household surveillance surveys. International Conference on HIV/AIDS and Food and Nutrition Security. Durban, South Africa: International Food Policy Research Institute, 2005.

90. Linneman Z, Matilsky D, Ndekha M, Manary MJ, Maleta K. A largescale operational study of home-based therapy with ready-to-use therapeutic food in childhood malnutrition in Malawi. Matern Child Nutr 2007; 3:206–15.

91. Manary MJ. Local production and provision of ready-to-use therapeutic food (RUTF) spread for the treatment of severe childhood malnutrition. Food Nutr Bull 2006; 27:S83–9.

92. LoPriore C, Guidoum Y, Briend A, Branca F. Spread fortified with vitamins and minerals induces catch-up growth and eradicates severe anemia in stunted refugee children aged 3–6 y. Am J Clin Nutr 2004; 80:973–81.

93. Collins S, Dent N, Binns P, Bahwere P, Sadler K, Hallam A. Management of severe acute malnutrition in children. Lancet 2006; 368: 1992–2000.

94. Shrimpton R, Tripp K, Thorne-Lyman A. Refugee nutrition and low birthweight in Nepal: report to United Nations High Commissioner for Refugees and World Food Programme. London: United Nations, 2002.

95. United States Agency for International Development (USAID). Wheat flour fortification program in Bangladesh: final report. Arlington, VA: MOST: The USAID Micronutrient Program, 2003.

96. Seal A. Evaluation of the nutritional impact of on-site milling and fortification in Nangweshi Refugee Camp, Zambia. Geneva: United Nations High Commissioner for Refugees, 2005.

97. van den Briel T, Cheung E, Zewari J, Khan R. Fortifying food in the field to boost nutrition: case studies from Afghanistan, Angola and Zambia. Rome: World Food Programme, 2006.

98. Ulysse P, Jarlyne J, Ivers LC. Ready-to-use-therapeutic food and accompaniment in the management of infants with malnutrition and HIV in Artibonite, Haiti [abstract CDD0131]. In: Program and abstracts of the XVII International AIDS Conference (Mexico City). Geneva: International AIDS Society, 2008.

99. Sadler K, Bahwere P, Guerrero S, Collins S. Community-based therapeutic care in HIV-affected populations. Trans R Soc Trop Med Hyg 2006; 100:6–9.

100. Duffield A, Reid G, Shoham J, Walker D. Evidence base for interventions in complex emergencies. Lancet 2005; 365:842–3.

101. Young H, Jaspars S. The meaning and measurement of acute malnutrition emergencies: a primer for decision-makers. Network paper 56. London: Humanitarian Practice Network, 2006. Available at: http: //www.odihpn.org/report.asp?idp2849. Accessed 27 March 2008.

102. Menon P, Ruel MT, Loechl CU, et al. Micronutrient sprinkles reduce anemia among 9- to 24-mo-old children when delivered through an integrated health and nutrition program in rural Haiti. J Nutr 2007; 137:1023–30.

103. Bonnard P, Cekan J, Schlossman N. Food, food aid, and HIV/AIDS programming. Washington, DC: Save the Children Federation, 2006.

104. Bell C, Devarajan S, Gersbach H. The long-run economic cost of AIDS: theory and an application to South Africa. Washington, DC: World Bank, 2003.

105. Strauss J. Does better nutrition raise farm productivity? J Polit Econ 1986; 94:297–320.

106. Deolalikar A. Nutrition and labor productivity in agriculture: Estimates for rural south India. Rev Econ Stat 1988; 70:406–13.

107. Edstro¨m J, Samuels F. HIV, nutrition, food and livelihoods in subSaharan Africa: evidence, debates and reflections for guidance. Brighton: Institute of Development Studies, 2007.

INDEX